THE RECEIVING

Also by Tirzah Firestone

With Roots in Heaven:
One Woman's Passionate Journey into the Heart of Her Faith

The Woman's Kabbalah:
Ecstatic Jewish Practices for Women (audio program)

THE RECEIVING

RECLAIMING JEWISH WOMEN'S WISDOM

RABBI TIRZAH FIRESTONE

May 2013

For Bonnie!
With love,
appreciation,
+ blessings for
deep fulfillment!
R Tirzah Firestone

HarperSanFrancisco
A Division of HarperCollinsPublishers

For the seven women who guide this book
And for the countless others who have gone unnamed

CONTENTS

INTRODUCTION

very Saturday morning when I was little, my father and I would walk hand in hand to synagogue. When we arrived, we would go directly to his special shelf, from which he took the purple velvet bag that held his prayer shawl. I remember this shawl as a sea of white wool with black stripes, soft fringes, and tiny silver mirrors sewn into the neckpiece. I clung to my father's leg as he swept the cape over his shoulders, and as it descended over us both my world was transformed. Suddenly everything around me glowed with a golden warmth. Following my father to his seat on the men's side of the Orthodox *shul*, I sat next to him for hours, floating on the Sabbath ritual and the Hebrew chants that filled the air.

One Saturday morning I confided to my father, "Daddy, I want my own prayer shawl, and I want to dance up and down the aisles with everyone dancing along, and I want to go up to the holy ark and sing." A long frozen moment followed. Then he whispered, "You know, you're getting too old to be with me here. It's time for you to go to the women's side."

That very day, my father took me to the edge of the wavy blue partition that kept the women at the back of the synagogue and shooed me over. I was shocked to find that it was a different world there. None of the women or girls, for instance, wore a magical cape. Removed from the holy warmth of the men's prayers, they sat behind the partition chatting and distractedly turning the pages of their prayer books. All that was sacred seemed to begin and end on the men's side. For the rest of the Saturdays of my childhood, I sat behind the plastic partition, wondering why I, along with all the other women and girls, had been cut off from the spiritual soul of our heritage.

It was, in part, this feeling of separation that drove me away from Judaism to look elsewhere for a more alive and accessible spiritual experience. I spent over a decade exploring other religious practices and mystical traditions around the world. Then, due to some remarkable people and circumstances, I returned to the Hebrew texts, chants, and mysteries that had first kindled my ecstasy as a little girl. This time as a rabbinic student, I felt the same shock and indignation I had experienced as a child when I discovered that the Jewish history books and encyclopedias were in large measure devoid of women.

Where in the world had all the women gone? Where were the wise women and community leaders, the seers and the sages? Was there not even one Jewish counterpart to the Hindu poet Mirabai, the Islamic saint Rabi'ah, or the Catholic guide into the soul's interior Teresa of Avila? I found that, sorrowfully, Judaism was entering the twenty-first century with no named women mystics or spiritual guides.

The apparent absence of women and a woman's mystical tradition roars with the injustice done to generations of women who were simply deleted from history. *The Receiving* challenges this inequity. It empowers women to reclaim their rightful connection to the ancient Judaic teachings and, perhaps more important, to their own inherent spiritual wisdom.

Of course, Jewish women have always been central characters in the Jewish story. Women made life happen. They bore and raised the children, kept the home running, and often had businesses on the side to allow their men to study Torah. But while men's path to holiness was fueled by study of the sacred word, most Jewish women did not have that opportunity. Women's connection to the Divine was necessarily found in the immediacy of their domestic experiences and in the powerful life questions that challenged their daily functions: What will save this ailing child? What ritual will promote forgiveness and purification after a violation or rape? How do we help midwife one another across the thresholds of marriage, motherhood, birth, and death?

As important as it was, the Jewish woman's role was forever seen as ancillary to the proclaimed central purpose of Jewish life: the sacred study of the Torah and enactment of its laws. Yet, in its attention to the moment at hand, the women's way necessarily bespeaks an approach to spirituality that sees every aspect of life as an opportunity for holiness. For men as well as women, just as essential as the transmission and study of sacred texts is the cultivation of a connection to the Divine, the ability to carve out an inner life and receive divine inspiration and guidance.

The feminine approach to spirituality, which incorporates the inner spiritual life and the value of *receiving*—the literal meaning of the word *Kabbalah*—has scarcely been valued or preserved within Jewish tradition. The little that does remain of the Jewish women's legacy comes in the form of women's prayers, known as *techinahs*, and scanty records of their spiritual arts, such as amulets, prescriptions, and other magical practices. As important as this historical legacy is, it is covered in greater detail elsewhere. My purpose here is to provide readers with a guide to the inner life, and to restore our connection to the ancient feminine wisdom that has been so deeply hidden until now.

At my ordination as a rabbi, I made two pledges. The first was public: I committed myself to helping remove the barriers, which I experienced so early in life, that have kept women shut away from the holiness of their own tradition. In this work I have much help. There has been a veritable tidal wave of enthusiasm on the part of women around the world who demand participation in the sacred study and rites of Judaism. Throughout the world, the bond between women and the Jewish tradition is reweaving itself in the form of women's prayer quorums, support circles, and study programs.

My second pledge was more private, and far more difficult. I pledged to uncover the jewel that I sensed must lie at the innermost heart of Judaism but that I had experienced only fleetingly: a wholeness that was composed of both the outer Torah and the inner receiving, the masculine as well as the feminine approach to God, a path that did not divide or exclude, but that brought opposites together in an inclusive life of holiness. Writing this book has been the first fulfillment of that pledge.

The wholeness of which I speak is, indeed, alive at the mystical core of the tradition. Although it has often been garbed in hierarchical, and even misogynist, terms, the essence of the mystical Jewish path, known as Kabbalah, is one that is intrinsically balanced and inclusive. It acknowledges not only the feminine aspects of life, but also the fact that neither the human world nor God can be whole without the marriage of its masculine and feminine parts, its light as well as dark, transcendent as well as earthly components. As you will see, the beauty of this mystical path is that it understands the human need to hold these opposites in tension in order for there to be wholeness and balance on earth.

Because the feminine path naturally honors all of life's experiences, from the most sublime to the most mundane, it easily supports this mystical model, understanding that God's presence can be found in all things. Tending to the simple yet profound moments of life is just as important as performing the most exalted of rituals. In the feminine approach, the heart bursting with prayer over a sick child is seen as no less valuable than the awesome invocations at a formal Yom Kippur service; caring for life in all its fragility is as important as safeguarding the tradition itself.

I began searching to find the treasures of wholeness that had been hidden, yet which I was convinced lay waiting to be redeemed. I surmised that the best place to start seeking was among the women whose lives might be secret caches of such wholeness. Despite the paucity of women mentioned in the history books, I found that throughout the ages there were indeed Jewish women mystics, sages, and miracle workers whose lives were richly balanced in masculine and feminine values.

In this volume I present seven such women whose chronology ranges from the second to the twentieth century. Each woman represents a different aspect of feminine wisdom, and each one guides us from across the ages by means of her own life story, to help modern women connect with crucial aspects of feminine spirituality. By presenting the surviving stories of historical holy women, it is my intention to begin reconstructing the feminine legacy that has been lost, and thereby open the door to a path of wholeness.

As I dug through the records, holy books, and annals, piecing together the information about these women that managed to survive, each woman seemed to push her way forward through the scanty print that bound her to brevity, bringing with her another approach to accessing the Divine. Each one opened a new door, pointing to yet another way of fulfilling a life of holiness.

I must admit that I began writing this book in a state of anger at the ways that women and the feminine path have been devalued and omitted from Jewish history. But as I continued to immerse myself in the stories of these holy women, I found their determination and positive attitude to be contagious. They were too busy to be angry! They had important work to carry out and were undeterred by the harsh conditions of the outwardly denigrating world in which they lived.

Like many women in our imbalanced culture, I myself had grown up identifying with masculine values, secretly considering feminine ways less worthy and less effective. All that has changed for me now. Through my study of these seven women, I have learned how truly potent the feminine path is. I understand now how much more skillful and powerful it is to calmly connect with the deep currents of life and act in attunement with them, rather than operate in the more self-aggrandizing manner I had always equated with success. As the reader may notice, *The Receiving* reflects my journey from initial anger to understanding and then to excitement and optimism about the receptive power of the Feminine to uplift the world.

Each chapter of this book begins with the life of one woman, her story serving as a springboard into a particular aspect of Judaism's mystical wisdom, showing us a way in which life's opposites can be wedded. The seven women I have profiled, like women of today, struggled within a masculine system to find their own unique way to God. Some were sanctioned as holy women; others were ignored, humiliated, exiled, or worse. No matter their fate, each of their stories represents a component of feminine wisdom that has been long submerged. By reconnecting readers to the slender yet powerful threads of Jewish women's mystical history that have survived, I hope that modern women will begin to remember and reclaim the rich mystical legacy that is rightfully theirs.

The past several decades have seen an unprecedented awakening of interest in ancient spiritual wisdom. For the first time in its three-thousand-year history, the mystical teachings of Judaism, hitherto guarded by the rabbinic elite and taught exclusively to Jewish men, have been translated and brought out into the public domain.

While many women have attempted to study and apply this venerable wisdom in recent years, a common complaint has been that it is shrouded in abstract terminology, remaining a cosmology difficult to apply to modern life issues. Therefore, with women in mind, I have attempted to extract the clear essence of the Jewish mystical vision to reveal its innately balanced perspective. Throughout the book I present practical teachings and techniques to help the reader apply the ancient mystical wisdom to their lives; no prior knowledge of Jewish mysticism or the Jewish tradition is necessary.

As both a rabbi and psychotherapist, I come into contact with numerous women who are working to create wholeness in their lives. I have used some of their stories to illustrate the teachings throughout the book. Although all of these scenarios are based upon actual people, the names and, in some cases, events have been altered in order to protect the identities of the subjects.

Researching, studying, and compiling the material for *The Receiving* has been a profound experience for me, and it is a great privilege now to share this material with you, the reader, so that you, too, can learn from it and allow its wisdom to enrich your life.

The time is ripe for women's wisdom to come into the world. All of us, women and men, Jews and non-Jews, stand together at a critical crossroads in human history. The mystical traditions of the world are calling us to avail ourselves of their ancient wisdom. Likewise, the feminine side of the human spirit, which has lain dormant and waiting, is reawakening from centuries of neglect, begging us to share in her riches. Together, both the mystical and the feminine paths can bring us to the necessary next step in our evolution toward wholeness. May *The Receiving* help move us forward on this extraordinary journey.

SEPTEMBER 11, 2002
5 TISHREI 5763

CHAPTER 1

TENACITY IN EXILE

Hannah Rachel of Ludomir (1815–1905)

F or over two thousand years, feminine wisdom has run through Jewish history like an underground stream. Submerged by a dominant ethic that did not know how to tap its riches, it was left to meander, discovering its own subterranean path to the ocean. In its long exile, unseen and unlauded, the stream has wended its way beneath desert and temple, glory and wreckage. Intermittently surfacing to the light, laughing out loud at human folly, it always returned to its hidden route, quietly nourishing the earth from below.

But in our time, the underground current of women's wisdom is rising to the surface for good, ready to pour forth its treasures, never to be pushed down again.

Hannah Rachel of Ludomir was one woman mystic who exemplifies this persistent current of feminine wisdom. Literally pushed out of the Jewish community by its male leaders, Hannah Rachel was humiliated and debased because she violated their narrow view of femininity. Nevertheless, this brilliant and tenacious woman succeeded in becoming a testimony to the enduring power of women.

Living in enforced isolation in a tiny green hut, Hannah Rachel had a profound relationship with divine forces, which gave her the strength to withstand the external condemnation she received while she studied, prayed, and made meaning of Judaism's deepest truths. Hannah Rachel's tenacity reminds us that we each must discover our own relationship to God and reclaim and make new meaning of our ancient heritage.

Hannah Rachel's story begins at the turn of the nineteenth century, in a village called Ludomir, on the Lug River in the Ukraine. Her father, a simple Jewish shopkeeper named Monisch Werbermacher, had been counseled by his local rabbi to divorce his barren wife, as Jewish law suggests when a couple have been childless for ten years or more. This would allow him to find a more fertile woman to provide him with children. But Monisch loved his wife, Leah, and Leah loved him. He could not bring himself to follow such advice.

Instead, Monisch journeyed to another rabbi, a sage and miracle worker known as the "Seer of Lublin" (Rabbi Jacob Isaac HaLevi Horovitz) to ask that, if Heaven would allow it, he bless his wife and himself with a child. Monisch stood trembling as the holy man closed his eyes. For a time it was as if he were absent from the room. Finally he said, "Go home. Your wife will soon conceive a child. A holy soul this one is." On his journey home, overflowing with gratitude and awe, Monisch vowed to raise his unborn child to become the learned sage he was meant to become. No effort would be spared.

The following year, Leah bore a daughter. Monisch reeled with shock. "A daughter?" he cried. How could a female become a rabbi or sage? What could the Seer have been seeing? Everyone knew that only male children could take their formal place in the faith. It was not even customary to educate girls in the sacred texts. Letters enough to read Yiddish, yes, and perhaps a little Russian to get along, but nothing more.

Nevertheless, Monisch resolved to fulfill his vow to raise a sage. Against the misgivings of his wife and the Seer of Lublin himself, when the girl, named Hannah Rachel, turned five, she was sent to take instruction in the finest schoolhouse in the area. There she began her career in sacred Hebrew and Aramaic texts, all the while sitting behind a screen to keep her apart from her male schoolmates.

Hannah Rachel took to her studies with aplomb. By the time she was eight years old, she had distinguished herself as a scholar, stunning everyone with her ability to memorize, understand, and penetrate the essence of the texts. But there was something amiss and even her father sensed it. Hannah Rachel was too precocious, too solemn; indeed, she seemed not a child at all. Disinterested in playing or socializing, she would withdraw to her room after classes and continue to pore over her tomes. Soon she began to ignore her parents too, speaking only when spoken to. Her mother, weakened from her pregnancy late in life and distressed over her daughter's long silences, grew sick and died. By then Hannah Rachel was nine.

Monisch, now a widower, questioned the wisdom of his bold experiment in raising a daughter to be a scholar. Finally he went to a Jewish court to have his vow annulled and pulled Hannah Rachel out of school. But this only served to aggravate the situation. Hannah Rachel refused to tear herself away from her studies. For days at a time she would not talk; instead, she stood swaying over her large volumes, intoning passages from them in ancient liturgical chant.

As happens in small, tightly knit, communities, the neighbors began to gossip, spreading malicious rumors about Hannah Rachel. Surely she was possessed, some whispered. She was queer and sexless, said others, neither woman nor man. Hannah Rachel was twelve by then and of marriageable age. But when her worried father broached the subject, she replied that she had no inclination whatsoever to be "as other females."

What was Monisch to do? He was a plainspoken man, and his adolescent daughter was getting to be too articulate a scholar for him to fight with. The Seer of Lublin had died the same year his wife had passed away. So he decided to consult the celebrated Hassidic rebbe Mordechai of Chernobyl.

Reluctantly, Hannah Rachel accompanied her father to Chernobyl to see the great preacher. In her presence, the rabbi reprimanded Monisch for having subjected the girl to the holy books. Hannah Rachel herself interrupted the rabbi and began debating on Talmudic grounds why it is indeed permissible for women to study the sacred texts.

"On the very same page of Tractate Sota that you are quoting is the counterargument, Rabbi."

"I see you know the text. But daughter, no one has the right to interfere with the tradition, which is God's intention for women. A woman's fate is marriage and children."

"But even Maimonides says that a woman is not bound by the injunction to be fruitful and multiply. And do you not remember the responsa—you have it there on your bookcase—that states when a woman asks to study Talmud, it is incumbent upon the sages in her generation to aid and encourage such a woman and reinforce..."

"You are going too far, Hannah Rachel. You will regret it," he warned.

Before dismissing the father and daughter, the rabbi took Monisch aside and whispered a plan. It was just after Czar Nicholas I had decreed that every Jewish boy over the age of twelve was to be taken from his home to be catechized, baptized, and trained for military service. Barracks were teeming with young marriageable soldiers in need of companionship and religious retraining. A uniformed Jew showed up at Hannah Rachel's door the following Sabbath. Because the situation implied an important religious duty—to clarify and help the man return to his own tradition—Hannah Rachel was happy to take him in and spend the Sabbath in Talmudic conversation. She was particularly relieved that the soldier, eight years her senior, never questioned her Talmudic interests or devotion. For many weeks every Saturday the soldier appeared and spent the day with Hannah Rachel in conversation and study. Her solemn mood lightened. One Saturday night, Monisch was amazed to find her crocheting a prayer shawl for her friend and putting aside a pair of phylacteries for him.

Before his next visit, however, Monisch was called to the barracks and curtly informed that their young Sabbath guest had been shipped to Omsk on a twenty-five-year tour of military duty. Hannah Rachel stalked about the house. Although she did not cry, her heartbreak was obvious. The next day she was gone.

Hannah Rachel, wrapped in her mother's woolen shawl, her hair pulled up under a babushka, slunk through the muddy alleyways of Ludomir, past the marketplace and the ruins of the historic church. There at the top of the hill was the cemetery where her mother was buried. Hannah Rachel prayed at her mother's grave all afternoon, invoking her spirit to intercede on her behalf. Night fell and the girl, emotionally drained and feeble, fell asleep near her mother's tombstone. After midnight she awakened frightened and disoriented. She took flight, tripping over the graves, her dangling shawl catching on a headstone and throwing her to the ground. Did she fall unconscious or was she simply terrified? Hannah Rachel lay there till morning, when a grave digger making his rounds discovered her quivering body.

For several days she lay in bed in a state of trance. Then one morning she called to her father and said in a feeble voice, "I have just come from the Heavenly Assembly and they have conferred upon me my oversoul." Having uttered these words, she slowly got out of bed and took out the crocheted prayer shawl and phylacteries meant for her soldier friend. Her father watched as she donned them and began to pray the morning prayers. Then, once again, she slid out a large tome of Talmud and resumed her studies.

Hannah Rachel was nineteen when her father died. After the thirty-day mourning period had passed, she sold her parental home and shop and moved to a tiny green hut near the Jewish marketplace. There her rabbinical career began.

As Hannah Rachel continued worshiping every morning in the prayer shawl and phylacteries normally reserved for men and immersing herself in her sacred study, word soon spread that the "holy virgin in Ludomir," who lived in a little green hut and whose behavior was like that of a male, performed miracles like the great Hassidic wonder-workers.

At first it was just women and then a few men who began to seek out Hannah Rachel to listen to her teachings on Sabbath afternoons. The *"grune Stubel,"* as the hut was named, soon became a meeting place of a sizable congregation. And then from beyond the Lug River, from Podolia and Galicia and Volhniya, came hundreds more: the lame, the blind, and the despairing, seeking out Hannah Rachel for blessings and intercession on their behalf.

The "holy virgin," as she was now called, held audiences with hundreds, always through the window of her hut. From there she would teach, bless, and hold her discourses. Her second room was reserved for her alone, as a chapel and sleeping quarters.

Once again, the rabbinic authorities lost patience with this anomaly of a woman. Hassidic circles across eastern Europe buzzed with rumors of her conduct, and the rabbis grew increasingly indignant at this woman's masquerading in men's religious garments and peddling kabbalistic teachings without authorization. Once again, the rumors flowed. The maid was possessed by an evil spirit.... She spoke the utterances of Satan....

The rabbis appealed to her first with a campaign of missives that always began in a conciliatory vein: "To the holy virgin of Ludomir in the name of all the disciples of the Besht and his saintly followers...." But the letters invariably turned rough and ended with a warning that she stop her unorthodox ways and return immediately to conduct befitting a Jewish woman.

Hannah Rachel's answers were calm. She simply refuted their claims with Talmudic citations. Their next move was to threaten her with excommunication, calling upon all good Jews to rise up against this "maid and her misguided illiterates," to not "come within four ells [about five yards] of her and her defiled assembly nor marry into the desecrated households of her supporters." The rabbis ended their call to action as a call to wage a war of God against "Satan now flourishing in the profaned community of Ludomir in the guise of a female."

The "holy war" came to a head one Sabbath afternoon when a small riot broke out in front of the green hut and rocks were thrown into the window of the maid's chapel. It was rumored that Hannah Rachel sought religious asylum in a nearby Greek Orthodox convent. The mother superior there was said to have offered protection on the pretext that the Jewish faith gave no official recognition to its holy women. At the time, a Jew entering a Christian house of worship was unheard of. Women of completely different theological backgrounds banding together to offer religious sanctuary to one another! This was surely the greatest heresy—and the most threatening of all.

It did not stop there, however. Hearing that the famous Chernobyler Rebbe had once prescribed marriage for Hannah Rachel, a committee of three prominent rabbis was formed to make the journey to Ludomir to insist that Hannah Rachel wed immediately. These men composed a court of law, with civil and religious jurisdiction that no one in the Jewish community would dare to repudiate.

When the court arrived, they announced themselves to Hannah Rachel's elderly scribe, who sat in the anteroom of the green hut. We can only imagine how Hannah Rachel felt as she invited these adversarial men into her sacred quarters. There they proceeded to discuss a woman's role in Judaism. The male rabbis were armed with foolproof Talmudic arguments, or so they thought, for they seemed to convince Hannah Rachel that her religious practice and marriage need not be mutually exclusive. However, once she was married, she would have to abandon her career as a public personality, because it was not proper for a married woman to come into contact with the male public.

Hannah Rachel must have been desperate to get rid of her guests, but they were not about to quit until they had been satisfied with an outcome they found acceptable. She consented to their appeal. Her pale, long-faced scribe in the front room would have to do. Although many years her senior, he was a man nevertheless. There and then, outside the green hut, in the shade of a makeshift wedding canopy, the three rabbis performed the marriage of the female rebbe and the scribe.

The next morning, as soon as her three guests had gone, Hannah Rachel drove her new husband out of the hut demanding a divorce document. When he protested loudly and threatened to call the three rabbis back, she told him she had never intended the marriage to be more than a formality. She had agreed to it for appearances only. Since Hannah Rachel had refused to live with her husband, the rabbinic court could say nothing. The marriage had not been consummated and so was null and void. But now the rabbis had no choice but to excommunicate her.

As soon as the decree of banishment from the Jewish community was made public, Hannah Rachel was abandoned by her followers. Except for a few kindly old women who secretly slipped in to check on her periodically, Hannah Rachel was left to herself, a lone and brooding figure in her little green hut. It did not take Hannah Rachel long, however, to throw off the yoke of her painful history, sell her hut, and buy a ticket to Palestine. She arrived there at the age of fifty-five.

Hannah Rachel lived the rest of her life in relative peace in the May'ah She'arim quarter of Jerusalem. There, once again, she established herself as a rebbe. Women and men followers flocked to her modest court and sat at her Sabbath table to hear her teachings. It was reported that her table was decked with twelve little *challahs*, as was the custom in the courts of the great Hassidic rabbis and Kabbalists of old. But Hannah Rachel was, no doubt, the first rebbe to bake the *challahs* with her own hands.

On holy days, dozens of pilgrims would come from Tiberius, Hebron, and Safed to pay tribute to the female rabbi and behold her with the sacred scrolls of Torah. And, before each new moon, Hannah Rachel would lead her female followers to the Tomb of Rachel to pray and deposit their tiny written prayers in the stones of the tomb.

Until the end of her long life, Hannah Rachel was seen every morning wending her way to the Wailing Wall, her prayer shawl and phylacteries bulging in the little purple bag she carried. It has been speculated that it was by the power of her prayers at the Wailing Wall at century's end that heaven's gates were opened to allow the great return of Jews to Palestine from around the world.

Hannah Rachel died in the early years of the twentieth century. If her teachings were indeed written down, they have been lost to us. No one knows where she is buried.

Female Saints and Sages

Through the eyes of a twenty-first-century woman, Hannah Rachel's story might look a bit ridiculous, a throwaway caricature from archaic times, of little relevance to our modern sensibilities. But it is precisely for this reason that I have put Hannah Rachel first: we must look squarely at her tragic life because it does not stand alone. Hannah Rachel's life resounds with thousands of years of history that went into its making.

Like the brief text on a page of Talmud, her life is surrounded by centuries' worth of fine print containing the background and commentary to the formation of Jewish attitudes and behavior toward women. And, just like a piece of Talmud, we cannot look at her life apart from the context that created her predicament. The echoes of Hannah Rachel's life are the myriad nameless women through the ages whose lives were unknown and unmarked, but who, like Hannah Rachel, rebelled against the tight mold made for them by men.

In another culture, Hannah Rachel would have been revered as a luminary rather than cast out as an intractable nuisance. In the Hindu tradition, women who are touched by the spirit are blessed to heal and inspire large numbers of followers, achieving public status as sacred teachers or gurus. Even early Islam claims a female mystic. It is well known that the Catholic tradition has been richly inspired by its female saints, women who felt called by God to take up a life of prayer and devotion. The church wisely gave these women a place within the Christian camp, once it became clear that not all women were cut out for a path of motherhood and homemaking.

But within the Jewish tradition, women like Hannah Rachel were considered aberrations of nature. Far from being a model of feminine wisdom about whom Jewish parents could proudly tell their daughters, Hannah Rachel has come down through history as an unknown or, worse, as a secret, hidden in the shadows because there was no legitimate place for her or women like her.

How ironic it is that we know more about Hannah Rachel's life than about any other women recounted in this book. The completeness of her biography is due, sadly, not to her courage and sagacity, but to the outrage that she generated among the rabbinic authorities of her day. What the rabbis experienced as a desperate and unprecedented dilemma had a fortuitous outcome (for us, if not for Hannah Rachel), for her journey was relatively well documented.[1]

From the Beginning

It is impossible to pinpoint how or when men became the dominant authorities within Judaism. It is a fact that is already ubiquitous throughout the earliest of Jewish texts. Still we must wonder: How did men come to assume sole leadership among the Jews? What caused the first prophet and priest, Moses and Aaron, and the hundreds of generations of priests and rabbis that followed them to treat women as secondary to the defined purpose of the people, which was to become holy through the study and practice of God's sacred Law? Why did women put up with being kept, from earliest times, on the outer circle of the formal tradition? More important, did women have their own ways of accessing the Divine that have remained unrecorded?

Open any Bible to the story of the giving of the Ten Commandments in Exodus and you will find the earliest signs of division. God has given Moses explicit details about the way the people were to prepare themselves for the imminent revelation at Mount Sinai. In turn, Moses tells the people to consecrate themselves, wash their clothes, and be ready for the third day, on which this great event will unfold. "And He said to the people, 'Be ready for three days. Do not come close to a woman.'"[2] It is to the men that Moses speaks. The women are the subjects of the speech, spoken about rather than to, a separate entity that might threaten the mission unless properly handled.

It is easy to read into the text a gender hierarchy. "The people" to whom Moses is speaking is clearly not the entire people; it is the men. Could the text be telling us that the experience of revelation was a male experience? Does it tell us that women were not part and parcel of the people, but considered a hindrance to the men's experience?

Women have told themselves many things about this verse over the generations. Perhaps the injunction was a sexual precaution: the spiritual power of the coming event required a kind of attention and physical reserve not possible in a sexually mixed camp. But then why did the leader not speak to both genders? Words such as "All of you, men and women, separate from each other now" would have served the purpose. It is undeniably the men who are spoken to. The men seemed to count in a way that women did not, at least on the page.

Women have consoled themselves with the thought that the verses before them today are a much later version of an event that actually did include women, written down and compiled centuries after the event of the revelation occurred. Yet if our verse from Exodus was indeed a late redaction, it still could not have come any later than the first century, when the canon of Torah was closed, according to scholars. That means that for around two thousand years, what is perhaps the most formative story of a nation was heard in a manner that focuses on the men as the major protagonists—a very long time for women to be on the outside, "listening in."

The Rise of the Masculine

When we move forward in time to see what the next writings show us on the topic, we find that the books of Judges, Kings, and the

Prophets also illustrate the life of a society based on male leadership. The new nation had entered and settled in the land of Canaan; the mandate from God was to "completely destroy all the places where the nations which you shall possess serve their gods, to tear down their altars, break up their sacred pillars, burn their Asherah trees, and chop down the statues of their gods...."[3] These holy sites and relics were, of course, those of the native Canaanite inhabitants, extravagant worshipers of gods and goddesses. Rich in shrines, deity figurines, and engraved images, this pagan culture was the undesirable element in the story of the developing Hebrew monotheism.

Typical of ancient Near Eastern and Mediterranean religions, Canaanite deities were couples and even families that spanned generations.[4] This made sense to the people who relied on their gods for the fertility of their crops and animals. The harmonious partnership of male and female divinities in the heavenly realms seemed to assure worshipers of success and productivity on earth below.

Ultimately the Canaanite religions gave way to the new culture of the Hebrews, whose one male God, YHVH, attempted to rise to dominance without the help of a female consort or the use of images so common to female deities. As we shall see in Chapter 2, however powerful YHVH was, the Hebrew leaders never fully managed to vanquish the polytheistic culture around them; the Hebrews quietly intermarried, adopted the local gods, and subtly integrated many aspects of the Canaanite belief system into their own.[5] Perhaps this was because the people's simple understanding demanded a more balanced deity, one that reflected the human experience of male and female coupling and families.

Nevertheless, the new religion officially paid homage to the one God, YHVH, who appeared in all the sacred texts as masculine. The elimination of the female element from the new cosmology inevitably led to the elimination of the woman from the circle of power.[6] As we shall see, primacy of the masculine principle in the divine realms translated into a dominance of the masculine principle in the regions of human control as well.

Where Are the Women?

Sprinkled through centuries of preponderantly male leadership we do find a few influential women leaders, clearly the exceptions to the rule. In Judges, we find Deborah,[7] a judge and stateswoman, whose prophetic word was known far and wide. There were other women prophets, but few were recorded. Noadiah is mentioned by name but nothing more is said about her.[8] Another is Huldah, whose power was acknowledged during Josiah's reign near the end of the First Temple period.[9] Besides Huldah, we sense that there were other influential women whose words and actions had clout, but we hear nothing about their leadership and barely the fact of their existence.

In a long line of kings, three queens stand out. Most notorious was Jezebel, the Sidonian princess who became queen of Israel at the side of wicked King Ahab.[10] Far more popular was Esther, the beautiful Jewish queen and heroine of the Purim story, whose reign with King Ahasuerus of Persia is historically questionable. Less celebrated but more historical is Salome Alexandra, the remarkable ruler of Judah during the first century B.C.E. Her nine-year reign was unprecedented for peace and prosperity during a time of bloody political intrigue.

Concurrent with the political development of the Jewish nation was its religious development. In this department, there is even less light on women's lives. The priesthood, a caste composed of the male bloodline of the tribe of Levi, was designated by Moses and Aaron in the wilderness to administer the sacred rites of the day. This was the work of animal and agricultural sacrifices—heavy, bloody labor, difficult to imagine today. Animal sacrifices were the ancient people's way of communing with the Divine, and the priests who officiated at these rites were the mediators of the sacred.

But the priests also wielded a great deal of political power. Dictating where and when the sacred rites were performed as well as who was considered pure and impure, the priests held the power to summarily disqualify the adult female population from sacred service due to the contaminating power assigned to their monthly blood. Against the backdrop of the temple cultures of the ancient Near East, which were largely populated by women priestesses to whom blood was considered holy, not vile, the male priesthood of the Hebrews stood out in stark relief. Perhaps as an oppositional stance to the cults that the Hebrew leadership had come to uproot, female participation in the ritual services of the Jewish people became severely restricted.

The Word as Sacred

With the destruction of the Temple in 586 B.C.E., the very basis of Jewish religious life was shaken. Forced into exile, their national identity at stake, their leaders decided to commit the people's oral tradition to writing, so that wherever the people went, they could take their sacred legacy with them in written form. Within a generation, the medium by which Jews related to the Divine changed completely, from sacrificial rite to the sacred word: prayer and study. Just as women's participation in the Temple rites had been denied, so too, now, when the sacred technology shifted to that of the written word, women were once again denied access and the opportunity for influence. No longer were the priests in control; the new authority was the rabbis, teachers of the law and guardians of the nation's sacred heritage, the Torah. The task of safeguarding the people's sacred treasures in the form of holy words was assigned to the men.

For the next two thousand years, the highest rung of holiness achievable in the Jewish tradition was by means of erudition. But all of the sacred Jewish writings were produced by men for men. Women who had the resources and time to study did so as outsiders. Formal daily prayer and Torah study became the spiritual currency of the day. It was a rare and peculiar woman who would enter the male world, one in which focus, mental precision, and unyielding intellectual effort was transmuted into the gold of the spirit.

But what about the woman's world? What was the gold of her spirit? Most certainly it was not the written word. Until the late modern period, it was highly uncommon for women to be familiar with the sacred language at all, let alone to study the sacred texts. Unless she hailed from a family of great wealth or rabbinic prominence (and her rabbinic relatives were advocates of female education), a Jewish girl before the past century would most often have grown up illiterate in the sacred languages of Hebrew and Aramaic, and sometimes in the common tongue. For centuries the sine qua non of the Jewish tradition—devotion through the sacred word—was largely inaccessible to half of the Jewish population.

In Jewish society knowledge equals power. More than wealth and political distinction, among Jews it is education that wields power. Quite simply put, to be excluded from textual knowledge meant to be out of the loop of power. Excluding women from reading and understanding the texts essentially meant excluding women from power.

Women's exclusion from the textual tradition and from participation in the sacred rites of the community affected not only women, however. Eliminating women from sacred study and ritual had grave implications for the tradition as a whole. More than women's participation and contributions were lost; the possibility for wholeness for all Jews was crippled. As you read on, you will see evidence that men too suffered tremendous impoverishment of soul as a result of their cutting off of what they could not understand.

Breaking the Contract

All of the foregoing history is the necessary context for Hannah Rachel's story. For Hannah Rachel to presume to step into the world of knowledge was a breach of her unspoken contract as a woman. Vital to understanding her plight was the community consensus that she threatened—the primacy of the written law and its guardians, the male rabbis.

Although her own father had defied the collective agreement, Hannah Rachel grew up studying such Talmudic passages as "Rabbi

Eliezer said: The one who teaches his daughters Torah is as if he taught her folly."[11] What did she make of this statement? What did she tell herself about the Jewish community who had taken Rabbi Eliezer's statement as an accepted fact? And what did she tell herself about her own passion for study being forbidden to other Jewish females?

Male scholars mistakenly believed that women would never read or study their words. Otherwise, why would they have continued to refer to women as if they were a separate and inferior class (as in the first passage in Exodus we spoke of earlier) rather than speaking directly to them? In the Talmud, the rabbis express their beliefs that women are intellectually incapable. They refer to women as light-minded, of unstable temperament,[12] and overly fond of talking.[13] Some of the rabbis equate women with the most frivolous and useless aspects of human existence. The most insulting of these references comes in Tractate Shabbos 152a: "Though a woman be a pot full of excrement, and her mouth full of blood, still men rush after her."[14]

Perhaps this last statement underscores a more general disdain for life in the physical body, which the rabbis assumed needed to be transcended. Women came to represent the state of being stuck in the mire of the material plane, as we shall see in the next chapter. But one must be curious: How was it that such foul creatures were worthy to carry men's children, but never the sacred Torah (which was literally prohibited from women's touch)? This is a paradox not easy to penetrate.

In a tragic underestimation of the power and ingenuity of their women, the rabbis failed to see that, in time, women's desire for wholeness would lead them to break down the barriers and attain the keys to the intellectual power in which the rabbis prided themselves. Could they not imagine that one day women themselves would discover these and other pejorative comments as they studied, and would finally demand respect and equality? This day has finally arrived.

Women, Slaves, and Children

One unfortunate phrase that runs through many of the Talmudic trac-tates like a chorus classifies women along with slaves and children. For a sampling: "Women, slaves and minors are exempt from saying the Shema."[15] "Women, children and slaves are not counted in the rit-ual of three inviting others to prayer."[16] "Women, slaves and minors shall not be made guardians."[17] And, "Women, slaves and minors are ineligible to testify as witnesses before a court of law."[18] This last, incredible as it may seem, does indeed mean that an eyewitness testimony by a woman does not officially count in a Jewish court of law.

What woman can read this refrain without feeling totally demeaned? Children grow up, after all, and slaves, according to ancient Jewish law, were freed every seventh year. But women, ah, women, they had a legacy all their own.

What exactly *was* the woman's legacy? After a broad review of rabbinic law, it becomes clear that women were mandated their sacred purpose by the men and the society of the day. Women were set apart in the domestic quarter, away from the sanctum of study and prayer, which was the exclusive domain of the men. Women were relegated to the bearing of children, care of the home, and providing for the needs of men, so that the latter could fulfill their sacred duty to bring holiness into the world.

To be fair, the Jewish division of labor between men and women was not at all remarkable; women's domestic role was common throughout the world from ancient times. In Judaism, however, unlike in other traditions, the role and responsibilities of women were understood to exclude her participation in the most sacred practices of her tradition. She was told that her domestic functions were her way of participating in the sacred because they sustained the life of the family.

Although it is certainly true that homemaking and child rearing are important ways to God, they are not necessarily the desired ways

to God for *all* women. However, there were no other means sanctioned
by the spiritual authorities by which Jewish women could attain holiness. The fact that Hannah Rachel had no taste for marriage was seen
as pathological by the rabbis, because, unlike their Christian counterparts, Jewish women did not have the choice of a scholarly or
monastic life. Still, as we shall see, some were exceedingly inventive.

"Free" from Obligations

Although Jewish men were obligated to fulfill as many of the 613
mitzvot, or sacred practices, as possible, women were legally exempt
from all positive time-bound commandments.[19] This means that
women did not have to bother with any commandment that specified a time frame. This included all of the ritual activities that exemplified Jewish spiritual practice, such as morning prayers, wearing the
phylacteries and the fringed prayer shawl, hearing the *shofar* blown
on Rosh Hashana, and the study of Torah.[20]

Women were released from all of these sacred obligations so that
they were free to occupy themselves with other things. There were a
few "other things" women had to do: gathering wood for the ovens
that cooked the food, drawing and carrying water to wash the clothes
and bathe the children and elderly, grinding grain for bread and weaving
flax for clothes—in short, everything that had to do with keeping body
and soul together, everything that took place on the material plane.

Rabbinic authorities take pains to point out that women's exemption from these positive activities was never meant as an official prohibition, only permission to desist in order to take care of domestic
duties. Hannah Rachel emphasized this point on numerous occasions
to her rabbinic colleagues: women were not *prohibited,* just *excused,*
from these rituals. Nevertheless, as her story makes abundantly clear,
women were not welcome in the men's world.

Women simply did not have the license to show up in the men's
territory, nor were they counted as members of a *minyan,* a holy quo-

rum of ten needed to pray together. How many times have women been forced to lower their voices when, overriding their exemption, they chose to fulfill their right to say the mourner's prayer, Kaddish, for a loved one? How many have been shooed out of temples and study halls with comments like "You don't have to be here. You're exempt! Now leave us men to our business!"

Most commentators, women and men alike, see women's exemption from performing a majority of laws as being supremely compassionate. It would have been unreasonable and even cruel, for example, to require the mother of small children to show up for prayers at dawn. The rabbis knew that a woman's duties were to the home and children and that it was these demands that came first, dictating her timetable.

Others take the stance that women's exemptions from Torah study and formal prayer are due to the fact that women are inherently elevated, "naturally spiritual," and do not need these formal daily rigors to uplift and purify them as do men. This backhanded compliment attempts to glorify women while keeping them functionally men's servants. Either way you cut it, there is a fundamental inequality in the practice of the Jewish faith. This deep-seated discrimination remains unresolved, leaving Jewish religious practice a less than desirable option for many women as well as for men who are sensitive to the issues of equality.

One fascinating medieval commentary on this subject serves to elucidate a rarely spoken view about men's interest in "freeing women" from time-bound positive commandments. It comes to us from the fourteenth-century Spanish commentator Rabbi Abudarham:

> The reason women are exempt from time-bound positive *mitzvoth* is that a woman is bound to her husband to fulfill his needs. Were she obligated in time-bound positive *mitzvoth*, it could happen that while she is performing a *mitzvah*, her husband would order her to do his commandment. If she would perform the commandment of the Creator and leave aside his commandment, woe

to her from her husband! If she does her husband's commandment and leaves aside the Creator's, woe to her from her Maker!
Therefore, the Creator has excepted her from his commandments so that she may have peace with her husband.[21]

According to Rabbi Abudarham, a woman is caught between the
commands of God and the demands of a husband. She is servant to
two masters. Perhaps not surprisingly, it is God who seemingly bows
out of the competition, leaving men as rulers of their wives and
women in a tenuous servitude, one that would have them serve the
secondary "master" rather than the highest object of their faith, the
Divine.

For women like Hannah Rachel, whose natural inclination was to
serve the Divine directly, not through service to a man but in a life of
solitude and scholarship, the rabbis' template of womanly service
was untenable. The combined duty of marriage, childbearing, and
homemaking was the one-item menu all women were given, like a
one-size-fits-all dress that you had to put on for the rest of your life,
no matter your personal shape or taste.

Bread, Blood, and Fire

Although women were exempt from many of the commandments
that defined the spiritual lives of men, over time they came to cher-
ish three special laws of their own. These were known as the laws of
ChaNaH, an acronym derived from three sacred activities: the making of *challah*, the Sabbath loaf, according to prescribed custom; *niddah*, keeping separate from one's husband during menstruation and
for seven days thereafter, culminating in a ritual bath; and *hadlakah*, the lighting of the Sabbath and holiday flames. We know little
about Jewish women's interior lives, but we do know from a wide
array of historical writings that these three rituals were the pillars of
feminine sacred service.

Many traditional Jewish women to this day will tell you that a woman's careful, loving performance of these three sacred commandments draws down divine power to safeguard her home and family. The three laws of *ChaNaH* were traditionally kept with such devotion that they became the hallmark of the female religious life, as evidenced in the special prayers they inspired.[22] In the light of women's pure-hearted devotion, it is particularly disconcerting to study the origins of these three cherished practices. They do not, as one would like to believe, stem from any precious feminine mandate, but from a rabbinic decree that declares, "For three sins women die in childbirth: For negligence with *challah*, with *niddah*, and with *hadlakah*."[23] What is the origin of this odious statement? Was it one man's ill-humored verdict or the improbable product of conclusive evidence? It is hard to imagine that such a fear-mongering statement could be divinely inspired.

The punitive, even hate-filled, nature of the decree is stressed in *Midrash Tanchuma*, a text from the turn of the first millennium that elaborates on the Mishnah, the earliest codification of the oral Torah:

> Why were women commanded these three commandments? The Holy One said, Adam was the beginning of My creation, and was commanded concerning the Tree of Knowledge.... "When the woman saw that the tree was good for eating and a delight to the eyes, and that the tree was desirable as a source of wisdom, she took of its fruit and ate. She also gave some to her husband...." Thus she caused his death and shed his blood.... So she sheds her blood and keeps her period of separation in order to atone for the blood of Adam that she shed. Whence comes the *mitzvah* of challah? She polluted the challah of the world.... Whence comes the kindling of the lights? She extinguished Adam's light....[24]

In an environment where such statements were taken at face value, and men who were immersed in such opinions came home daily to partake of the nourishment provided by the objects of their contempt, one wonders, What did women think of themselves? Did women believe these things or, worse, internalize them? We hope not. But then how did they succeed in staying immune to such mental violence, and how did they manage to nourish their own souls?

Given the deep division that kept women responsible for men's mortal needs but alien to their eternal pursuits; given the near absence of opportunity for female scholarship and given what they would find if and when they cracked the code and studied for themselves; given the extreme condescension and even loathing that threaded itself through the texts that men consumed for hours each day, one must ask, From what wells did women drink to quench the thirst of their spirits? Finally, how do we, today, deal with an injustice of such magnitude that it threatens our reliance on the ethical vision of Jewish law?

The Woman's Way

Denied access to the main artery of Judaism, women were left to find and cultivate a different kind of spirituality. If they were not allowed to connect to the great chain of tradition through their teachings, then the female ancestors were still there. Women could reach them with their ardent cries, could penetrate the heavens with their tears and pray for their presence in their lives.[25] If they did not understand the evolution or meaning of the laws they were asked to perform— why they salted their meat just so, why they were not allowed to sing out loud, or why their blood was anathema to men—they followed their husbands' instructions anyway and, ultimately, the rabbis' dictates.[26] But within the boundaries of the law, women had their own rituals: summoning the angels of the food to assist in its transformation before cooking; casting protective circles around birthing beds and sickbeds; communing with the ancestors for advice and guidance; and creating their own prayers and rituals for fertility and an abundance of milk.

Just as knowledge of the sacred word filled their men's lives, I propose that women were filled with a different kind of knowing. In the kitchens and in the woods, at the birthing stones and before the fire with babes suckling, in bathing the elders and helping them pass out of their tired bodies into eternal life, women's knowing was born. It is a knowing that comes from handling the physical world and sensing the divinity that infuses all aspects of it, even the basest parts. It is a knowing that arises from dreams that come to us at night and the signs and omens that wink at us from the natural world.

The woman's way is a communion with the Divine born not of letters but of the tangible wholeness of life. It is a knowing that has long been discounted and neglected by the history books, but it has never gone away. It is in the blood of women, in their cooking and artistry, and in the way they relate to others. One of the tasks of this book is to help us understand that this way of knowing and receiving the Divine exists and to recover it in our lives.

The woman's way of knowing and relating to the divine wholeness in all things was never sanctioned by the rabbis of the Talmud or the texts of the Middle Ages. Yet women persisted, throughout the centuries, in efforts to seek and find nourishment within their tradition. And, over the ages, a small number of women found their way inside the doors to the very heart of the tradition, barely slipping by the sentries of rabbinic authority and community approbation. There is a reason why women like Hannah Rachel persisted. She was connected to the living power of the mystical legacy within the tradition.

The Mystical Heart

From the days of the oral tradition, the rabbis evolved their concept of God's will into a system of laws and regulations known as *halakha* (literally, "the way to go"). Although *halakhic* practices derive from the revelation at Mount Sinai that occurred over three thousand years ago, the mystical approach dips into the fiery stream of divine consciousness that is ever present. Mysticism is a stratum of the Jewish tradition—or any tradition—that issues from an experience of divine immediacy, an ongoing revelation, eternity in every moment.

It is here at the mystical core of the religion that many find the intrinsic wholeness within Judaism. This core is known as Kabbalah, a word that means "the receiving," "receptivity," or "that which is received." Far from being one book or teaching, Kabbalah is more like an evolving movement. Some claim that its esoteric doctrines date back to Adam, some to Abraham. In any event, Kabbalah reached its literary zenith in the thirteenth century with the publication of its central treatise, the *Zohar*, translated as the "Book of Splendor." Gaining great popularity in the sixteenth century, it finally rooted itself strongly in the teachings and stories of the Hassidic masters of the modern age.

The very term *Kabbalah* is nebulous and often misunderstood. This is because its teachings were traditionally transmitted from teacher to student in oral form and by means of sacred texts. But, in whatever form, true Kabbalah always includes the personal experience of receiving wisdom from the divine realms.

It is in the rich mystical texts of Judaism (although they themselves are not immune to male distortion and misogyny) that one can discern truths of a universal nature and begin to see clear of the heavy historical baggage of gender imbalance otherwise so ubiquitous in Judaism. Far from the legal codes of *halakha* and the more mainstream understanding of Jewish cultural purpose, the mystical voice of the tradition speaks on a universal level of the reunification of masculine and feminine principles, the journey that all souls make toward their highest purpose, and the ways in which both men and women can learn to receive spiritual wisdom.

This is spiritual information for which many of us have yearned. Here at the mystical core of the tradition, women can find a foothold in what is profound, beautiful, and nourishing in the most ancient tradition of the West. Once one touches the mystical heart of the tradition—which is all about the wholeness born of masculine and feminine union and the divine wholeness mirrored within us—one can see through the disparaging attitudes of the rabbis and begin to peel off these nonessential layers to get to the treasures beneath.

The Feminine Presence

One central metaphor that runs throughout Jewish mysticism and is especially well developed in the *Zohar* is that of the feminine element of God, which complements and completes the masculine element, the "Holy One Blessed Be He." After all the centuries of false publicity, we are relieved to find that the self-contained, male-affected God that dominates Jewish scriptures also has a feminine essence, with whom He yearns to be joined. She is known as the Shechinah, a name that comes from the Hebrew root *sh'chn,* meaning "to dwell." In its actual usage, Shechinah means "She who dwells within," or the imminent aspect of God that can be apprehended through our senses. In the words of the great scholar of mysticism Gershom Scholem, the Shechinah is "one of the most important and lasting innovations of Kabbalism. The fact that it obtained recognition in spite of the obvious difficulty of reconciling it with the conception of the absolute unity of God, and that no other element of Kabbalism won such a degree of popular approval, is proof that it responded to a deep-seated religious need."[27]

Deep-seated religious need, indeed. The highly unnatural portrayal of God as a single *masculine* unity failed to go over well for generations of Jews throughout history who knew enough to question such a flawed cosmology. No wonder the Shechinah has been popular for centuries.

Never actually occurring in the Bible, the term *Shechinah* and the concept of God dwelling here and now, the very essence of the feminine presence, is hinted at when God tells Moses, "Let them [the people] make for Me a sanctuary so that I may dwell [*v'shacahanti*] within them."[28] Throughout Talmudic literature, the rabbis endowed the Shechinah with physical and emotional acuity. Feeling what people feel, aching as people ache, She is the aspect of the Divine that lives within the human experience, rather than being separate from it. Wherever deeds of kindness and hospitality are performed, wherever words of truth are spoken between people, and whenever lovers are in harmony with one another, there the Shechinah is found.[29]

Over the centuries, the Shechinah came to personify the feminine, loving aspect of God. From biblical times, when She was merely the dwelling place of the Divine on earth, the Shechinah evolved into a powerful and real experience of God's presence, a personal and loving face of God who is deeply devoted to people and to whom people, especially women, have been deeply devoted.

The Mystical Marriage

The God of Judaism was once pictured as a lone and lofty father figure; His feminine counterpart existed in His shadow, relegated to a lower plane. But the people's "deep-seated religious need" to know and experience the wholeness of Divinity, in both its masculine and feminine aspects, simply could not sustain the division between the lofty male God and the suffering feminine presence below. Despite the schism between genders on earth, in which males had dominant status and females were ancillary, the popular imagination kept pushing toward a greater unity in the divine realms.

This unending striving for unity is reflected in the sacred texts of the Middle Ages as the yearning of the Divine Beloveds.[30] In the mythological terms of the *Zohar*, as long as the Temple was standing, God the King sought out His lover and wife, the Shechinah (also called Matronit), daily; their joyous uniting was a regular ritual, a repeated *hieros gamos*, a sacred marriage of a cosmic order. When the Temple was destroyed and the People Israel were sent into exile, the Shechinah, the mystical embodiment of the sacred community, went with the people,[31] and the two cosmic lovers were separated. The exile of the Shechinah was a divine catastrophe, a disruption to the essence of wholeness and unity of God, bleeding away the vitality and power from life itself. However, there is a resolution, if only temporary. And it is here that we humans come into the story, as we shall soon see.

The metaphors of royal lovers are not meant to be taken literally. Rather, they point to archetypes, living patterns that are found in the human psyche and in life itself. Archetypes are universal; they live deep within us and surface in the form of individual dreams and collective myths. Archetypes are important because they point us to the potential wholeness within ourselves, as well as the wholeness in the world around and beyond us.

However it is viewed from culture to culture, the mythical union of masculine and feminine powers is a universal archetype that is seen as having cosmic significance and healing power for the world. The archetype of the mystical marriage is powerful and pervasive in Jewish mysticism. We have seen that God and the Shechinah are the supreme Divine Couple and the mystical, spiritual parents of the people Israel. Throughout Jewish mystical texts and later in Hassidic teachings, we find that the reunification of these Divine Lovers is the chief concern and goal.

Paradoxically, this union depends not upon the will of God but upon the will of humanity. One of the most remarkable innovations of Kabbalah is the idea that human beings can help to repair the split in the godhead. In fact, not only are humans able to do this, Kabbalah teaches that it is our supreme obligation to bring about the reunification of the masculine aspect of God, the King, and His lost lover, the Shechinah. In this way, Kabbalah is given to the path of wholeness.

Yichud: *Making Life Whole*

Human beings have an intrinsic need to reconcile the polarities of masculine and feminine. There are numerous ways of doing this, externally by means of partnership with a mate or in community and internally by means of reconciling our various intrapsychic natures. But if wholeness is our objective, then the work of unifying opposing forces must be done.

In the same way, the image of a masculine deity must have a complementary image of the feminine principle if the image of God is going to inspire and heal. Likewise, for the sacred marriage to take place within the human soul, both feminine and masculine energies must be present.

In the Jewish mystical tradition, bringing fractured parts together as a whole is symbolized in a ritual known as a *yichud*. The term *yichud* (pl. *yichudim*), or "unification," is a ritual of intention used in Kabbalistic and Hassidic circles to bring together the broken unity of God and the Shechinah.[32] Of course, by virtue of taking on the healing of forces on such a grand scale, one is also enacting a more personal rectification too.

In the classical tradition, a *yichud*, or mystical intention, would preface every sacred act of one's day. Before donning a prayer shawl in the morning, lighting the Sabbath candles on Friday evening, or immersing oneself in the ritual bath, one would say a special incantation such as the following ancient prayer: "(I do this act...) For the sake of the unification of the Holy One Blessed Be He and His Shechinah, in awe and in love, to unite the (holy letters) Yud and Heh of the Holy name into a complete unity...."[33]

Of course, merely reciting the words of an incantation does not in itself have the power to heal the godhead. The words serve to focus our attention so that we are completely present, intent that the action that follows be for the purpose of healing life's polarities. The prayer reminds us that we are part of a much greater whole and that everything we do has an effect on that whole. Hidden in the *yichud* prayer is the understanding that there is no limit to the healing power we have to affect change and repair that which has been broken.

The *yichud* prayer also underscores how central the healing of feminine and masculine principles is in Jewish mystical life. That the world is broken is understood. But it is not only we who are fragmented; God too is broken. For this reason, the act of reuniting the Sacred Lovers is a ubiquitous theme in Jewish mysticism. The practice of *yichud* is a way of focusing our intention to reconcile opposing forces in the world that keep us from living whole and balanced lives.

This is a dazzlingly simple, yet profound, concept. The implications of the *yichud* ritual are immensely empowering. Many of us are aware of the clarifying effect of setting an intention before beginning an important business meeting, say, or setting out on a journey. To use the same focused intent in a spiritual vein is a tremendously provocative thought. What if we were to set an intention to heal and unify our own selves? What would it mean to translate the mystical metaphor of unifying Sacred Lovers into terms that are more relevant to our own lives?

Bringing It Home

As we shall see, each woman in this book was a master of *yichud*, unification. Each woman accomplished this mystical marriage in her own domain, whether it was by receiving the Holy Spirit within herself, marrying vision to action, joining forces with her husband in a true and equal meeting, or, like Hannah Rachel, enacting the sacred mysteries of prayer and study to effect healing in others. Although our modern lives differ outwardly from the lives of the sages, we too are able to enact unifications that balance and heal ourselves and those around us. Every time we engage in a genuine meeting of opposites, we are performing this sacred marriage and literally sewing the world together.

When we walk in nature and deeply experience the physical world as a face of the Divine, we are making a *yichud* between form and essence. In the act of lovemaking, when we allow ourselves to be fully present and merge with our partner, we are unifying the seeming opposites of body and soul, self and other. A *yichud* is also performed any time we transcend the boundaries of our individual egos to make peace with another person, as when we let go of our anger and hurt and reach out in a gesture of forgiveness and reconciliation. At the very deepest level, though, enacting a *yichud* is a lifelong alchemical process undertaken in the laboratory of our lives. This is the mystical work of healing those parts of our own selves that have been torn or broken. For many women, this is the lifelong journey of becoming whole.

I would like to share with you a story of a woman whose healing journey exemplified such a *yichud* process. From a young age, Margot was a gifted pianist. The only daughter in a prominent Southern family, Margot was groomed by her parents for the life of a concert musician. As a girl, she practiced piano for a minimum of four hours a day, the music of Bach, Mendelssohn, Brahms, and Chopin pouring through her with ease. But, above all, Margot adored composing her own music. She would sit at the keyboard and grow very still, imagining a clear pool of water. Then she would let her fingers find their own way, rippling over the keys like water, the deepest passions of her soul unleashing themselves in breathtakingly beautiful compositions.

When I met Margot in her twenties, she had already been on tour for ten years and was showing signs of physical and psychological fragmentation. She had a serious sleeping disorder and was extremely thin. The pressures of her concert schedule were so rigorous that she often did not know where she was or even who she was. Her days were dominated by hours of practice, performance commitments, and Margot's own need to play impeccably. She pushed on, never missed an engagement, and won several competitions. But Margot's soul was tearing in the process.

At twenty-eight, Margot had a nervous breakdown. She was hospitalized for three months before she was moved to her mother's home. Her break with reality had been so severe that it took Margot many more months to rediscover her identity, and when she did, it was from the inside out, as if viewing the world from a small, dark, and very interior cave. From her internal refuge she slowly began to look out at the world again, to see, as if from a distance, her parents' need for her to be a celebrity, her teacher's urgency that she get back on tour, her own habit of regimenting her creativity to make it yield in just the right way. Struggling with all these forces, Margot did not sit down at a piano for over two years.

Margot's life had grown so desperately out of balance that the only way she could save herself was through the slow recovery of that part of her that had been exploited, one might say, her feminine side. The feminine soul within us connects us to our deepest feelings. It speaks to us through the spontaneous imagination, responding to a source of creativity that our conscious selves cannot prescribe or control.

Margot had a wise doctor who helped her mother create a healing environment free from all the subtle pressures that kept Margot spiraling downward. For a long time the doctor visited Margot daily, helping her to relate to her dreams, which gave her hints about what her soul needed to heal. Margot took long walks with her dogs, knitted, stared out the window of her room, was silent, did nothing, slept when sleep came, and read cheap novels when it would not.

Slowly Margot began to recover. She began to realize that her penchant for hard work and self-discipline had grown monstrously out of proportion, while her love of music, friends, and the simple pleasures of life had atrophied. It did not take long for Margot to see that she did not want to be a celebrity at all; she had simply adopted her parents' desire for her. She didn't even know if she wanted to play piano. But she wondered about her childhood pastime of sitting at the keyboard until something within her stirred and her hands delivered the music of her soul.

Margot's personal *yichud* took years. Approaching fifty now, she is a woman whose face is a map of her journey toward wholeness, her eyes and mouth lined from her struggles with success, failure, and self-compassion. Margot never returned to being a concert pianist. In fact, she changed careers entirely. But, perhaps most important, Margot was finally able to return to the piano to express herself. She now composes her own music for the joy of it, sitting quietly until the creative spirit takes over and flows through her spontaneously.

Margot has rediscovered her formidable sense of discipline, but now uses it in the correct measure, both in her outward life and to help her bring forth and translate her internal experience. Margot's music tells the story of her feminine soul, which has become an equal and honored partner in the marriage of her inner parts.

When we study and reclaim Jewish mystical principles for ourselves and then put them to use in our lives, it is clear how far-reaching and personally applicable they are. The principle of *yichud,* unifying opposites, is one example. It is a life principle particularly relevant for women, who are inherently given to the work of sewing, healing, mending, and reconciling.

Hannah Rachel of Ludomir was a unifier of opposites. She studied the mystical tradition, necessarily in seclusion, and put the principles to work in the form of understanding for herself and healing for others. Ultimately, she was able to shore herself up and access the inner strength she needed to stand in her power, publicly becoming the rebbe she had always been. Whether or not we relate to Hannah Rachel's particular story, we can drink from the immense wellspring of faith that fed her throughout her life. Through her faith, she was able to maintain an ongoing relationship with God and with the Jewish tradition, despite those who claimed to represent it.

We can follow Hannah Rachel's lead by working with the mystical principles that lie at the core of the venerable tradition that she so loved. Although the seeds she sowed in her life were watered with the tears of rejection and exclusion, we who come after her have both the good fortune and the moxie to harvest her crop in joy.

Women now have the freedom to study the sacred texts, and they are pouring en masse into educational programs at every level, becoming rabbis, theologians, and scholars in their own right. Although the nominal authority still rests in the hands of men who deem themselves to be the guardians of the official tradition, the next stages of Judaism will involve the reintegration of women and the feminine principles, the contemplative, the mystical, the interpersonal, and all that pertains to our earthly lives. This *yichud* on a grand scale remains to be fulfilled.

How will women's new awareness and involvement influence the evolution of this great religion? What will come as women graft their deep spiritual knowing with their new erudition? Perhaps it is too soon to tell, but I believe what will come forth is the wholeness for which individuals have been hungering, and the healing for which the Jewish people have been waiting.

CHAPTER 2

RECLAIMING EROS

Beruriah (Second Century)

In second-century Palestine there lived a female sage by the name of Beruriah, a brilliant woman of God who was supposedly defeated by her own feminine nature. Beruriah, whose name means "the clarity of God," has been associated throughout Jewish history with both spiritual wisdom and sexual disgrace. We will use her mysterious tragedy as a springboard from which to delve into the areas of female sexuality and the larger topic of eros within Judaism.

Beruriah was a brilliant Talmudic scholar, about whom her male compatriots spoke with awe for the breadth of her legal knowledge.[1] She had the keen ability to draw out of Jewish law its most penetrating meaning. Her place was in the House of Study, and her passion was to immerse herself in sacred texts, applying what she had learned to life in an unusual and wise manner.[2]

But the stories from the Talmud that surround Beruriah teach us about more than her sagacity. They teach us that for the rabbis of her day, the forces of godliness, family values, and purity were set squarely in opposition to the sexual, salacious, and forbidden parts of life. Beruriah managed to position herself in the middle of these, refusing to be subject to the men's dichotomies. This is precisely why the story of Beruriah is still important—her tragedy was the result of a split that still gapes painfully within us, begging to be healed. Almost two thousand years after her drama is purported to have taken place, Beruriah's tale still reverberates.

Because Beruriah, defying the dichotomy that the men had laid out for women, attempted to enact a *yichud,* or unification, of colossal proportion, she is a model for women today. She teaches us that the woman's way to God is to bring together all of our parts—the scholarly, the erotic, the light, and the dark—into a unified whole, no longer allowing ourselves to be compartmentalized. Beruriah's legacy is the knowledge that there are many paths to God, and all of our many natures are doorways to that path.

Although it was the country folk who told the tale of Hannah Rachel, Beruriah's story was handed down to us strictly by men, the rabbis of the Talmud and later generations of rabbinic commentators. In looking at her story, we need to remember that the facts as they have come down to us have been colored, as all stories are, by the view of their reporters. In this chapter we shall explore the rabbis' worldview, along with the assumptions built into it, with a mind to freeing the story—and Beruriah—from the tradition's narrow interpretations.

Who indeed was this enigmatic woman who mastered the Law, refusing the strictures set out for women of her day? More than any other nonbiblical woman referenced in the Talmud—and there are not many: Rachel, the self-sacrificing wife of Akiva; the nameless maidservant of Judah the Prince; and Yalta, the outspoken wife of Nahman—Beruriah stands out for the lucidity with which the rabbis speak of her. Other women are referenced merely to make the rabbis' points, but Beruriah *is* the point. They take pains to describe her as a three-dimensional character, and their ambivalence is clear: for her scholarship, acerbic wit, and femininity, Beruriah was both revered and feared.

The picture of Beruriah's life is derived from numerous tales and references scattered throughout rabbinic texts. These are found in various tractates of Talmud, one in Midrash, the nonlegal commentaries, and still another handed down by the eleventh-century French commentator Rashi (Rabbi Shlomo Yitzchaki, 1040–1105). About her life from a woman's perspective, we have almost no information. Her male chroniclers, for example, never mention Beruriah in the context of other women or uniquely feminine tasks. Nor do we have exact dates for or a chronology of her life events.

The Talmud first introduces us to Beruriah standing beside her father, Hanina ben Teradyon, as the Romans are torturing him to death. Hanina, a prominent rabbi of second-century Palestine, had defied the Roman ban against studying and teaching Torah in public places. He was arrested and condemned to public torture and death. The guards were ordered to place bundles of dry branches around Rabbi Hanina, who was wrapped in his own Torah scroll, and to set them on fire. To ensure and prolong his suffering, wool sponges soaked in water were continuously placed and replaced over his heart.

The Talmud reports, "His daughter exclaimed, 'O my Father, that I should see you in this state!' He replied, 'If it were I alone being burnt it would have been a thing hard to bear; but I am burning together with the Scroll of the Law. God, who has regard for the plight of the Torah, will also have regard for my plight.' "[3] Nothing more is said here about Beruriah, but we cannot but feel the enormity of her pain and helplessness as she stood watching her father burn to death. Hanina's students crowded around their teacher as well, and they asked him how he was. He declared that he saw the letters of the scorched Torah parchment rising up and soaring on high.

This mystical moment, filled with both cruelty and transcendence, surely captured every soul who witnessed it. Even the executioner, overcome by the holy rigor of his victim, yelled to Hanina, "Rabbi, if I raise the flames and take away the tufts of wool from your heart, will you assure me entrance into the World to Come?" Hanina assured him, and the executioner then removed the wet sponges and stoked the fire; Rabbi Hanina's soul quickly departed. The story ends by telling us that the executioner too jumped into the holy fire, whereupon a voice erupted from heaven announcing, "Both Hanina ben Teradyon and his executioner have been welcomed into the World to Come!"

As a consequence of Hanina's rebellion, the Romans also condemned his wife to death (although we hear nothing more of her) and his daughter to serve as a prostitute in a brothel.[4] Could this have been Beruriah? We know from the rabbis' accounts that she was married to Rabbi Meir, a Palestinian rabbi famed for his sacred scholarship and mystical powers. Here the Talmudic legends converge in such a way as to cause their authors trouble. After all, how can a prominent rabbi have a wife in a brothel without bringing upon himself the greatest humiliation? Indeed, reading a bit farther, the story shifts to accommodate this problem and we find that Beruriah suddenly has a sister.

According to the Talmud, Beruriah, ashamed to have her sister placed in a brothel, asks her husband for help. Rabbi Meir complies, taking a bag of gold coins and setting out to free his sister-in-law. Disguised as a soldier, he enters the brothel, finds the woman in question, and pretends to be a customer.

" 'Prepare yourself for me,' said Meir. The sister of Beruriah replied, 'The manner of women is upon me.' 'No matter, I am prepared to wait,' he said. 'But,' said she, 'there are here many, many prettier than I am.' "

Seeing that she is avoiding his advances and thus proving herself innocent, Meir goes to the warden of the brothel to demand her release. But, fearing the Roman authorities who ordered the woman there, the warden demurs. Bribing him with gold coins, Meir tells him that if he finds himself in trouble, he should simply pray. " 'Say, "O God of Meir, answer me!" and you will be saved.' "[5]

The story of a pious man mucking around in a house of sin may sound strange, yet it is not an unfamiliar theme among the stories of the Talmud.[6] The rabbis who find themselves there are usually wrestling with their physical drives and the *yetzer hara,* the instinct to fulfill personal passion. The point of these stories is usually made handily, that, even under such tempting conditions as being surrounded by a house full of wanton women, it is indeed possible for a man to overcome his physical urges and emerge unscathed.

The theme of a helpless virgin in a brothel, less familiar in a Jewish context, is, however, more common in the literature of the rabbis' day. It is hard to tell whether the story is factual or not. We do know that the rabbis of the Talmud are, at least, borrowing the theme to illustrate a lesson. We never hear of the "sister of Beruriah" again, and we realize that she has been a rabbinic device, a useful stand-in that splits off Beruriah's erotic side from her holy side. The "sister" plays the damsel in distress, saved from the hands of depravity by a brave rabbi in shining armor. As long as the feminine is hidden and helpless, the story seems to be saying, it is clear what to do with her: remove her from danger, save her from her inevitable doom, get her back into her rightful place.

But what of the "other sister," the one who is not in trouble, but who is outwardly capable, self-assured, and savvy? This theme is less clear, has few parallels in world literature, and certainly has no play in the ancient literature of the Jews. Beruriah does not seem to need any help. She is clear about her purpose and intention and finds them in the House of Study. She wants only to study and apply what she has learned.

Beruriah's husband, who so valiantly braved the "dark side" to champion his innocent sister-in-law, was questioned by the rabbis for so readily entering into the forbidden territory of a brothel. He was also pursued by the Roman authorities for his insurrection; his likeness was posted on the gates of Jerusalem with a proclamation saying that anyone seeing a man resembling it should apprehend him at once. One day, a Roman guard recognized Meir and ran after him. The Talmud reports,

Rabbi Meir ran away and entered a harlot's house. Others say he happened just then to see food cooked by heathens and he dipped in one finger and then sucked the other. Others again say that Elijah the Prophet appeared to them as a harlot who embraced him. God forbid, said they, were this Rabbi Meir, he would not have acted thus! He then arose and ran away and came to Babylon.[7]

We are not told why Meir had to flee the country. For now, the reader is satisfied that Beruriah's husband has escaped to safety. One figures that she is with him. But that is sadly not the end of the story, or even the middle of it. The only thing that is clear for now is that the theme of sexuality seems to permeate the stories of Beruriah and her family like a stain. With her "sister's" ill repute and her husband popping in and out of brothels and having the kiss of a sacred harlot on his lips, one gets the distinct feeling that the authors of her stories are working out their own sexual conflicts here.

What indeed was the nature of Beruriah's sexual life? We know only that, along with being a scholar, she was the wife of Rabbi Meir and the mother of two sons. But you can hardly be a wife and mother without being sexual and, to some degree, aware of the domestic world. That meant Beruriah was indeed a woman! And didn't women's lives revolve around physical objects and tasks, the plucking of birds, the kneading of dough, and the wiping of messy floors and baby bottoms?

To the rabbis of the Talmud, who in the wake of the loss of the Temple and its priests were now the elite class, women were associated with blood and bodily secretions, sexual smells, and the impurity of all of those earthly things. How could it be then that this sexual woman, Beruriah, was also a scholar, one who had studied and committed vast scrolls to memory?

Hadn't the rabbis wanted to ban women from the study of Torah on the grounds that it would foster in them "lasciviousness"?[8] In fact, it had even been whispered that Beruriah's father, Hanina, had been tortured to death as a punishment for having allowed his daughter to study like a man.

Yet Beruriah sallied between the two worlds of men and women without apology. Even in the domestic realm, Beruriah proved to be almost eerily aware of a spiritual life. The following poignant story about Beruriah's motherhood is a classic in Jewish literature. Although it never mentions Beruriah by name, it is clearly her, in all of her shining wisdom.

Every Sabbath afternoon, Rabbi Meir would go off to teach in the House of Study. One Sabbath it happened that both of his sons died suddenly. Beruriah placed them on their beds and covered them up, then returned to greet her husband when he returned home. When he asked for their sons, Beruriah demurred, not wishing to disturb her husband's Sabbath peace.

"They have gone off and will return soon enough," she replied. Then she handed Meir the wine goblet and lit the candle for the Havdalah ceremony, which concludes the Sabbath day. Again, Meir asked for their sons.

"Don't worry," Beruriah assured him. "I am certain they are safe." Then she continued.

"Meir, I have a question for you."

"Ask."

"Some time ago, a man came and left an object with me for safekeeping. Now he wants it back. Should we return it to him or not?"

"What a question! You surprise me, Beruriah. You well know the law: anyone who keeps a pledge must return it to its rightful owner when he calls for it."

Then Beruriah took Meir gently by the hand and led him to the room where the boys' lifeless bodies lay upon their beds. When her husband began to lament their loss, Beruriah reminded him, "Did you not say to me that we must return the pledge to its rightful owner?"

Meir responded by chanting, "The Lord has given, the Lord has taken away. Blessed be the name of the Lord."[9]

In this story, like many others about her, Beruriah's virtue and talent lie in her ability to apply Jewish law so sensitively that it preserves rather than diminishes the dignity of the people around her, in this case, her husband. By reframing the death of their sons in the legal metaphor of an owner coming to reclaim his possessions, Beruriah not only guards the peace of the Sabbath from being marred, but also helps her husband to remember his faith in God. Although some have criticized Beruriah for being inhumanly stoic in this legend, it demonstrates once again how her faith in God's providence infused every occasion.

Living in Two Worlds

For the rabbis of second-century Palestine, life was a struggle between the powerful forces of the erotic world and the ideals of spiritual purity, intellectual discipline, and the rewards of a world beyond. The women's world was moist and sensual and smelling of the earth's richness, and the men's world was dry and crisp, soaring ever higher through logic and complexity. Beruriah refused to limit herself to either camp and defied the boundaries of the neat category that men had laid out for her and her gender.

How did Beruriah manage to live in two worlds, one foul and full of the physical and the other sublime in spirit? For Beruriah, life depended upon a safe passage between these two worlds. As daughter, wife, mother, and outspoken scholar, she melded typically masculine and feminine polarities in one person. However, because the distance between the physical and the spiritual planes was a dangerous abyss for the rabbis of her day, Beruriah became a target of their confusion, fear, and ultimately their hatred. Her demise, if we are to believe the legend handed down by Rashi, was as sordid as it was tragic.

Once Beruriah mocked the rabbinic dictum "Women are flighty" (also translatable as "Women are easily seduced"). Her husband, deeply troubled by such insurgence on the part of a woman, set out to put her in her place, saying, "By your life! You will end up proving the rabbis' words to be true."

The medieval commentator Rashi tells us that Meir then set his wife up by having one of his students attempt to sexually seduce her. If Beruriah fell for the seduction, then Meir had the proof he needed that the rabbinic dictum was correct. For many days Meir's student courted Beruriah. Finally she gave in to him. We do not know exactly what that means or how far the seduction went. But when Beruriah realized she had been had, she lost all hope in life and committed suicide by strangling herself. This is the reason Rabbi Meir fled to Babylon in disgrace.[10]

Many women feel shock and outrage upon hearing this story. Perhaps this is because it is so devoid of humanity, a quality that abounded in Beruriah herself. Whether this medieval story is factual is not known. Sophisticated scholars have disputed its verity for generations, claiming that such behaviors were far from thinkable in the world of the great Torah scholars. Yet the story has nevertheless survived, and with a vigor that few other Talmudic stories have. Like a despised tabloid, it seems to whisper to us from the shadowy regions of our most revered sanctum, telling us what we most dread, that men's fear of women is so compelling and so unconscious that it is allowed to grow into a hatred that supplants our most cherished values.

The ugliness of the story, then, is not in its farce, but in the deeper truth that it belies, not in its contemptuous moralizing, but in the show of values that finally wins out among its authors. We are left with two unfortunate messages: One, that tragedy is what happens to a woman who dares embark on the path of learning reserved for men. And two, perhaps even more distressing, that the values espoused by the Torah—the sanctity of the marriage covenant, the pledge of selfless service by its students—may be abandoned in order to vindicate the power and honor of its "rightful" scholars.[11]

Men's warning is clear: women such as Beruriah—smart, forthright, and able to best a man at his own game—come to no good. Women, take heed! Know your own nature and keep to your own functions. It is men and men alone whose domain it is to be holy, who are meant to ascend to God through their scholarship. Women, whose sexuality is powerful and ubiquitous, must be bridled and kept separate, their chastity the sole measure of their worth.

In this sense, whether or not Beruriah literally succumbed to the seduction ploy does not matter. The fact that this legend was ever conceived of and the fact that it has endured in the tradition of a people are tragedy enough. Its cautionary message is clear: it is dangerous for women to study Torah. Beruriah and the seemingly unfeminine values she stood for—fearlessness, unapologetic brilliance, unswerving loyalty to one's goals—were indeed felled by those who insisted that the world of the sacred belongs solely to men.

What became of Beruriah? Did she truly die at her own hand? Was she finally strangled by her own truth, a truth that could find no outward expression or context in a world damaged by dichotomies? How else could a woman already so devastated by the loss of her immediate family—father, mother, sons—have born this final blow of betrayal by her husband? It is difficult to imagine the loneliness of a life that could hardly have afforded her many women friends or much female support. Her world was the world of the House of Study and her peers were the elite class of male scholars to whom she was a suspicious, albeit revered, "other." Beruriah must have hungered for an authentic friend, one who could see beyond her female exterior to her complex essence, a friend who could meet her at her own level and behold her as a soul who loved the discourse of truth and wished only to soar beyond the narrow dualities that her era dictated. In the end, no matter how high we soar intellectually, we each must return to reckon with the depths of our own human loneliness.

Whether or not Beruriah took the bait that her husband set out for her is not clear. Nor do we know why this man who was so willing to rescue the virgin in the brothel condemned his wife to the fate from which he saved her sister. What we do know is that when

Beruriah learned of her husband's treachery, her world collapsed. She no longer had a loyal partner as a husband, and her colleagues from the House of Study had also shown themselves as rogues. The holy House of Study had turned out to be a house of sin, and the small and untenable piece of ground that Beruriah had carved out for herself finally slid from beneath her feet. Beruriah no longer had a place in the world from which to continue.

We leave our legend with no remedy. The rabbi in shining armor who braved the dark den of immorality to free the lost damsel is, in the end, himself lost, and to a far more pernicious darkness. Sadly, there is no one virtuous enough in the story to dash back in and rescue Beruriah, to understand, console, and make meaning of her husband's ruse. That job falls to us.

Would that Beruriah had fled to Babylon with her beloved, a husband who believed in her and unswervingly defended his wife's dignity. Would that Meir, refusing to hear his colleagues' jealous rumblings about the woman who muddied their stereotypes and dared to transcend them, had sacrificed his own honor and spirited her away to freedom. Would that Beruriah could have fled into a gentler circle of souls, one that had no need to split the feminine side of life off from the world of ideas, and one that held her sexuality to be not a foul danger, but a fountain that feeds and fortifies one's most sublime humanity. The latter is something that we aspire toward and must create for ourselves. It is definitely not out of reach.

Beruriah's Paradox

In Chapter 1 we discussed the practice of *yichud* to heal the polarities in life. The idea of joining or marrying opposites is a central theme in Jewish mysticism and essential to the ancient tradition. Remember that, from the mystic's vantage point, this work is a human being's supreme task and privilege. Mythically speaking, this was done through the intention to join the Holy One, the Divine

Masculine, whose abode was in the heavenly realm, to the Shechinah, the Divine Feminine, whose home was in the earth plane and in people.

Although we may not subscribe to the *Zohar*'s picture of celestial King and earthly Queen, we have seen how the union of opposites depicted in this imagery is nevertheless at play in each one of us in a psychological sense. The struggle that Beruriah carried out in her own life belongs to us as well: the effort to marry within ourselves the two sides that had been split asunder, the spiritual from the material.

Despite her colleagues' confusion about these warring elements within the human psyche, the deepest Jewish wisdom warns us to guard against simpleminded dichotomies that would have us divide life into categories of pure and impure, good and bad, high and low. This is the kind of thinking that professes easy ways to manage the world but butchers all sense of subtlety, the hallmark of true wisdom.

Mysticism, in whatever form it comes, is a subtle art, given to nuance and paradox. It arises from an ability to hold seeming opposites or contradictions in hand and treat them respectfully as equals. The mystic, for this reason, is one who is given to paradoxical thinking, the ability to think beyond (*para*) the commonly held opinion (*doxa*).

Beruriah was the ultimate paradoxical thinker, and one whose world could not tolerate the level of contradiction she imposed. In this sense, she was far ahead of her time. She may have been groomed by men to be a rationalist, but by virtue of Beruriah's being a woman, her life leapt ahead of her training to the mystic's conclusion: that both the linear/rational and the circular/erotic approaches are necessary to live a whole life.

Intrinsic to the mystical path within Judaism too is the idea that the masculine and the feminine not only complement but need one another to be themselves, that heaven requires earth and earth heaven, that polarities can and must be united. Opposites, whether we are talking about them in mythic terms or in relation to our own personalities and perceptions of reality, require one another in order to fulfill their natures and destinies. Just as one cannot draw just one side of the Chinese yin-yang symbol without the other and one cannot really know light without having known darkness, so the intrinsic nature of the masculine cannot be whole without the feminine, and vice versa.

The Seal of Solomon

The idea that opposites require one another for wholeness lies at the very heart of the ancient Hebrew tradition. Its central symbol, the Seal of Solomon, also called the Star of David, is found on the flag of the State of Israel and all manner of Jewish insignia. But few realize that this simple six-sided star is a profound mystical symbol.

The Seal of Solomon consists of two interpenetrating triangles of equal size, one planted on earth and pointing upward toward heaven, the other suspended from heaven and pointing downward toward earth. It is interesting to note that in the ancient Sanskrit chakra system, the six-sided star symbolizes the heart center. The heart is seen as a kind of alchemical vessel in which the two forces of high and low, spirit and earth, come together and act upon one another, bringing about a dynamic and balanced personality.

In the Jewish tradition too, before the heaven-focused era of the rabbis, the ancients knew that both heavenward and earthward orientations were necessary for wholeness. They realized that neither approach alone was sufficient; rather, both are mutually dependent and have an affinity for one another.

However, as we have seen in the time of Beruriah, the rabbis did not honor this approach, and their imbalanced view had an enormous influence on the evolution of the Jewish tradition. They emphasized looking upward to the unbounded heavens for inspiration, for a sense of cosmic mystery and the sublime.[12] Their ascendant and transcendent perspective, symbolized in the upward-pointing triangle, is broad and visionary, given to clear, logical thinking and mental acuity. Command of the sacred word, the Law, and the ethical codes is represented by this aspect of the star. The aspect of God found here, traditionally pictured as a heavenly father, king, and judge, was wise and beneficent, cognizant of all that transpires from above and prepared to mete out justice on earth below.

Judaism is filled with references to a heavenward orientation and numerous allusions to a God that lives above and beyond it all. But what about the downward triangle, the earthly orientation, the force that pulls us to the sensual, embodied life? Far less emphasized in official Judaism, this God is found in the wisdom of the earth, the power of the present moment, the life force that fills our bodies when we breathe in the fragrant earthly air. It is the downward triangle that points to the mystery and ecstasy of our sexuality and the miracle that we can create new life through our physical bodies. It is the feminine principle that is unafraid to proclaim the holiness of the earth itself, and that encourages us to relish our bodies and find sanctity in what our senses would have us enjoy.

Nothing Lost

How is it that women allowed their vantage point to be omitted from the oral and written tradition to the point of no mention? One wonders in what ways women were in touch with their own unique wisdom after hundreds of years of exclusion from the central teachings, liturgy, and practices of Judaism. Until very recently, for example, no official Jewish liturgy had mentioned that there even *were* female ancestors, never mind any feminine aspect of God. Even today many synagogues are still in an uproar over the notion of changing the liturgy as it has stood for "all time."

During the many centuries when women were not allowed to participate in intellectual pursuits, they necessarily channeled their feminine gifts into stories, parables, songs, and remedies. Sadly, because women's wisdom was largely kept among the women and was rarely written down, and because male historians over the centuries did not concern themselves with these facets of Jewish life, a large body of women's contributions was lost.

But women are women and, as Carl Jung has told us, nothing in the psyche is ever lost.[13] The cumulative power and wisdom of centuries of women's thinking and feeling about the mystery of life could not have simply disappeared. Any psychologically aware person can tell you that a vital thing suppressed in one quarter will find its way to the surface with a vengeance in the next. And, as we shall see, the feminine power in Judaism has been doing just that.

The ancients well knew that to be whole we must become like the balanced six-sided star. They knew that any image or belief that does not embrace both male and female, both high and low, both earth and heaven is not a true image.[14] Wholeness comes from the mystical work of holding both orientations in tension and balance.

What Lies Below

There is a fine old story about a student who came to a rabbi and said, "In the olden days there were men who saw the face of God. Why don't they anymore?"

The rabbi replied, "Because nowadays no one can stoop so low."[15]

The rabbi knew that much wisdom lies beneath us, just under our feet, and that it requires great humility and a change in perspective to glean it. Whatever happened to our ability to listen down low? How can we rediscover the face of God that lives below?

As we have seen from Beruriah's story, the Hebrew tradition, too, developed in such a way that it became unquestionably one of ascendance and transcendence, no longer the balanced model represented by the beautiful Star of David. What happened to the earthly focus of the downward triangle in Judaism? When and why did the power and influence of the feminine principle decline? To understand these questions, we must look back to the cultures and myths that foreshadowed the Hebrew tradition to discover the matrix in which it originated.

An Era of Balance

The dawning of the Hebrew tribe took place in a world immersed in the worship of fertility and the power of the feminine to bring forth life. At the time of transition from a hunter-gatherer society to a more stationery, agricultural one, people were extremely aware that their very lives were dependent on the mercy and generosity of the land upon which they lived. Mother Earth in all her potential fullness was worshiped in the form of the Great Goddess in numerous depictions. Religious rites revolved around the goddess and her male consort, who together were understood to fertilize the fields, the sheepfolds, and the marriage bed.

The first patriarchs of the Hebrew tribes came onto the scene somewhere between 1900 B.C.E. and the beginning of the Iron Age, around 1250 B.C.E.[16] Many scholars see the strong monotheistic ethos of the new religion as a reaction to the ancient Near Eastern matriarchal worldview, which had by then begun to decay.

The advent of the Iron Age was the point of one of the most radical changes in orientation known to religious history, some say the history of consciousness. It was at this point that the feminine, image-based cultures and religions of the ancient Near East came under the heel of a sweeping new vision, that of a male-dominated monotheism, in which the written word and a more linear approach to life prevailed.[17] The shift from a worldview in which the body of the Mother Goddess gave forth all parts of creation to one in which a male deity ruled and an ethic of "power over" became the norm took hundreds of years, roughly between 1900 and 1250 B.C.E. This is precisely the period during which the new Israelite tribe rose to power in this area of the world.

As always, one can look to the myths of a time period to discover the ways in which the people of that era experienced the universe.

During this particular period, one can see a drastic change in the stories and mythology of the ancient Near East. These stories clearly tell of a revolution that was taking place in the way people were viewing life. In the earlier mythology of the Fertile Crescent region, the powerful creator goddess always had a male lover who provided seed, pleasure, and partnership. Suddenly, a change occurs, not in one area or tradition, but throughout the ancient Near East. We begin to find the goddess yielding to her male consort, ultimately evidence of a new dynamic. The male god begins to break away, struggles for autonomy, and is finally granted sovereignty by the goddess.[18]

The Defeat of the Feminine

The transition from the earlier feminine worldview to the new masculine paradigm can be clearly seen in the Babylonian creation story called the *Enuma Elish*. This epic is important because it bears the mythological roots of all three patriarchal religions, Judaism, Christianity, and Islam. It is here that we can graphically see the shift in worldview, from one in which the Mother Goddess is the source and fabric of all life to one in which the Father God takes over, establishing a position of supremacy and ultimately becoming the sole ruler of the universe.

In this Babylonian story, Tiamat, the ancient Mother of the Universe, had long before generated creation as part of herself. The heavens and the earth and all that lived therein were divine, not because she made them, but because she *was* them and they were her, her very body. At the dawning of the Iron Age, all of this changed. Tiamat was overtaken by her great-great-great-grandson Marduk, who chopped her into two halves and violently took over her rule, remaking creation all over again.

The goddess who had birthed heaven and earth from the very substance of her own body is now replaced by an arrogant man-child who refashions the world by manipulating her slain body as if it were so much cosmic Play-Doh. Once the Goddess issued life, and her divinity was imminent in that life. But now the God *makes* his creation by fashioning life out of a substance different from himself, inferior to divinity and, so, dispensable.

In this way, a fundamental dualism was first born between the male Creator and his world. One might even say that this was the beginning of the dichotomy between spirit and matter. Until now, nature was spiritual and spirit was natural because the Divine was inherent and imminent within creation. With the myth of the male god, all of this was changed. The Divine now transcended creation; that is, spirit was no longer inherent in nature, but lived outside or beyond it. Spirit was now the creator and nature was the created. Under the new male god, the stars and sun came under the rule of one Lord who had refashioned all of creation from the dismembered body of the Great Mother. In time, She became the representation of destruction in the form of the evil serpent, while Marduk came to represent the power of creation and order. The impact of this new myth was formidable: the defeat of the feminine sensibility marked the end of a culture and hailed a new worldview.

This tale must have met some profound collective need, because it spread in popularity across the entire ancient Near East, altering the gentler creation myths of the region and the societies that embraced them. In its wake, a new ethic took root, one that would reign for thousands of years. It was an ethic of war, expansion of territories, and the aggressive heroics of warriors, one in which the violation of life seemed justified.

A Solo Act

It was within the foregoing broad matrix that the new culture of the Hebrew tribes was fostered. All of the various male gods of previous cultures—Ptah, El, Dummuzi, Marduk—seem to collapse into the one great Father God of the Hebrews, YHVH, who arrives on the world stage as a solo act. Having cast away any vestiges of feminine influence in the form of a mother goddess, divine partner, or the web of creation, the Torah's creation story, in unprecedented fashion, also makes no mention of a divine lineage or family. There is now only one God who stands alone and independent of any other, transcending nature and creation.

As if the idea of a feminine deity had never existed, the new all-encompassing God creates with His words. "Let there be light!" says He, and there is light. There is little surprise that even thousands of years later, the dominant ethos in the Jewish culture (and perhaps in the Western world that emerged from its overarching mythology) is that of the Word, written, studied, and spoken.

In the oldest stories of the Hebrew scriptures, God is unquestionably transcendent, that is, beyond nature, rather than one with it. The creation of life was the result of a divine act that brought order out of chaos. And what became of the earlier power of the feminine? As in the Babylonian culture, which preceded the Hebrew, it came to be associated with darkness, the moon and earth, chaos, and nature devoid of spirit.

The feminine sensibility is almost invisible in the Jewish Torah, unless you are trained to look for it. In Genesis, it appears in the form of the dark void. Elohim brings forth creation out of a deep abyss of waters called in Hebrew, *Tehom*,[19] usually translated "the Deep." Clearly, *Tiamat* and *Tehom* arise from the same root word. Another term from the same root, which tells us that the suppressed feminine is just below the surface of the Hebrew creation story, is the term *Tohu vaVohu*,[20] the "formless void," or nasty chaos, out of which the earth was called into order by Elohim.

Here is the foundation of that familiar duality that has entrenched itself in the psyche of the West. The feminine takes her assigned place in the dark void, to live there as an underground power for roughly three thousand years. The masculine principle, in contrast, basks in the light of the sun and heaven; it comes to represent clarity, omniscience, and spirit devoid of nature. Forgotten for now is the fact of their innate need for one another, that a whole life can come forth only through both of these mutually dependent halves.

The repercussions of this ancient dichotomy of values are, of course, phenomenal. Only in the past century are we beginning to accurately acknowledge and measure them. Perhaps the greatest tragedy of this mythic dichotomy is the overly literal assignation of these values to men and women. Instead of being seen as principles or energies that live together within each of us, they were taken as wholesale categories in which to lump each half of humankind— women in the camp of darkness and men in the camp of light.

Taking all of this into account, it comes as no surprise that there is no term for "Goddess" in the Hebrew language, nor any direct reference to the feminine face of God in the Hebrew scriptures (remember from Chapter 1 that such terms as "Shechinah" and "Matronit" were postbiblical appellations, originating in the Talmud and later). Yet, to trained readers, the Divine Feminine litters the landscape of the Torah and is far from gone, externally or in the psyche of the people.

Taking a less prominent role in the cosmic pantheons of the tribes, the feminine principle still showed up in the popular religion for several hundred years. Her name was Asherah, Astarte, or Anat. She is mentioned in the Five Books of Moses only as the deity of the Canaanite people, who depicted her in small wooden forms and planted her at their sacred sites in oak groves, temples, high places, and shrines throughout the land. She is most often called Asherah, and it was her form that the Israelites were charged repeatedly throughout Deuteronomy to take down, destroy, and eradicate upon entering the holy land.

As we have said, when the Israelites entered their newly inherited land, they did not, as Jewish legends often picture it, find the land populated with primitive, godless inhabitants. Instead, they came upon a well-developed religious culture, one that would in time be absorbed into their own. Although their judges, kings, and prophets continued the campaign to eliminate the Canaanite rites for hundreds of years, archeological evidence shows that they never fully succeeded. In numerous passages the Bible itself tells us that the ancient Hebrews worshiped the Goddess down to the days of the Babylonian exile in 586 B.C.E. And, although Jeremiah and other prophets railed against the people's unending loyalty to the Queen of Heaven, the First Temple in Jerusalem actually hosted a statue of Asherah.[21]

From Joshua to Josiah, the prophets and rulers chastised the Israelites for their tenacious loyalty to the neighboring gods and goddesses and their worship in the shrines, temples, and oak groves. For the better part of a millennium, from their penetration into Canaan until their return from the Babylonian exile around 500 B.C.E., the feminine principle was pictured in the Hebrew tradition as the devious serpent or snake trying to usurp man's best intentions to aspire to God and godliness. Implicit was men's fear of women's mysterious powers as life-givers, those connected to the earth's cycles of blood, sexuality, and fertility. The biblical myth of the snake that tempts Eve in the Garden of Eden is an important example because it stands at the very beginning of the Hebraic tradition and, as such, has immense psychological power.

The Power of the Snake

In the myth of the Garden of Eden, the snake, often associated with the deceitful nature of human sexuality, may be seen in two ways. It can be viewed as a symbol of our basest instincts, which continuously tempt us to take, to have, and to keep for ourselves, urging us to build ourselves up immodestly and ultimately to steal into the upper realms and "be like God." If we listen, then we are, as Jewish and Christian preachers have railed at us for centuries, truly, suckers, sinners, and spiritual fools who need continual whacks to keep us humble.

Other viewpoints, as ancient as the Gnostic sects and as modern as Carl Jung and the modern depth psychologists, see the snake not as evil, but as the principle of knowledge or emerging consciousness.

The snake comes not to get us into trouble but to goad us to know more, to uncover our eyes, and, through knowing, to become more than we have been. In this alternate sense, the snake is the part of ourselves that seeks self-realization.[22] The snake, which continually sheds its own skin, is an apt symbol for metamorphosis and that which constantly urges us to outgrow ourselves, to shed old points of view, reformulate our beliefs, and revitalize ourselves. In this approach, the story of temptation at the base of the Tree of the Knowledge of Good and Evil signifies an initiation in which we are tempted by our inborn desire to raise our consciousness, to transform ourselves, and, like the snake, to shed our skin and partake of higher consciousness.

As a culture, though, we have approached the snake not as a messenger of growth, but rather as a sort of demon who sets before us the impossible sexual temptation and then watches us struggle and succumb to it—not unlike what Meir did to Beruriah! In order to avoid what we assume will be an inevitable fall, our tradition has chosen to remove the snakelike peril as much as possible; we separate ourselves from temptation and make sexuality a taboo, placing it at the bottom of the ladder of importance, for how could our physical nature lead us to heaven? Centuries of having our fears stoked has led us to view our sexuality as the most insidious and cunning of forces, bent upon bringing us down and mastering us. So we choose to preempt it, to squash the tempter before it can squash us.[23]

Although the Judeo-Christian culture has relegated the feminine principle to the realm of the serpent, it is clear that the deep feminine principle, albeit never completely lost, was hidden from our sight. From the first injunctions to destroy her form upon entry to the Promised Land, she has been targeted in the form of all nonrational and intuitive practices and wisdom.

Nevertheless, there resides in the human psyche a relentless striving for wholeness that will simply not brook a one-sided approach. The need for a healthy relationship between masculine and feminine energies is archetypal, a pattern found in all peoples and in all aspects of creation. This need insists upon finding God, not only as pure spirit, but also in our connection to the earthy, sensual here-and-now aspects of our lives, and it is as insistent now as it was in the days of the prophets.

Eros: The Flame of Desire

How do we begin to heal the ancient split between the so-called higher and lower elements of life? How do we reclaim our sexual power, which is so central to our feminine wisdom? Perhaps the answers to these questions are the keys that will unlock Beruriah from history's prison, restoring her dignity and bringing us one step closer to healing our torn tradition.

Women know innately how powerful sexuality is. Far from belonging exclusively to the genital region of the body, our sexual energy is a powerful force that nourishes everything we touch in life, from our relationships with our lovers to the food we cook, the gardens we plant, and the way we do our work in the world. And, although intimacy and interconnection are paramount for a sexually vital person, in this broader understanding our sexuality does not need a man or any partner to fulfill it, because it is our own; it influences every aspect of our lives and is the very source of our sensuality and aliveness.

One word that describes a life fueled by earthly sensuality is *eros*. You may remember the story of Eros from Greek mythology; he was the son of Aphrodite, the goddess of love and beauty. But you don't need to believe in gods and goddesses to understand that eros is a quality of human relatedness that lives within us all. To awaken the eros within ourselves is to live alert to oneself and to relate to those around us with a willingness to see and be seen, touch and be touched.

Living with the quality of eros does not mean to live promiscuously or with the goal of gratifying one's own pleasure, but to live connected to one's fire. And lest we make the mistake of thinking that eros resides strictly in the physical world between sensual people, let's remember that eros is the flame of desire that warms *everything* we do in our lives. Without it, every relationship and every undertaking is dull and arid. So too must our deepest spiritual longings to connect with something greater than ourselves be fueled by our eros; without it, they are nothing but the dry tinder of mental meanderings.

The discounting of the feminine principle, and with it the rounder side of life, has harmed not only women but men, cutting all of us off from our wholeness, our life force, and our earthly wisdom. It is easy to imagine Beruriah, with her pithy speech, audaciousness, and ability to cross boundaries, as a woman of eros. Sadly, Beruriah lived at a time when these full-bodied qualities were unseemly for a woman. For this reason, the stories split Beruriah and her eros into two women, one in the House of Study and one in the House of Ill Repute, the latter requiring a savior. Still, Beruriah's story was at least recounted by the rabbis, and for this we are grateful. One shudders to think how many hundreds of dynamic, outspoken women who lived after Beruriah were censured, discounted, or thoroughly ignored by the leaders of their communities.

Hinting at Wholeness

The rabbis of first- and second-century Palestine who created and acted in the drama of Beruriah did not live in a vacuum; they were greatly influenced by the philosophies of the Greco-Roman culture in which they lived. They too were aware of the formidable power of sexuality and that the ancient Jewish tradition did not wish to submerge this powerful human force, frowning upon celibacy and the single lifestyle. Ultimately, they evolved a philosophy not dissimilar to that of the early Greek Stoics and Christian fathers: sex was not a sin in itself if it was seen as a holy partnership between man, woman, and God for the purpose of procreation.

Of all the prevalent philosophies of their day, of which there were many, perhaps the rabbis' own biblical tradition created the most confusion for them. Their own tradition was filled with an ambivalence all its own. The wisdom of the ancient Hebrews was in many ways simpler and less neurotic than that of the Judaism of Beruriah's day, which was so deeply influenced by the dualism that came with the Greek philosophies. Although the Hebrew God was depicted as masculine, with respect to human instincts He was not at all puritanical. This was a God of fertility who had commanded humans to be fruitful and to multiply and had continuously promised the ancestors a profuse progeny, symbolized by the sands of the shore and the starry heaven, and the abundant fruit of womb and breast.[24]

Yes, there was an entire scroll of priestly prohibitions and purity laws explicitly restraining men from incest, homosexuality, bestiality, and the impurity of menstrual and other bodily fluids. But, then, what was actually practiced seems to have been another story, for the ancestral narratives of the Torah themselves contradict many of these laws. For instance, if we look at the Israelite nation's most lauded hero, King David, and the dynasty that came through him, we find dozens of strange deviations from the law of the land. The great Davidic dynasty, for example, comes through the line of a Moabite girl, a young widow by the name of Ruth, who sought to perpetuate her family line by brazenly putting herself at the bedside of her kinsman Boaz. One might easily take a *halakhic* attitude and call Ruth's "immodesty" unfit for the ranks that came forth from her. But the rabbis see Ruth as a heroine, despite her sexual forwardness, and, more, as a noble carrier of the kingdom of David despite the fact that intermarriage between the Israelites and the Canaanite nations, and particularly the Moabites, was explicitly forbidden by the Torah.[25]

King David was a man for whom eros was a powerful motivating force; his desire for women and for God were both consummate. His legendary rise to power and reign over the Hebrew nation were entangled with all manner of passions, and the Torah is forthright about both his lustiness and his zeal for God. For example, his desire for and appropriation of two married women, Abigail, the wife of Naval,[26] and the famous Bat Sheva,[27] mother of Solomon, are both reported in detail. Marked by repeated scandal, David's political career was far from pure in the *halakhic* sense. Still, in his story, we find light and shadow, glory and disgrace intermingling in scripture itself.

Why did scripture choose to unambiguously tell these stories of ancestors who repeatedly took the law into their own hands, violating sexual norms and behaving in unexpected, unconventional, and far from legal ways? Are these contradictions or simply the paradoxes of life, woven together in one fabric? Perhaps it is in itself a message to find tales of deviance alongside lists of sexual prohibitions and the consequences for disobedience of those laws all in one text.

The rabbis who redacted and canonized the Hebrew scripture were surely aware of these inconsistencies. They seem to be hinting to us that the straight way alone is not always the way of the hero. The way to wholeness must include the rounder way, the way of eros. Throughout the Torah, we find that the path of the godly person, from Abraham to Ruth to King David and ultimately to Beruriah, necessitates going to the point of subverting or at least defying the established order. Paradoxically, even with all the laws set forth to regulate our lives, this defiance does not mean failure, but a different kind of success.

Including the Sensuous

All of the Torah's stories of intrigue and unpredictable behavior are stories of eros, the unabashed desire to connect, to love spontaneously, to follow a calling and thereby step into one's destiny. The most erotic of all stories in the Torah is the luscious Song of Songs, filled with the sensual imagery of unrestrained sexuality between young lovers. This most voluptuous poem was canonized side by side with the laws of priestly purity, the misogyny of Ecclesiastes, and the proclamations of the doctrinaire leader Ezra, who forced all Jewish men to divorce the non-Jewish wives they had married during the

Babylonian exile and send them packing! Nevertheless, the Song of
Songs survived the rabbis who wished to throw it out, and it remains
an unabashed proclamation of the sublime nature of our physical
existence:

> *And oh, may your breasts be like clusters*
> *Of grapes on a vine, the scent*
> *Of your breath like apricots,*
> *Your mouth good wine—*
> *That pleases my lover, rousing him*
> *Even from sleep.*[28]

The sensuous and blatantly sexual Song of Songs obviously raised
the temperature of the first-century rabbis. It was only upon the insis-
tence of Rabbi Akiva, the famous second-century Palestinian sage
and martyr, contemporary of Beruriah's father and forerunner of Rabbi
Meir, that the Song of Songs was included in the canon at all. Ultimately, this highly erotic text was entered into the canon as a metaphor
for the love affair between God and the Jewish people; in this way it
was fully accepted by all. As Rabbi Akiva said, "The whole world only
existed for the day on which the Song of Songs was given to it. Why
so? Because all the Writings are holy, and this is Holy of Holies."[29]

One might argue that a metaphorical reading detracts from the
Song of Song's sensual nature and discounts its earthly holiness.
Nevertheless, it remained in our Torah rather than falling into disuse,
and brings forth, once again, the mystical theme of *yichud,* the
union of feminine and masculine. Once again, we bump into the
paradox that it is in the mystical core of the tradition that we find
recognition of eros as a necessary ingredient for a life of true spirit
and wholeness.

The rabbis of the Talmud believed that it was man's nature to act
with sexual abandon, that without will and the containment of the
Torah's precepts, the *yetzer hara,* the instinctual passions, would win
out. Morality needed training and boundaries, the rabbis taught, and,

above all, willpower. The struggle for control of sexuality was seen not as a battle between body and soul but as an interior struggle of will. It is interesting to note how the men's beliefs about their own nature were often projected onto women, as we have seen in the case of Beruriah and the bet about her sexual vulnerability.

Given their ambivalence toward women and their understanding that the libidinal drives presented grave dangers, Jewish men directed their passions into the study of Torah. The House of Study was (and still is) the place where eros reigned without restriction. Here men could be unabashedly ardent in their love affair with the Torah. Ben Azzai, the one bachelor of the Talmud, when confronted by his colleagues for advocating the necessity of procreation while he himself was unmarried, said, "But what shall I do, since my soul lusts for the Torah?"[30]

The rabbis knew that the instinctual inclination, or *yetzer hara,* was a force to be reckoned with. They fought with themselves about how to restrain their urges. As we have seen, speaking with women was kept to a minimum. Even looking should be avoided. "Anyone who looks at the little finger of a woman is as if he looked at her genitals."[31] But the strictures that the rabbis placed upon themselves and the time and energy allotted to keeping themselves protected from exposure may have been measures that arose out of awe for the sheer power that sexuality has, not only to corrupt our lives but to exalt them. We know this because peppered throughout the twenty-six volumes of Talmud, admittedly few and far between, we find alternate passages that hint at this awe and appreciation and bespeak a recognition of a more balanced approach, inclusive of the "rounder" way of life. How lucky we are to find these threads of ambivalence, the necessary minority voices that could be picked up later in history and woven into the mystical tradition, which speaks of wholeness.[32]

According to the Talmud, "Three things are a taste of the world to come: the Sabbath, sunshine, and sexual intercourse."[33] And, along with traveling, hot baths, and wealth, sex is listed among eight things that are harmful in large but beneficial in small quantities.[34] In the end, the rabbis knew, we are not here to torture and subdue our humanity, but to choose life. "In the world to come, each person will have to account for the earthly pleasures which were allowed to him but which he neglected to enjoy."[35]

Prescriptions for Wholeness

Beruriah would have been greatly aided by the views of wholeness that are expressed in the *Zohar*. The *Zohar*'s teachings abound with feminine images of ocean and moon, apple orchards in full, fragrant blossom, and secret gardens. Completely unambiguous about the ultimate importance of the union of feminine and masculine principles, the *Zohar* sees the masculine and feminine aspects of God as mutually dependent and their affinity for one another as the sublime ingredient enabling potential wholeness and holiness to spread throughout all of creation.

As for sexual intimacy, the *Zohar* is emphatic that relations between man and woman reflect the loving activity of the masculine aspect of God, the Holy One and the feminine Shechinah. Sex is far more central to our human purpose than one would expect, given the laws and prohibitions governing it. Animal instinct? Yes. An impulse rooted in our most physical nature? Yes. But sex, the *Zohar* teaches, reaches far beyond our animal selves, our *yetzer hara*, which pushes for its appetites to be satisfied. In fact, it can create ripples that affect the divine forces, inducing union in the cosmic realms.[36] Through the sexual act, a couple not only mirror the Divine Union, but help to bring it about and attract a flow of blessing to the physical plane.

We may see this differently in our times with changing sex roles and same-sex marriages. But however we view marriage and sexuality nowadays, the essence of the teaching is irrefutably given to wholeness, for we are no longer limited to the literal perspective of ages past. We know that the feminine principle does not live exclusively in female bodies, but in all people, men and women, as well as throughout creation as the energy of receptivity, relationality, and warmth. Likewise, we know now that women are gloriously endowed with what were once deemed masculine qualities: focused intent, worldliness, and the ability to penetrate to the heart of a situation. The crux of the matter is to unite these qualities within ourselves so that we and our relationships may live in balance.[37]

Beruriah would also have been fond of the view of passion brought forth by the Hassidic movement, which originated in the second half of the eighteenth century in eastern Europe. This movement, given to joy and heartfelt worship, succeeded in breathing new life into Judaism. It is clear from its texts and stories that what we call eros was solidly recognized by its proponents.

The movement's founder, Israel ben Eliezer (1700–1760), lovingly called the Ba'al Shem Tov, "Master of the Good Name," by his followers, understood that without the warm and personal connection between people and ardor for the Creator, religion is dry and suffocating. The Ba'al Shem called the spirit's fire *hitlahavut,* the flame of ecstasy and longing. He knew that the future of Judaism and the life of the spirit depended upon igniting this flame of desire in each of us.

With the notion of *hitlahavut* came the idea that it is our longing for God that creates connection, rather than, say, a ritual done to perfection but without much personal feeling. Above all, the Ba'al Shem pointed Jews back to a forgotten adage in Talmud, *Harachamana liba ba-ee,* "The Compassionate One requires of us only the heart,"[38] for it is in our heart that we feel the warmth of connection and the passion for God. The Ba'al Shem gave people the permission to know God through all aspects of their lives, through their passions, longings, joys, and heartaches. This was a great gift, especially to women, who some say find it easier to relate to God through their hearts than through intellectual rigor.

The idea that all aspects of life are intrinsically holy was deeply embedded in Judaism long before the Ba'al Shem, and, despite the rabbis' ambivalence toward sexuality, women, and the material world, it has remained at the mystical core of the religion. *B'chol dracheha da'ay-hu,* "No matter what path you take," said King Solomon, "you can use it to know God."[39] The verse tells us that we *can know* the Divine intimately, as a lover knows the beloved, by keeping ourselves awake to our own longing and spiritual fire.

Bringing It Home

Healing the ancient split that divides us from our sensual knowing is the work of many women today. As a culture, we have lost touch with the mysterious wisdom dormant in our bodies. Rather than learning to listen to the subtle rhythms of our monthly tides and attune ourselves to our bodies' intricate signal system, many of us grew up relating to our cycles with the barest tolerance and drugging ourselves when the signals got too strong.

There is a widespread movement to recover the divine mystery of our bodies, to join the physical and sensual with that which is spiritual. One client, upon discovering the power of her own sensuality, declared, "And all these years I thought my body was just there as a lamppost to hold up my head!" This thinking—that our bodies are just necessary equipment for our mental faculties—is the same ancient division that could make no allowances for Beruriah and her earthy approach to the sacred. But eros, living connected to one's fire and sensual wisdom, can bridge the gap.

Kabirah was a woman I knew whose journey exemplified the struggle to integrate eros into her life. Growing up in an ultra-Orthodox Jewish home in London in the 1960s, Kabirah had attended religious schools all her life, where she was immersed in a rigorous double curriculum of secular and Hebrew studies. Kabirah's father was a dedicated rabbi and the principal of her Jewish girls' high school; her mother taught in the Jewish elementary school. Ever the good student despite a rather rote religious training, Kabirah also had a devout side, a love for God that was deeply personal.

Kabirah, whose given name was Ettie Rochel, was the consummate obedient Jewish daughter; whatever her parents told her to do she did, never thinking twice about their instructions. She had never worn a pair of slacks, bared her arms above her elbows, or dared to put on makeup. These were the accepted standards for girls of her religious ilk, and she never felt a need to question them.

But then everything changed for Kabirah. The spring after she turned eighteen, she fell into a kind of fever. Although she was not physically sick, Kabirah experienced a bodily heat that she likened to a volcano erupting throughout her torso and arms. The internal fire was accompanied by extreme restlessness. Suddenly her parents' London flat was intolerably small. She started slipping out at night to take long walks alone, an unthinkable act for a religious girl.

Kabirah also contacted Sandra, a girl she knew whose parents had divorced and who had left the Orthodox community. Sandra went to public school now and had friends who were boys. She drank beer and wore jeans and knew about life. The girls got together. Although at first Kabirah was extremely nervous about her clandestine life, in Sandra's presence she began to feel her freedom, and rapidly became acquainted with the secular world of boys and sex.

Living a double life did not last long. Kabirah's parents, agonized and feeling out of control, futilely tried to clamp down on her. Finally Kabirah ran away, making her way to an urban commune on the other side of London, where she was able to find a room in exchange for household duties. This was a huge house where followers of an Indian guru lived, danced, ate, and made love together. Their spiritual practice was called "chaotic meditation," in which the devotees were given free rein to move, breathe, and dance wildly. This freedom seemed like the perfect medicine for Kabirah, who threw out her demure Jewish lifestyle along with her wardrobe to don the flowing, provocative clothing of a free woman.

For the next six years, Kabirah was on a journey of self-liberation. Still rebelling against her regimented childhood, she was hell-bent to try anything that would help her experience her own passion. She fell in and out of love with both men and women, got pregnant, had a baby, changed lovers, lost lovers, got married, got divorced, and finally moved away from the spiritual community to live alone with her daughter.

Over the years, Kabirah had gravitated to yoga as a spiritual practice, and she was now a proficient yoga teacher. She could support herself and her daughter on her earnings, and, just as important, she was learning to use the yoga to work with her physical passions and the inner heat she had first experienced in her late teens.

It was then that Kabirah's journey began to make sense to her. She understood that she had had to experiment, to taste life deeply, to express herself fully in a way that would never have been permitted in her parents' world. But despite her radical lifestyle, Kabirah had never lost her love of God. Underneath the Orthodox life with all its trappings, the central teachings of Judaism had made their mark on her.

Slowly Kabirah began to rediscover the devoutness she had known as a little girl. The Orthodox Jewish community and lifestyle had many profound truths, but it did not have a copyright on devotion. Combining the discipline of her yoga practice with the rediscovery of her desire to love and serve God was the next frontier for Kabirah.

Kabirah knew that her spiritual practice was one that required a strong body awareness, which is why she gravitated to yoga. Yet she also longed for the sincere religious devotion that she had been raised on and the rich essence of the Jewish tradition. She began to pray again, spontaneously at first and then from her old prayer book. She taught her daughter Hebrew songs and prayers from her childhood, slowly reconnecting to Jewish practices that felt harmonious with her newfound beliefs. Ultimately, the life that Kabirah charted for herself was one in which her physical passions could coexist with her devout love of God without compromising either one.

Kabirah's journey is another example of the need to create a *yichud* in one's life. In Kabirah's case, the work was to marry a fiery temperament with a spirit of devotion. The wholeness that is the synthesis of these two seemingly divergent natures is the goal of all of us who are working toward integrating eros into our lives.

Women are learning what a powerful force their sensuality is. When we liberate it from the rusted shackles of men's control, reclaiming the fire of eros in our lives without shame, every aspect of our lives is warmed and enlivened. This fire is the fuel behind our ardor for God, our love for our children, our sexual passion, and the zeal with which we do the work of becoming whole people.

In this chapter, Beruriah has been depicted as a fiery woman who fought to be whole. In truth, we cannot say who she was or what fate actually befell her. But we do know that she had the wisdom of a sage, the eros of a woman, and the brazenness of one who would not be silenced.

Beruriah's story is an extreme example of the struggle for eros and what happens when we are cut off from it. Beruriah's need to be included, listened to, and honored is our need as well. On our journey to becoming whole people, Beruriah teaches us that we must struggle to claim what is ours. A woman's bodily wisdom, use of intellectual rigor, and passion for God are not those of a man—nor should they be. Beruriah reminds us to take pride in our feminine gifts, to take down the walls that compartmentalize and diminish them, and to bring our distinctly feminine voices back into the tradition.

What can we do to repair the division of worlds that destroyed Beruriah? How can we help restore her honor? Our contribution is surely to resurrect and live the radical path of the Star of David, the path of Jewish wholeness: to explore, revere, and exalt the nameless mystery of heaven above and, equally, to "listen down low," following the holy wisdom of the earth, our bodies, and our sensual knowing.

CHAPTER 3

PRACTICAL SPIRITUALITY

Malkah of Belz (ca. 1780–1850)

Wwe come now to a very different story about a robust woman who, by all accounts, knew true joy and fulfillment in her life. Malkah of Belz lived in the latter part of the eighteenth and first part of the nineteenth century. She was the wife of the famed Belzer Rebbe, Rabbi Shalom Rokeach, and the matriarch of the Hassidic dynasty that he founded. It is primarily through stories documenting her husband's life that we come to know of her.[1] By means of these tales, scattered through Hassidic literature, we have several good, albeit sideways, glimpses at Malkah, long peeks into a world of unabashed, practical spirituality.

In contrast to Hannah Rachel and Beruriah, Malkah seems to have fully lived the life she was created to live. A jovial figure, she is an example of the wholeness that comes from living comfortably and skillfully in the material world. A true expert in the art of homemaking, Malkah opened doors to the sacred by means of her cooking and her attention to physical space. She, like Beruriah, attempted to erase the damaging dichotomy that had been artificially created between the physical and the spiritual realms. But Malkah's passion, unlike that of Beruriah or Hannah Rachel, was rooted in her home.

Malkah was a woman who was clearly happy to be alive and to possess a physical body with which to serve God. She was famed for her good spirits and her ability to nourish others through her superb cooking, but her world did not end at the boundaries of her earthly domain. Malkah was well traveled in the realm of spirit and was, in fact, what one might call clairvoyant. Her ability to see beyond the veil of this world and yet remain down-to-earth allowed Malkah to move back and forth from the literal dimension of life to the timeless world of the soul, as if moving matter-of-factly between two rooms.

Because of her remarkable ability to bridge and balance the material and spiritual planes, in this chapter we will use Malkah's story as the starting point for our exploration of the Tree of Life, the central motif of mystical Judaism (see the Appendix). This image will help us understand how to reconcile and heal life's polarities. Standing at the center of the tradition, the Tree of Life, like Malkah, is deeply rooted in the earth, making room for all of life's stations and experiences. More than just a sacred symbol, it contains within it an entire philosophy of inclusion and wholeness, which we will use in our reintegration of the feminine principle. We begin our study of the Tree of Life in this chapter because the Tree, like Malkah's story, teaches us that every aspect of life, even the most mundane, can lead us to God.

Malkah's skill at homemaking was one example of her practical spirituality. Her home was known for being a sacred environment filled with good smells and a feeling of *shalom bayit*, a palpable peacefulness; everyone who entered Malkah's home felt its healing power, and hundreds came to be nourished there, both physically and spiritually. The atmosphere in her home was in part due to the relationship Malkah had with her husband, a famous rabbi who was known to consult her in all matters, both personal as well as rabbinic.

The love affair Malkah and Shalom enjoyed for almost forty years stands out in a history in which the segregation and disregard of women was the norm. Men, and in particular public figures and community leaders, were careful to keep their relations with their wives extremely private. Rarely would they converse in public, and never would they show signs of affection. In this male-centered milieu, what man would want to undercut his power by openly showing his need or affection for his wife?

For this reason, the unrestrained respect and admiration that Malkah and her husband showed one another was highly unusual. Stories about their mutual devotion are well known among Belzer Hassidim to this day, who see it as a reflection of the love between God and the Shechinah, the masculine and feminine faces of God. For those of us who choose spiritual partnership as a path to wholeness, Malkah and her husband stand out as models.

One well-known Hassidic story actually attributes her husband's greatness to Malkah. Shalom, who was actually Malkah's second cousin, had come to live with her family in Sokol after the early death of his father, Rabbi Eleazar Rokeach. It was clear to Malkah that her cousin was a genius, someone meant to be a spiritual leader. But for a long while, even after their betrothal and some time into their marriage, Shalom doubted his aptitude for being a rabbi and attempted other businesses.

Malkah persisted. Every night at midnight she would wake him up with the words, "Shalom, get up from your bed. It is time to serve God." As everyone else in the house slept, she helped her husband into his clothes and spirited him out the window to the House of Study. One legend tells that this ritual lasted for one thousand nights. On the thousand-and-first night, a great lightning storm arose, threatening the modest structures of Sokol and any creatures who dared to be out of their beds. Nevertheless, Shalom ventured into the storm and made his way to the House of Study. On that awesome night, with thunder, wind, and lightning all around, Shalom was visited by Elijah the Prophet himself, who initiated the young man into his spiritual leadership role. Shalom's self-doubts were finally vanquished; Malkah's clarity of vision had triumphed.

After a time, the couple left the village of Sokol, and Shalom sought out the teachings of the great Seer of Lublin, who, like Malkah, saw in him the light of greatness and urged him to move to Belz to take up the role of leader. It was there in Belz, in western Ukraine, that Shalom's teachings became renowned and the couple's dynasty became established. Jews and even non-Jews came to visit their court, from Hungary, Poland, and elsewhere in the Ukraine, to bestow gifts of all kinds in exchange for sacred study and, if possible, time with the rebbe.

Given the way that women were marginalized in that culture, it was astonishing that the now great rebbe did not turn away from the woman who had set him on his path, but rather raised her up and recognized her publicly for her wisdom.[2] To understand the anomaly of Malkah and Reb Shalom's relationship, though, we might take a look at the sociohistorical context of their lives.

In the late eighteenth century, village life in eastern Europe was simple and the Jewish community lived in close quarters. Men held jobs that were permitted to them by the state; they were merchants, tanners, millers, lens grinders, butchers, and so forth. Most every man took time, however, to sit and study Torah.

Women kept to their own tasks of bearing offspring and tending to life's physical requirements. At times, a woman would run the family business and support her family as well, freeing her husband to learn Torah all day. But, as we saw in Hannah Rachel's story, it was almost never the case that a woman dared enter the men's world of study, although within Hassidic circles women were permitted to seek private guidance and council from the rebbe. In the main, women would rarely have been seen in public in the domain of the rebbe or his students.

Due to the affinity of Malkah and her husband, an unusual break with the women's tradition was found in the Belz court. A famous story told by Rabbi Baruch Halberstam[3] illustrates this break and the palpable harmony that existed between the two.

Baruch was still a young boy when he first visited the Belz court with his father, Rabbi Hayyim of Zanz. It was a time-honored custom for rabbis as well as students to journey great distances to visit the courts of other rabbis of distinction, to receive blessings, guidance, and answers to their questions. Normally, the visitor would be announced and have to wait in a hallway or sitting room until being called in for his private audience.

Instead of waiting in a deserted vestibule though, the father and son came upon the rabbi sitting at a table with Rebbetzin Malkah.[4] The couple were eating their meal together, simply enjoying one another's company in a plain, undecorated room. For a rebbe to be found sitting with his wife was highly unusual. One might see him seated with his Hassidim perhaps or with other rabbis, but not with his wife, and surely not in public!

The father and son were taken aback. Malkah, being who she was, remained at the table and invited the guests to sit down, continuing to eat and speak with the men. Later, on their way home, Reb Hayyim asked his son his impressions.

"Tatti, it was like visiting the Garden of Eden itself. I experienced sitting with Adam and Eve when they were still wholly pure, before they ever ate the apple," his son said.

Rabbi Hayyim responded, "I swear, that is exactly how they appeared to me as well."

The story speaks of their intimacy. The Belzer Rebbe consulted Malkah with his every problem and concern, and often, if he was not available to counsel a student or visitor, Malkah would do so in his stead.

Once a man came to the court with great pain in his feet. The rabbi was away and so Malkah listened to his plight. "What can I do for my feet, Rebbetzin? I am in constant pain and it grows steadily worse." After a moment's contemplation, Malkah responded with an antidote and the man left. The following month, the man returned to the court, walking sprightly and filled with confidence. This time he spoke to Reb Shalom himself, regaling him with the story of the miracle that Malkah had performed. He reported that his pain was gone and his feet were now as healthy as those of a young man. She was a rebbe in her own right, he declared, one who could both see and heal.

"What kind of healing did you administer? And how did you know what to give him?" Reb Shalom asked Malkah later.

Malkah chuckled and replied, "I didn't give him a thing! He gave to us! When he told me of his foot ailment, the verse 'Your words are a lamp unto my feet'⁵ popped into my head. So I told him he needed to go buy a year's worth of candles and bring them as a donation to the House of Study. It was by the merit of his generosity that he was healed!"

Simple miracles like these were commonplace in the Belz court. They were based upon inward listening and the faith that one had access to the voice of inner wisdom at all times. Malkah was known to follow this inner voice and to do so with a good bit of *chutzpah,* or audacity. Her husband learned over time to respect her advice, even when it ran counter to his own judgment.

Near the town of Belz there lived a man who was generally disliked for his evil business dealings. Yet he was a patron of Reb Shalom and traveled to see his teacher regularly. Reb Shalom had compassion for the man despite his unpopularity.

It happened that the man came down with a life-threatening disease, and just afterward his wife gave birth to a baby boy. The father wrote to the Belzer Rebbe inviting him to come to the boy's circumcision in the honorary role of *sandek.*⁶ As Reb Shalom prepared to go, Malkah warned him to rethink his trip. Seeing beyond the simple appearances of the day, she knew that her husband's holy presence would somehow tip the scales for the man, hastening his end. Nevertheless, the rebbe was intent upon traveling and did not allow Malkah to dissuade him.

No sooner did Reb Shalom enter the house than the man grew deathly ill and died. The circumcision took place, but there was a pall of calamity around the event. When the despondent rebbe returned home, Yehoshua, the son who would eventually become his heir, asked him, "Why did you not listen to Mama? She told you not to go."

"My son," he answered the boy, "I have long known that your mother is exceedingly intelligent. But I did not know until now that she had the gift of prophecy."

It was because of Malkah's depth of insight that her influential husband taught his students to respect and draw out this deep knowing from their own wives. He recognized that women often had a kind of sagacity that a man was slower to achieve on his own and that men did well to listen to their women's advice.

Because the Belzer Rebbe visibly demonstrated this respect for the woman's way of knowing, his example was followed by his Hassidim, and honor for women has been passed down to this day. Although all the Belzer wives may not have been on the spiritual level of Rebbetzin Malkah, their husbands' attention and willingness to draw them out undoubtedly helped to elevate the women's own sense of worthiness, thereby encouraging them to let their inner wisdom come forth and be articulated.

Sacred Sexuality

Given what we know of their love and devotion for one another and Malkah's enjoyment of the physical realm, we might go one step further and imagine that Malkah and her husband enjoyed their sexual union together and used it as a shared religious experience, practiced with care for one another and great devotion to the divine forces.

The importance of conscious sexual relations was stressed throughout Jewish legal tradition itself.[7] As was discussed earlier, celibacy was not an acceptable long-term practice within Jewish tradition, and being married was part and parcel of fulfilling oneself as a human being.[8] Moreover, it was among a husband's legal responsibilities to his wife to engage sexually with her and to give her pleasure. That a woman could expect "conjugal rights" with her husband was based upon scripture itself.⁹ These laws, in addition to women's laws of ritual purity, created a kind of sacred container for the union of husband and wife that stood at the foundation of their lives together. Although the laws were far from universally observed, the holy couple of Belz most likely held to these traditions and, in turn, were held by a container that allowed them the ecstasy of a loving sexual life together.

In Jewish mystical terms, sexual union is seen as a door to the most intimate spiritual experience possible. Because of the procreative potential of sex between a man and woman, it has been seen from ancient times as an opportunity to join together with God as partners in the greatest, most astounding undertaking available to humans: the bringing forth of new life. The idea that bringing forth a child requires a three-way partnership between mother, father, and God is referred to in the Talmud. So sacred is the act of parenthood, in fact, that the parental partners are considered co-creators on a par with God.¹⁰

Beyond producing offspring, though, sex is a vehicle by which a couple can unify themselves through shared pleasure, and the sheer power of two people's joined pleasure can go further and raise and unify other energies beyond themselves. With practice, a couple can learn to direct their thoughts and energies, not only to the outcome of orgasm, but toward the goal of drawing forth other kinds of blessings such as the healing of loved ones, the lifting of heavenly decrees, and certainly a blissful communion with God.

The theurgic nature of sexuality, that is, the use of sex as a vehicle to bring about cosmic change, is taken up particularly in the *Zohar.* As already discussed, the act of making love reflects and embodies in this world the intercourse of the divine emanations in the world above. But the sexual act done as a holy act not only helps to bring about cosmic intercourse, it attracts a flow of blessing down to the physical world.

For students of the *Zohar,* of whom Reb Shalom was one, it was important to coordinate one's lovemaking with the precise time of intercourse in the divine world.¹¹ When is that? "The right time for people in general is at midnight throughout the week," the rabbis taught, "because it is at that time that the Holy One takes His delight with His Shechinah in the Garden of Eden."[12] However, we also know that scholars who were devoted to the mystical life rose regularly at midnight to engage in sacred study, and Malkah awakened Shalom nightly at midnight to do just this. The *Zohar* made allowances for such couples, saying, "Sexual union might take place at another time, the time of another, more exalted intercourse, and this is on Sabbath night."[13] For hundreds of years, Friday night has been known by mystics to be the auspicious time for sexual relations between husband and wife, for it is filled with the sacred energy of the Sabbath candlelight and was the mythical time of the Shechinah's return from exile to reunite with Her Beloved.

Any two partners who share a path of holiness can direct their sexual energies with prayerful intent, not for personal pleasure alone, but also as a means of bringing blessings of healing and peace into the world. In the Jewish mystical tradition, the couple consciously become a conduit for the divine forces, channels for the flow of blessing from the upper realms into the physical world and, conversely, from their own union, a mirroring in the worlds above. First in words and then in action, they consign their loving union to effect a *yichud*, unification for the healing of this world and the world beyond.

The success of such a joining lies in a couple's seamless commitment to a power greater than themselves. Malkah and Shalom were partners whose entire lives were dedicated to God and to creating holiness in their home. Their mission was the same: to build a *dirah l'matah*, a sacred dwelling place on earth in which to host God, and one way they were able to align their energies to achieve this mission was through their loving union.

Although this healing aspect of sexuality lies at the foundation of the Jewish mystical tradition, it has been kept so secret that it has been all but lost to mainstream Judaism, which focused on the more outward, rational aspects of the tradition. Hindu and Buddhist traditions have numerous teachings about the spiritual use of this most powerful energy, usually known as Tantric wisdom. But the sacred teachings about Jewish sexuality, kept for the exclusive use of the mystical elite, have been tragically lost to most Jews. Perhaps it was feared that in the hands of simple people these teachings would be misused or confused with lascivious behavior. Nevertheless, censorship of such teachings has yielded negative consequences, leading to the dilution of a rich tradition. For Judaism to become a viable path to spiritual wholeness, the wisdom of sacred sexuality must be reclaimed.

Alchemist in the Kitchen

Despite their remarkable harmony, Malkah's and Reb Shalom's approaches to living a holy life were vastly different. The kitchen was the setting of Malkah's personal spiritual ecstasy and holy service, and she spent most of her day there, up to her wrists in fleshy white dough in the kneading trough, vigorously chopping fish and onions at her cutting board, or standing over the woodstove tasting a broth for an unwell child or Hassid.

Out of Malkah's kitchen came food each day for her seven children, scores of students, visitors and *schnorrers*, indigent beggars and holy men who came to Belz to learn from her husband, the great rebbe. The kitchen and adjacent dining hall were her personal domain, the worldly hub of the Belzer court. The great hall's benches filled to capacity every evening with male students of all ages, and it was Malkah's job to fill their bodies with warmth and nourishment that would produce nothing short of joy.

Certainly Malkah must have had help, perhaps the wives and daughters of the rebbe's Hassidim and *melamdim* ("educators"). The women's work under the watchful eyes of Malkah was holy work. If the men had their House of Study, then the kitchen was the women's House of Prayer. Rather than their mouths, it was their hands that did the praying, all day long. Just as the men had to guard against idle thoughts entering into their study, so the Rebbetzin would have instructed the women firmly that their thoughts and words permeated the very food they washed, chopped, stirred, and mashed. If their cooking was done in an atmosphere of holiness and pure thoughts, then the life that their food gave forth would also be holy and pure. It was that simple.

Malkah was an alchemist. She knew the sacred art of combining ingredients—each with its own particular potency and purpose—to create a thing greater than their sum. Each herb, root, and cut of meat was important, but the most important ingredient of all Malkah knew to be the power of her own thoughts, the shape and quality of which would, on any given day, determine the outcome of the soup or the meal, the disposition of the Hassidim, and the day itself.

Prayer in the Batter

Because of the importance of the thought behind the deed, no day would have begun for Malkah without specific rituals by which to set her mind in order. Before sleep, Malkah prepared *neggelvasser*, two small pitchers of water with bowls, and placed them at her bedside as well as her husband's so that they could both begin their day with the *mitzvah* of self-purification and blessing God's name before their feet even touched the ground.[14] With her first blessings, she dedicated her day and all of her energy to God's service.

Malkah would never have dreamt of donning a prayer shawl or *yarmulkah* ("skullcap") as women would one day insist upon doing. Wearing these was considered to be exclusively the men's commandment. The women had their own way. Malkah had used an ample head covering since the day of her wedding. And as for prayer, while the men prayed three times a day in their *minyan*, poring over their prayer books, Malkah had no need of all those pages. There was too much to be done. Malkah had found her own way to pray throughout the day, from her first blessing as the cold water hit her fingertips to the final prayer of forgiveness before she laid down her weary head.

Women were commanded to pray in their own way at least once a day. The rabbis, after all, were no fools. They knew what woman's work consisted of and that it did not allow a woman to stop. For this reason, Malkah prayed as she moved through her day, drawing the household water, swaddling babies, putting out feed for the animals, and cooking. She had learned most of the formal prayers by heart as a young girl, the morning blessings, the Shema Yisrael, the prayer before and after eating food and after elimination.

There were, of course, the blessings of *ChaNaH*[15] and the informal women's prayers, called *techinahs:* before putting the bread in the oven, before her monthly women's immersion, and before lighting the Sabbath candles. These and other snippets of sacred verse put to her own little tunes served to focus Malkah throughout the day, to draw down strength, to call upon divine powers to help her accomplish all that she had before her.

In this way, humming and whispering her way through the day, Malkah could have an ongoing discourse with God and, at the same time, invest all of her tasks with *kedushah,* "holiness." The sight that she had been given, to see behind the veils of the outer world, was only by the grace of God. She had learned to thank God for it, to attend to it diligently even when she did not like what she saw, and on special occasions to ask for it pointedly.

One story tells of Malkah looking into the future and seeing that a blight would be hitting the young fowl in the region. Because these birds, called capons, were the favorite dish of a visiting rebbe and friend, Meir of Premishlan, Malkah used her powers to intercede, successfully diverting the plague to a wilder, nonedible species, one that was more heartily able to withstand the disease. Malkah's spiritual talents were not limited to seeing alone. She was also able to use her power of focus and of prayer to change the laws of nature.

A Wound That Won't Heal

Unlike Malkah, most women don't immediately associate domestic activities with success, a term that tends to emphasize material productivity, intellectual rigor, and a cerebral orientation. Have women been socialized into believing that a feminine approach is inherently devoid of power? One wonders how much of modern women's adoption of male standards has been the result of buying into men's largely disdainful attitude toward women, being co-opted by a power far more popular but less balanced than their own. Have we abandoned our own feminine wisdom before ever discovering the power intrinsic to our own feminine ethic? Most important, have we adapted an either/or, black-and-white approach to our understanding of holiness? Whatever the answers to these questions, the division between masculine and feminine that has given rise to a degradation of feminine values begs to be healed first and foremost by women themselves.

Until the past century, when women formally entered the world of scholarship, the Jewish woman's spiritual contribution had been the material health and viability of her family and those around her. For Malkah, who saw the physical world as nothing less than the materialization of divine energies to be enjoyed as gifts from God, these contributions were clearly equal to the work of the ancient high priest, who had once consecrated the sacrifices of the people and then fed them meat with which to sustain themselves. But for those men and women who held a worldview that oriented itself upward and out of physical life, placing the highest value on transcending the constraints of the physical plane, women's work was seen as janitorial and their world as devoid of spirit.

To appreciate Malkah's gifts and to allow her nondualistic philosophy to help us repair the split in our cultural thinking, it is, once again, important to understand her historical context, for it is still influencing us today. The tasks to which Malkah and most women gave themselves wholeheartedly—the keeping of the home, providing of food, bearing and nurturing of the young—were unquestionably valued, at least outwardly. After all, women were directly responsible for the survival of life and the continuity of the people—what could be more important?

Yet there was another standard at work during much of Jewish history, a vestige of the one discussed in the preceding chapter, which held women in their necessary roles of keeping body and soul together while simultaneously despising them for doing just that. The same ideology we saw developing in Beruriah's post-Hellenistic Palestine, dichotomizing spirit and matter, had continued through medieval times. Especially for the elite scholars who were revered by the people for their sagacity and spiritual idealism, the ultimate standard of holiness lived outside this world altogether.

By Malkah's day, at the precipice of modernity, women had been kept out of the rich intellectual waters of the tradition for hundreds of years. They had made their own way, but because so few were educated enough to dip into the wellsprings of Torah, they dipped instead into the prevailing superstitions and magic of the times. This, of course, won them no honor. Women, mired in the physical and emotional realms, were often seen by men as the personification of what must be avoided; they were irrational and often hysterical females who foolishly placed their faith in such things as amulets, herbal concoctions, and strange rituals against the evil eye.

Concealed within the disdain for all that constituted the physical world—the blood and guts of material life—was the unspoken yet fervent belief that God lives, as all men should, far above and outside this world.

Take the words of the Vilna Gaon, preeminent sage of the eighteenth century, whose writings and discourses are to this day sacrosanct among most learned traditional Jews. Ardently anti-Hassidic in ideology, the rabbi of Vilna here describes the highest virtue of the Torah scholar as one that categorically excludes any attention to the worldly needs of one's family:

True heroes are men of noble heart with the fullest trust in God, constantly doing *mitzvot* (sacred precepts), and meditating on the Torah day and night even though their home be without bread and clothing and their families cry out: "Bring us something to support and sustain us, some livelihood!" But he pays no attention at all to them nor heeds their voice...for he has denied all love except that of the Lord and His Torah.[16]

The Gaon of Vilna apparently succeeded in living out this black-and-white ethical system because he is extolled by his sons for not hesitating to leave home to study Torah in isolation, even though his then only son, Shlomo Zalman, was deathly ill. Only after a month had passed did the father return home to inquire about his son's health. The son, already won over to the devaluation of the physical plane, deemed this spiritual superiority.[17]

Could this imbalanced worldview be God's will? An ethical system that splits the world of Torah study off from the human world of family, physical sustenance, and health would be considered by many practicing Jews to be antithetical to the tradition. The very essence of Judaism, they would say, is about sanctifying earthly life through enjoyment, blessing, and thanksgiving. Yet the subtler and more subliminal voice within the tradition has made transcendence of the earthly plane the highest spiritual rung on the ladder to God.

The Tree of Life

The belief that one's mortal ties to earth, body, and family are secondary to the cause of spirit subtly pervades our tradition to this day. It is a still unhealed schism, a wound in which the disparagement of women and women's practical way in the world has festered for centuries.

Malkah of Belz helps us to heal this wound. For her there was no dichotomy. Malkah knew well that the highest and holiest human task was not to leave the earthly world behind but rather to connect earth and heaven by making of one's life a conduit through which the river of spirit can flow, downward as well as upward. From a non-hierarchical perspective such as Malkah's, no creature, no circumstance, and no aspect of life is irrelevant or merely discardable. All phenomena in time and space are aspects of God's creation and portals that lead to potential holiness.

It is here that we begin to examine the teaching of the Tree of Life, undoubtedly the most important motif of the mystical Jewish tradition (see the diagram in the Appendix). It is the Tree of Life that provides us with the way out of the either/or perspective presented by the mainstream culture. Growing on the surface of the earth, with roots below and branches reaching to heaven, the Tree of Life symbolizes the great pillar that unites earth with heaven; through it the energies of the cosmos continuously pour into earthly creation and return back again to heaven.

Although the Tree is central to the Hebrew legend of the Garden of Eden, it did not actually have its origins there. For roughly a thousand years before the Hebrew creation myth was ever written down, the Tree of Life was one of the primary images of mythologies of the ancient Near East. The Tree embodied the feminine face of God, in whose presence the tension between all opposites was neutralized.[18] Seen as the spine or axis of the world and variously called the *axis mundi,* the world tree, and the alchemical tree, the Tree of Life is found in traditions the world over. It was believed that the person who came into contact with this life-giving creation would be transformed, made whole, by the power of eternal life that emanated from it.

Long before it became the central symbol for wholeness in the Judaic tradition, the tree was a universal symbol, originally representing the Divine Feminine and later coming to mean eternal life. But the Hebrew tradition did not just borrow this magnificent, mystical symbol. It took and developed the meaning of the tree, using it to bring forth a unique and profound philosophy about the dynamic complexity of life. This is its teaching: *to arrive at wholeness and eternal life, one must first encounter the multiplicity of opposing forces in the world and contend with the nature of dualism that is the principle feature of consciousness and life on earth.*

Back to the Garden

The Bible tells us that the Tree of Life sits in the center of the Garden of Eden. But it is not the fruit of this eternal tree that is withheld from humanity. It is another tree that holds the forbidden fruit around which the drama of Adam and Eve unfolds. This tree, called the Tree of the Knowledge of Good and Evil, represents the dualities of mortal life.[19]

For many people, these two trees are easily confused. Was there one tree at the center of the Garden or two? If two, are they connected? Although many readers think it is they who have misread it, the story itself is unclear. Adam is commanded to eat freely of every tree except of the Tree of the Knowledge of Good and Evil; disregarding this prohibition will result in mortality for Adam.

It is, of course, Eve who first puts her hand out to pick the forbidden fruit. Is it hubris or a desire for consciousness that drives her to the inevitable? She picks the fruit, tastes it, and passes it to her husband. It is only after they have both eaten from the Tree of Knowledge that the world's polarities—good and evil, mortal and immortal, self and other—even begin to exist.

With their vision of life now radically altered, the Tree of Life and its promise of eternity become mysteriously closed to Adam and Eve. What had been a state of pristine, unconscious oneness with God is now gone, and they are banished into a real, conscious life in time and space. It is only after living a humbling and hard-working life outside of the Garden that we, Adam and Eve's children, are ready to return to the other tree, the Tree of Life, and partake of its eternal fruits.

The Hebrew creation story is a template of the psychological and spiritual development shared by us all. It is not the story of a woeful fall, but the story of the birth of the ego, necessary for the work of consciousness to begin. Some say it is a story of young childhood development, describing the emergence of a child from preconscious oneness into separate individualism. I believe it is the story of humanity that occurs not once, but many times throughout our lives, as we make choices that take us farther and farther away from our primal innocence.

Paradoxically, these choices ultimately lead us into greater and greater degrees of consciousness. Though we may mourn the blissful yet unconscious state of unity that most of us enjoyed early on—symbolized by the Garden—it is only when we are thick into the conundrum of life's dualities that our hunger for the unifying source beyond opposites strikes us. It is then that the journey back to the Garden begins, to discover the Tree that heals opposites and to enjoy the fruit that is the product of our journey.

Two Trees in One

The kabbalistic Tree of Life is the synthesis of both the trees of the creation story: the tree that leads to consciousness through the path of opposites, called the Tree of the Knowledge of Good and Evil, *and* the tree that goes beyond opposites, the eternal essence of being, called the Tree of Life. This synthesis of duality and eternity is the mystery of the kabbalistic Tree. In this one dynamic, healing image, both of our natures are encompassed: the dialectical nature of our time-bound, dualistic lives here on earth *and* our eternal nature.

The kabbalistic, or unified, Tree has three pillars (refer as necessary throughout the following to the diagram of the Tree of Life in the Appendix). The central pillar may be seen as the *axis mundi*, the central axis that runs through the world and all of life, including through each one of us. The two pillars to the right and left of the central pillar are classically known as the Pillars of Mercy and Severity, respectively.

Although the mystical Tree of Life may look flat and unmoving on paper, it is in reality far from two-dimensional; and it is never still. It is, rather, a ceaseless dance of energy that pulses with life force. The outer two pillars may be seen as the poles of electrical energy that host a constantly moving, balancing, and rebalancing current between them. They come to full peace, for a time, in the central pillar, also known as the Pillar of Equilibrium, the place that transcends the dance of opposites and connects us to the timeless essence of life.

In mystical terms, each of us is an entire world or garden unto ourselves. And just as there was a healing tree at the center of the Garden of Eden, so each of us has a healing core of energy at the center of our individual psyches. Just as the archetypal Tree of Life has the power to unify and heal opposites, so we have, at the core of our beings, a connection to the universal power that can bring together all of our disparate sides and conflicting voices into one unified and peaceful whole.

The Sephirot

Coursing through the Tree, up and down the central axis and into its right and left branches, is a powerful flow of energy known as *shefa Elohim,* the "divine abundance." This energy circulates and flows, collecting in vortexes throughout the Tree. These vortexes might be seen as lenses positioned throughout the Tree, each lending its own particular viewpoint to the vital life current as it passes. The vortexes, of which there are ten, are called *sephirot* (sing., *sephirah*). To the *Zohar* and other mystical texts, the *sephirot* are understood as ways of describing God's various attributes, faces, and names.

For people who are familiar with yoga or Eastern traditions, including Chinese medicine, the Tree may be correlated with a map of the vital energy known as *prana* or *chi.* The *sephirot* may be seen as chakras, energy centers flowing throughout the body along designated pathways. In the Judaic system, just as in the Eastern systems, each of the *sephirot* is unique and purposeful and must remain unblocked so that energy may flow throughout the whole system.

Each *sephirah* has a masculine and a feminine quality and is associated with a body part on both male and female bodies. However, because Jewish mystical texts have been, until now, interpreted exclusively by and for men, little if any attention has been paid to how each *sephirah* relates to women's experience. For this reason, our study will emphasize the *sephirah* system from the perspective of a woman's body and psyche.

The Middle Pillar

The middle pillar of the kabbalistic Tree of Life immediately connects us to the central axis of vital energy flowing through our own bodies and through all of creation. This central axis is a balancing point between the dualities in our world—light and darkness, good and evil, energy and its implementation—which are represented by the outer pillars of the Tree. To a woman's sensibility, the central pillar can be seen as a sacred birth canal, a conduit through which humans bring forth the divine will onto the earthly plane and by which heaven itself is blessed by the gifts we offer up.

The beauty of the Tree of Life is that its dynamic is circular, flowing from heaven downward like rain and moving upward like sap rising. We can enter it at any point we wish. Although it has traditionally been studied from the top down, from a woman's perspective, it is perhaps best studied from the ground up—with roots firmly in the earth, the physical earth and our flesh-and-blood bodies.

Malkhut: Physical Manifestation

Of all the *sephirot*, Malkhut is most universally seen as feminine. For this reason, the name of God that corresponds to Malkhut is Shechinah, the Divine Feminine or the indwelling spirit of God. The feminine personage classically associated with Malkhut is the beautiful and modest Rachel, the beloved of Jacob. Rachel, who died in childbirth, is equated with the Shechinah Herself, who suffers the pain of childbirth and the loss of Her children into exile.[20] The great King David, divine poet, warrior, and lover, is the male figure representing Malkhut. This is because David, as we have seen, embodied both earthiness and human passion at the same time that he was a true servant of God. Although he was a man of lust and adventure, he strove to harness his energies and turn his love of God into action.[21]

Malkah of Belz also personified Malkhut. To her, earthly life was one lens through which to perceive and enjoy God's presence and abundance. So too the first of the *sephirot*, Malkhut, is about the physical manifestation of the Divine. The word itself means "queenship," just as Malkah means "queen." As Queen of the earthly realm, Malkhut pulses upward through the living earth, bidding us to grow into our skins, to partake of life's bounty, and, at the unfortunate times when we have been devastated, to begin again. Perhaps for this reason the rabbis also called this *sephirah* Faith.

Malkhut is life's urge to continue itself. It lives in our instincts and in the elements of our bodies, urging us to seize life now and live it to its fullest. It is Malkhut that quickens the hearts and bodies of new lovers and fuels a woman's urge to conceive. It fuels our pulses, our appetites, and our physical desires. At times, Malkhut is almost mechanical, as when the body keeps pumping ferociously even after consciousness has left it. Malkhut is our connection and pull to life on earth.

Seen by the *Zohar* as a particular face of the divine world, Malkhut is described by the rabbis in the most poetic terms. As the Shechinah, this *sephirah* was seen as the ocean, which receives and transforms the many streams of life into a unified whole. Malkhut was also depicted as the moon, a bride, and an apple orchard in full blossom.

Women may experience Malkhut in a more grounded way, as their physical bodies, senses, and sexuality. This *sephirah* connects us to our most primal urges: to live and to foster life. The food we eat, the milk that swells in our breasts, our blood cycles, and our bodies' encoded wisdom that tells us how to live on the earth—all this is Malkhut. Like Malkah, in Malkhut we touch, smell, handle and raise up the ingredients of the world around us. Here, food, sex, and physical work are all important and open the doors to the higher dimensions.

As every one of the *sephirot* is associated with a body part, Malkhut is located in a woman's feet, which serve as her roots to earth, or alternatively in her vagina, the root of her physical trunk. Like the lips of the vagina, Malkhut is the gate between inner and outer, self and other. At Malkhut, we face the reality of the physical world and make sense of it.

Meditation upon this *sephirah* will open one to experience the fact that, no matter how seemingly mundane, every situation, every moment of our physical existence is an opportunity for holiness. To connect with Malkhut, the roots of the Tree of Life, one must cultivate awareness of the physical plane through one's senses and bodily experiences. There are numerous ways to do this, as we shall discuss in Chapter 6.

Yesod: Creativity

Farther up on our Tree of Life, at Yesod, lies a more internal mystery. Here at Yesod is the taproot of our creativity, the very foundation of our being, which for women is often doomed to invisibility, for its very nature demands surrender. It is at Yesod that we begin to understand the spiritual conundrum of why women have remained hidden in the shadows for such a long time.

Remembering that the Judaic mystical system was transmitted exclusively by men, we must now carefully unwrap its masculine outer casing in order to discern the teachings that are universal, balanced, and also true for women. Through a *masculine* lens, Yesod is understood to be the center of generative power, usually seen as sexual or personal power, located for men in the male reproductive organs. In fact, in many mystical texts, the word "Yesod" is synonymous with "penis."

Yesod literally means "foundation." The personhood that a man acquires in harnessing his drives and the power to generate implied by Yesod's sexuality are seen as his foundation. Because Yesod has always represented the locus of personal will, which in a man is greatly affected by the output of testosterone in his body, Yesod has also come to be equated with the ego.

For this reason, Yesod is classically represented by the biblical character Joseph, who was endowed with an abundance of ego, but who was ultimately able to rise above himself to serve his people.[22] Joseph was also able to resist what might be considered the greatest temptation to a man, that of a gorgeous and sexually hungry seductress, Potiphar's wife, who pressed him repeatedly to sleep with her.[23] Joseph's sexual self-restraint and his ability to transform his ego from self-centered to God-centered are the model and goal of Yesod in the classical masculine understanding.

For women, Yesod takes on a different shape and quality altogether. It is the center of women's creative and procreative energies. Rather than an arrow of lust that directs our attention and must be trained to desist like the penis, for women, whose reproductive energies lie within, Yesod is the locus of interior creation, symbolized by that power-packing, fist-shaped organ, the uterus.

Whether or not we choose to have children, the uterus, or womb, root word of "woman," identifies us as women. It is the only part of a woman's physical anatomy that has absolutely no corollary in the male body. Even the clitoris, the amazing sensory organ created with the sole purpose of providing female pleasure, may be compared in function to the tip of a man's penis. But the womb is an extra thing, unlike any organ or faculty of a man, and as such it is unique and special.

Hidden deep within the pelvic cavity, the uterus is a stretchy, hollow muscle that, empty, weighs a mere two ounces; full of baby, it grows in weight to sixteen times that and expands in volume a thou-sandfold. Constantly in flux, this organ collects and fills itself rhyth-mically every month, making itself a plump nest in which to cradle a possible offspring. For most months of a woman's generative life, unless it has actually become that nine-month cocoon, the uterus automatically lets go, letting the blood that filled its potential home flow back into the earth, releasing any evidence of its dream, and returning to a state of empty readiness.[24] For women who do become mothers, the uterus is the place of that electrical meeting of seed and egg, of implantation and holding, stretching and containing, stretch-ing and more stretching, often to inconceivable proportions. Here in the Yesod center of a woman's Tree of Life is the locus of true devo-tion, of giving oneself over to another who is no other, of feeding and transmitting life with only hints of the boundaries that will nec-essarily come at birth.

Women have their own mysteries, which are borne out in their bodies, just as men's truth is borne out in theirs. Whether it is the urge to bring new life into the world in the form of a flesh-and-blood child or a piece of music or writing, medical research, or community ser-vice, women know in their cells and organs the work of creating, of inward carrying, giving over everything, and stretching to the point of disfiguring themselves to nurture a creation and bring it to life.

The female figure associated with Yesod is Tamar.[25] Tamar was a widow living within the family of Judah. Both her husbands, Judah's sons, had died. According to the ancient laws, a widow could not marry outside the family if there were marriageable brothers. Judah had one last son, Shelah, but withheld him from Tamar. This meant that Tamar, still a young and beautiful woman, was left in a helpless situation, at the mercy of the men in her family who refused to relate to her beyond her black widow's attire.

In her desperation, Tamar disguised herself as a sacred prostitute from the temple of Asherah and loitered on the roadside where she knew her newly widowed father-in-law, Judah, would be passing. Indeed, when Judah caught sight of the harlot on the road, he proposed to go off with her. But Tamar was cunning. She asked for collateral payment in the form of Judah's signet, bracelets, and staff before she allowed him to have sex with her.

In three moons' time, word came that his daughter-in-law Tamar had played the harlot and was pregnant. Judah angrily demanded that she be brought out and burned. But as Tamar was taken from her tent, she sent word to her father-in-law, saying, "By the man whose these are, am I with child. Please tell me, I beg you, whose are these signet, bracelets, and staff?"

Judah was caught. To his credit, he acknowledged his fatherhood as well as Tamar's righteousness (for he had indeed discredited her by not allowing her to marry) and took her for his wife. Tamar gave birth to twin boys, one of whom was the progenitor to King David. Tamar's will to fulfill herself at any cost is an expression of the *sephirah* of Yesod, which can be seen as the deeply ingrained instinct to create. Don't try to thwart Yesod; it will only go underground and come up more powerfully than before!

The feminine approach to Yesod demands that we, like Tamar, be endlessly creative. To connect with Yesod, we must listen to our creative urges, take risks, and cultivate our belly as a center of deep knowing.

Tipheret: Harmony

The energy continues to rise up the Tree, making a pathway from uterus to heart. These two organs know one another; they are different octaves, so to speak, of the same wisdom. Both share the same drive to connect, serve, and surrender.

Tipheret lies at the heart of the Tree. Just like the organ at the center of our bodies that pumps blood to our extremities, so Tipheret nourishes the entire Tree with its intelligent compassion. Tipheret is the one *sephirah* that directly converges with each of the other *sephirot*. Inside of us, it is the point of intersection between all of our parts: the connection of upper self and lower self, inner self and outer self, and self and other.

Although in Yesod we privately gestate our dreams and creations, in Tipheret we come out to meet the world, to touch and be touched, to reach out and to receive, to join our own inner world with a bigger reality.

Tipheret means "beauty," but not in the conventional sense of the word. As we have said, the *sephirot* of the middle pillar are all about balance between opposites. Tipheret is the beauty born of finding one's personal balance in the world. In Tipheret one balances a multitude of complexities that go hand in glove with the business of relationship. Here one negotiates a myriad of tensions between oneself and others, giving and receiving, finding and losing one's boundaries, and maintaining one's inner truth while acknowledging outer truths.

Another name for Tipheret is Rachamim, or "womblike compassion." Like Yesod, which we have correlated to the physical womb, Tipheret, at the heart center, is a kind of spiritual womb, one that belongs equally to men and women. This is the place in which the depths of our existence—our deepest feelings of pain, yearning, and connection—are transformed into our loftiest ideals. Like the *rechem*, Hebrew for "womb" (and root word for "compassion"), Tipheret is a secure and all-loving container in which our sense of self and our purpose in the world evolve.

In fact, everything we need to grow is here in the heart. But Tipheret is interested in liberation, not dependency. Like a womb at the point of its fruit's ripeness, Tipheret will begin to heave and contract at the first signs of readiness, squeezing us out into a more autonomous life. This might come in the form of a painful breaking away from our family or society's expectations of us in order to follow our own inner guidance.

Tipheret is the alchemical crucible in which our lives are transformed—sometimes despite our own protestations—in the service of our greatest potential. Tipheret's power is love, but not a soft and boundless love or a love of the unconditional sort. This is a love that seeks to help us grow, to liberate us from the dependencies of our small selves.

Each of us has a small self and a great self, and Tipheret is the link between them. The mystics entitled our small-minded ego orientation the *mochin de katnut,* and our less frequent cosmic awareness, *mochin de gadlut,* or "great mind." It was understood that the former was a necessary state of consciousness enabling us to live in time and space and take care of our worldly existence. In Tipheret, we can learn to shift gears between our two selves with some degree of control.

Jacob is the biblical figure who has classically personified Tipheret, and for good reason: he struggled intensely to form a bridge between his small self and his greatness. Jacob started his journey as a straight-laced mama's boy who snatched his brother's birthright and the lauded progenitor's blessing. It was only by being tricked himself and suffering a reversal of roles that he was able to grow up. After twenty years, the twin brother whom Jacob had duped came to call on him. Jacob suffered greatly at the thought of facing his brother, for in confronting him Jacob had to confront his own greed, arrogance, and fear, the dark elements of his own personality that, like his filial relationship, had never been dealt with. The night before their fateful meeting Jacob was met by a dark stranger and struggled with him all night long.[26]

This is a story of transformation. Jacob is given an opportunity to move from his small-minded or egotistical self to the much larger perspective of the higher self. But his greatness does not come by way of loving transcendence but rather out of his starkest fear and wrestling with the truth of his character. Paradoxically, it is through this descent into his humanity that Jacob finds the doorway out of his smallness, symbolized in the story by Jacob's new name—Israel, "he who wrestles with God." Through his struggle with his heart's darkness, he becomes the father of a people and can touch the heart of humanity.

Transforming the Jacob-self into the Israel-self, our small mind into our great mind, requires a lifetime of work. Focusing one's attention on Tipheret can be very beneficial in this regard. Meditation on this *sephirah* might be as simple as breathing deeply, directing the breath flow into and out of the heart area, or calling on God using the name fitting for this *sephirah*, which is HaRachaman, the "Compassionate One." Or the Tipheret focus may be a prayerful intent to stand in the threshold between one's small self and larger self, witnessing the play of consciousness between the two.

Whatever our focus, meditation on this *sephirah* will immediately provide us with information. Most commonly, it will bring us home to our own inner work, directing us to clear up specific relationships, tell the truth, or let go of old wounds. Clearing the heart of personal baggage may take a while! But until one's own house is in order, open and empty enough to receive clear signals, the voice of God will not be heard.

Then there is grace, Tipheret's gentler component. The experience of grace is not the result of personal work or mastery, but rather a spontaneous gift from God that swings open our heart's doors unexpectedly and gives us a glimpse of the Heart of all hearts, the Love behind all love. This kind of experience we cannot plan for, or even hope for. Grace may touch us at night in a dream or in the morning on the subway. When it does, it shows us the big vista just beyond the door, and, like Jacob, we are left with some memento of the occasion.

In Hebrew, Hannah means "grace," and it is the biblical character Hannah who is the female personage equated with the *sephirah* of Tipheret.[27] Like so many biblical heroines, Hannah was barren. In ancient times, a woman's worth was integrally tied up with her ability to produce offspring, and Hannah suffered greatly. She made a pilgrimage to the Temple, there to weep and pray to God. She made a bargain with God that if her womb opened, the male child that came forth would be offered to the holy work of the Temple.

Sitting alone in the Temple, Hannah was praying rapturously, her petition pouring out of her heart with abandon, when the priest entered and chastised her for being drunk! Hannah defended herself, knowing that her prayer was the overflowing of her troubled heart. When she returned home, she conceived a son and named him Samuel, which means "God has heard." As she had promised, Hannah brought Samuel to the Temple, and he ultimately became a prophet of the Israelite nation.

The rabbis of the Talmud extol Hannah and derive numerous teachings from her story. In fact, Hannah is discussed at greater length than any other female figure in the entire Talmud! The rabbis recognized that she was a person who knew the inner secrets of prayer. She had within herself the ability to reach from her heart to God's heart and, by so doing, to change the path of her destiny.[28]

Tipheret is both the personal and the cosmic heart, and from this place we can go to the utmost of our human powers, exerting every effort and doing whatever must be done. But our powers must not lead to hubris. It is a dangerous form of self-inflation to think that we alone have the capacity to storm heaven's gates. We do best to offer our works, as Hannah did her prayers, with abandon, letting them render us empty rather than full, for it is not into our fullness but into our emptiness that God can pour Her grace.

Da'at: The Flash

Tipheret delivers us to the upper realms of the Tree of Life, where the branches dissolve into the sky and our personalities become diaphanous. At the top of the middle pillar, we find a region beyond substance that can be experienced only by a self that is of no substance.

The door that leads into this region of Ayin, Divine Nothingness, is called Da'at. More like a flash or a mercurial dot than a door, Da'at is not a *sephirah;* it moves too quickly. Da'at is not a thing or even an energy, but a fleeting experience of insight, of *satori,* of cellular understanding that propels us out of ourselves into the beyond. In Da'at (which means "knowing" in Hebrew) we suffer a final death-blow to our concepts, to our ideals, to any vestige of our self's sublimity. Da'at is a momentary enlightenment that leads us to our truest selves.

One characteristic of Jewish mysticism that differentiates it from Eastern philosophies is that there is no indication of an ultimate personal enlightenment, no final liberation. Yes, there is an ancient belief in a collective redemption and a utopian era that will come in the days of the Messiah. But in reference to the individual, one finds no end to the oscillation between states of consciousness, from *katnut* to *gadlut* and back again. It is understood that the work of enlightenment is never ending. Just as Jacob returned to being Jacob even after he inherited the great name of Israel, so the *tzaddik*—the Jewish equivalent of a saint or *bodhisattva*—returns periodically to the ordinariness of personal needs, the mundane ingredients of life.

This is precisely where we find Malkah. In her seemingly ordinary way, Malkah knew how to immerse herself in the material world of Malkhut with such loving focus that her personal self dissolved, leaving her in a state of *gadlut,* expanded consciousness. From there, she was able to see into the future, receive guidance, commune with the divine forces, and then return to administer her wisdom to her family and community. In this way, Malkah navigated up and down the Tree, beginning with the most mundane tasks, moving through the revolving door of Da'at, into unchartable realms, and back to seven children and dinner on the stove.

Keter: Oneness

After Da'at, it is wisest to be wordless. What "comes next" is the great Oneness (also called, among other things, Ayin, the Divine Nothingness). It has no form or content or dimension, nothing around which words can take shape. One might figuratively call this territory the Mind of God, the infinite divine space from which all existence arises and to which all returns. Keeping in mind that Oneness is ineffable, we still need to approach it, knowing that our words will be necessarily limited. Keter means "crown." Within this infinite spaciousness, Keter is the first stirring of the cosmic will to take form.

Although we cannot grasp this dimension in any linear way, Jewish mysticism understands that this infinite dimension actually lives within each one of us in small measure. Practicing Jews regularly affirm in prayer and Torah study that God has sown a seed within us from this eternal realm. The object of the spiritual work from this vantage point is to sprout and cultivate this seed within our consciousness, bringing our innate divinity into the light of awareness.

It is clear that although the Tree of Life is a Jewish system, it charts a territory far beyond the purely Jewish worldview or, for that matter, any particular creed. Rather, it points us to a reality that includes all ideas and orientations: both masculine and feminine, East and West, light and dark. Here lies the sum total or unified field of all the polarities of our world. In this realm of Oneness, all things exist in a state of inherent *yichud*. It is heartening to know that at the core of the Jewish religion, we find an unfathomably broad view, unbiased as to gender or particular orientation, because it includes and transcends everything.

Keter, Oneness, does not live in our physical bodies, as do the other *sephirot*, but as a crown or halo just above our head. This *sephirah* connects us to our heavenly source, just as Malkhut connects us to our home on earth.

Initiates on the mystical path may experience the realm of Oneness, most for seconds only, but some for days on end. If you are fortunate enough to experience this vast and pulsing field, you may not be allowed to linger here for long before your personal structure— your body, mind, and personality—call you back to your singularity.

Bringing It Home

How does one personally apply this all-encompassing model of reality? Can we use the idea of the middle pillar of the kabbalistic Tree of Life to help bring our own lives into balance?

Charlene was a woman who did just that. I first met Charlene at a time in her life when she was struggling to cope with three small children and a husband who traveled extensively. She had come to my Jewish meditation class hoping to learn some coping techniques. In her personal introduction Charlene described how, in the evenings when she was alone with her children, she would feel engulfed by the children's endless demands on her. This feeling would lead to Charlene's shakiness, angry outbursts, or fits of crying, all of which scared the children as well as her.

The class began with a simple sitting exercise I called "Roots," in which the students imagined the bottoms of their spines elongating and extending downward, like a root into the earth. Then I asked them to imagine, upon inhalation, drawing their breath up from this root along the interior axis of their torsos, clearing out a passageway all the way up to the crown of their heads and slightly beyond, and then, upon exhalation, releasing it back down to the earth again.

Charlene took to this meditation easily, savoring her time in silence. At the end of the first class she reported seeing an image like an elevator shaft deep in her body, cluttered with all kinds of debris, children's toys, and dense fog. As she breathed, Charlene was able to begin clearing out this passageway. This gave her a sense of personal strength.

Charlene took this exercise home with her and practiced it daily, first rooting herself to earth, breathing long and slow breaths through her trunk, and connecting herself through the crown to heaven. The more she practiced, the easier it was to steady herself, even amid the chaos of childcare.

Using this exercise over several months, Charlene reported far more patience and loving feelings toward her children. She also experienced two sets of roots: one connecting her to heaven and one to earth. Whenever she felt overwhelmed or disoriented, she would begin carving out her interior column with her breath, anchoring herself above and below.

Charlene knew nothing about the Tree of Life or the middle pillar; she didn't have to. She was tapping an interior channel of energy that lies dormant within each one of us. The middle pillar is more than an idea; it is a power supply that, once open, can nourish, energize, and steady us. This is because it is connected to endless reserves of energy on each end, earth and heaven.

The Tree of Life, and in particular the middle pillar, is an axis upon which our personal balance may be achieved. It might be said that Malkah of Belz lived a life that expressed this rare state of balance, the result of a profound connection below and above. We will never know exactly how Malkah attained her remarkable state of joy and harmony, but we can use her as a model of what is possible, in addition to studying the Tree of Life for its profound teachings.

CHAPTER 4

RECOVERING FEMININE WISDOM

Asnat Barzani (1590–1670)

In the Middle East, in the mountainous region of Kurdistan, lived a seventeenth-century sage named Asnat Barzani. Asnat, who came from a life of outward poverty but who lived like a princess, was a true anomaly. In her own lifetime, she was referred to as Rabbi and Tanna'it, or Lady Tanna,[1] an unthinkable honor for a woman of her day and culture. But Asnat was not only a great sage; she was renowned for performing miracles and healings. Many believed, and Kurdish legends emphasize, that Asnat was one of the rare human beings who knew the secret pronunciation of YHVH, the Four-Letter Name of God.[2]

Asnat's life, which was devoted to study and teaching, exemplifies the feminine approach to Divine Wisdom. Asnat teaches us that the power to tap the Divine Imagination belongs to all of us. By opening ourselves to the highest levels of intuition and using the skill of discernment, we can bring our dreams into form.

Asnat may be seen as a master of the uppermost *sephirot* on the Tree of Life called the Wisdom Triangle. In this chapter, we will continue our exploration of the Tree of Life, studying this triad in particular. Beginning with Ayin, Divine Nothingness, we will delve into the divine functions of Emptiness, Wisdom, and Discernment to understand how these archetypal *sephirot* act within us. We will see how both our intuitive and analytical modes are critical to being a whole person and why they are depicted as the inseparable Divine Couple. Once again, the theme of *yichud,* the uniting of disparate parts, is central, as women's wisdom is reintegrated into the Jewish tradition.

Although we know far too little about Asnat, as her own writings have not survived history, her life of solitude, study, and community leadership glows with a special radiance. She lived in desperate poverty, but her love of Divine Wisdom clearly sustained her to the end of her outwardly difficult life.

The Jews of the Kurdish region—which spanned southeastern Turkey and adjoining parts of Iran and Iraq—were distinguished for their own particular music and food and for their religious poetry and spiritual legends. Although it was highly uncharacteristic among Mizrachi Jews (Jews from the Arab regions of the Middle East, northern Africa, and the Iberian Peninsula) for women to be lauded as leaders and sages, Asnat was accepted and greatly honored by the male leaders of her community.

This stands in sharp contrast to the story of Hannah Rachel, who was virtually banished from her people. The Mizrachi Jews, like their European cousins, depended heavily upon their women to be the keepers of the home and maintained a strong and unequal division in areas of domestic labor and religious practice. We can only surmise that Mizrachi Jews had a greater acceptance of women's ability to access Divine Wisdom.

Tradition dates the Kurdish Jewish community to the eighth century B.C.E., when the Ten Tribes were first exiled by the Assyrians. For centuries, the population of Jewish Kurdistan rose and fell in number, suffering religious persecution, poverty, and political instability. Today barely any Jews remain in the area, most having made their final pilgrimage to the State of Israel in the early 1950s.

Scattered through the towns and villages of the Kurdistan mountains and plateaus, Asnat's religious community lived humbly. Most Kurdish Jews lived spartan lives as craftspeople, peddlers, and merchants; many lived off the land. Their houses were rough and their cuisine was rustic, based on cracked wheat, legumes, and *kubba,* meat-and-wheat dumplings cooked in stews. Physical survival was a constant preoccupation for these Jews, second in importance only to preserving their faithfulness to God and the Jewish people.

Kurdish Jews worked hard to center their lives around their religious institutions—their synagogues, Hebrew schools, and *yeshivot,* schools of higher learning for boys and men. They were careful to marry among themselves. When the instability of their economic and political situation forced them to do so, they moved as an extended family in caravan formation until they found a safer location.

Unlike the Ashkenazic communities of Russia and Europe, who looked upon the rabbi as their chief authority, each Kurdish community furnished itself with a leader, or *nasi,* who was in charge of raising taxes to fund Jewish community needs, and a wise man, or *hakham,* who served as the ritual butcher, cantor, educator, scribe, and writer of amulets. These roles were always assumed by men.

Asnat's father, the legendary Samuel ben Nethanel HaLevi Barzani, fit into neither the *nasi* nor the *hakham* category, yet he was renowned for his scholarship and piety. Barzani was the unofficial yet acknowledged leader of Kurdish Jewry of his day. Although there was no printing press in Kurdistan during his lifetime and many of his writings, like those of his daughter, have been lost, what remains shows the work of a sage of Kabbalah.[3] So devoted was Barzani to sacred study, in fact, that he spent his life traveling from town to town, establishing *yeshivot.* He was famous for the saying "Any community that does not have a religious school is as if it did not have God."

When the itinerant saint Barzani came home from his travels, he spent his time training his daughter Asnat, grooming her to be his successor. The training Asnat received from her father—comprehensive study of the Torah, Talmud, and *Zohar,* along with sacred poetry in Arabic and Hebrew—was permeated with his mystical perspective.

Mystical Iconoclasm

For these two scholars, father and daughter, the study, memorization, and contemplation of holy words took them directly to God's door. Theirs was the mystical path to God known as Wisdom. They knew well that the hidden power of words can open one to a direct experience of the Divine. Their ardor and devotion to learning as a way of life teach us that sacred study is far more than a mental process.

To help Asnat establish and protect her mystical practice, her life was extremely sheltered. In fact, Asnat rarely went out of doors. Asnat Barzani's life was cloistered in much the same way that the monastic Christian orders structured themselves to protect their nuns from the distractions of the secular world. Cutting down on the pressures and stimulation of the mundane world enabled the nuns to cultivate a relationship with God that was strong and unimpeded.

Set apart from the small and impoverished world that surrounded her and untrained in the domestic work to which the women of her community committed their lives, Asnat must have been a source of wonderment in her town of Amidya. In a letter to her community, she wrote about her growing up, "Never in my life did I step outside my home. I was the daughter of the king of Israel.... I was raised by scholars; I was pampered by my late father. He taught me no art or craft other than heavenly matters."[4]

By "pampering," Asnat could not have meant material treats; the records describe her family as being extremely poor. The heavenly matters to which she refers as her sustenance were the words and concepts of the Torah and the doors of consciousness that they unlocked for her. It is clear that Asnat participated in an experience that might be termed mystical communion, or in Hebrew, *atzilut,* "mystical nearness," in which the separate self is utterly silenced and temporarily absorbed into God's Oneness.

Asnat was fortunate that her father gave her the means to live in spiritual solitude. One can imagine how much more fulfilling her experience might have been had she had a circle of like-minded women around her to share the journey! Unfortunately for Asnat and others with a similar mystical calling, there has never existed a monastic order for women in Judaism. Jewish women have throughout history been the workers and sustainers of the home, those who made it possible for men to do their spiritual work. Asnat's life flew in the face of this model, which was the only option for both Mizrachi and Ashkenazic women.

Particularly in the Arab world, at a time when women were barely educated and there was no hint of feminine liberation on the world's horizon, one wonders how it was possible for a girl to be raised as a scholar and saint! Despite the fact that Jewish women in Asnat's day claimed a higher status within their community than the Muslim women of the surrounding populations, they were still deeply bound to the domestic norms that had been imposed upon them centuries earlier by their own cultural matrix. Outside of their own womanly domain, Mizrachi women, like their Ashkenazic sisters, were rarely trained to attune themselves to God in any formalized fashion.[5]

The "Gift" of Superiority

Instead of the permission to commune with God that Asnat was given, most Jewish women receive a backwards kind of exemption, one that has been reiterated throughout the ages and in traditional circles to this very day. With minor variations, it goes something like this. A woman's relationship to God is inherently more intimate than that of a man's. Women naturally have within them the ability to shape and generate life. Unlike men, they are born sensitive and attuned to the Creator. Therefore, women require far less formal maintenance in the form of ritual, study, and prayer to keep them holy. It is because of their "natural spirituality" that so little has been asked of women by the rabbinic authorities in the way of religious praxis.

This idea and the division of roles and labor that proceeds from it are largely unquestioned in religious circles. It is understood that because a woman's spirituality is already so deeply ingrained, she needs less discipline than a man to keep her on track. Although this is a winning idea that speaks to the integrated nature of women's consciousness, it is also quite dangerous, for it has served to perpetuate the psychological *mechitza,* or divider, between men and women, with ritual practices predominantly happening on the men's side only, that has proved so damaging to both.

Thinking of women in such a "laudatory" way, men are free to dismiss the entire issue of the woman's portion in a legacy that was meant to be shared; they are free to spiral loftily away from the daily rigors of earthly existence, for their female counterparts have been divinely commissioned to serve as their ballast, the ultimate women's goal being that of holding together the body and soul of the family. Not a small goal, perhaps, or even an inconsequential one, but one without much prerogative, range, or room for self-discovery!

Ultimately this reverse chauvinism has succeeded in separating women from the mystical potential within their own heritage, harnessing them to serve as champions of the mundane world. All this because they are "naturally elevated" and "inherently spiritual"! In the end, this way of thinking has devolved over centuries into cultural standards that prohibit women from pursuing their own disciplined inquiry into the nature of the Divine.

Many Jewish women today prefer to avoid such proclamations of their superiority, choosing not to be excused from the "burden" of consistent spiritual discipline that involves a daily practice.[6] The sad truth is that, until recently, Jewish women with a mystical inclination have had to shape their own destiny outside of the established grid and to struggle in isolation to glean the riches of their own tradition. This has meant a huge loss of creativity and wisdom for the whole Jewish tradition.

Fortunately for modern women in search of inspiring models within Judaism, Asnat's life was utterly extraordinary. We will never know why her father chose for her what might be termed a monastic path. Did he see early on that Asnat had a predilection for words and ideas and required silence to contemplate them? Was he guided from on high to help this one daughter and not his others? Or was this sage who had only daughters and no sons simply determined to create a successor? In any event, his choice enabled Asnat to become a scholar, linguist, and miracle worker, and, perhaps more important, a woman with the unusual permission to develop a constant and intimate relationship with the Divine through the path of solitude and study.

Asnat's Mystical Powers

Asnat's closeness with God, which her Kurdish compatriots understood to be magical, gave birth to a legend about her and her pet dove. The white bird built its nest in a tree just outside the door of Asnat's house. On one particular day, as Asnat's dove soared joyfully through the heavens, a hunter aimed at its lovely body and shot it down. When the bird fell to the ground, all the children in the area came running. They loudly bemoaned the hunter's deed. How could he have shot down Rabbi Asnat's beloved dove? The ashamed hunter took the dead bird to its mistress and begged her forgiveness. Asnat took the bird from him and closed the door of her house. A few moments later, a fluttering was heard and the bird flew out of Asnat's door back into its nest. Asnat was able to heal and even call the dead back to life.

In Jewish mysticism, the white dove is symbolic of the Shechinah Herself. The legend tells us of Asnat's closeness with the Divine

Feminine Presence. Her life was devoted to bringing the beauty and the freedom of the Shechinah back into life, and the people of Kurdistan knew Asnat as the Shechinah's champion.

But a true relationship is never a one-way affair. Asnat's love for and protection of the Divine Feminine was reciprocated fully. Kurdish legends tell us of the faithfulness of Asnat's pet dove, who also watched over her mistress. Asnat, who was not only wise but beautiful, was once hanging laundry on her rooftop. A Gentile spied her and, smitten with her lovely form, lusted after her. Late that night, the man had vile thoughts and stalked Asnat's house, climbing up toward her room. Sensing the danger, Asnat's dove wailed out a foreboding cry. Hearing her bird, Asnat arose just in time to find the man outside her window. Without hesitating, she pronounced a sacred incantation and instantly the intruder found himself hanging from the beams of Asnat's roof, frozen in place.

The next morning, the townspeople gathered around to see the odd spectacle, but no one could so much as approach the man to remove him; the magnetic field of Asnat's spell was impenetrable. Only days later, after the governor of the township swore that the man would be tried, would Asnat consent to release him from his spell, saying, "Had he only intended to steal my possessions, I would have done nothing. But the man intended to do an evil deed to me, and this was the result."

Because of this and other stories like it, which were probably based upon true occurrences, it was common knowledge that Asnat had the power of the Holy Name. People flocked to her for her blessings, for with this power it was understood that Asnat could change the shape of one's destiny. Women who were heartsick and those who wished to conceive, men who were impoverished and those in need of healing all came to Asnat. Whether her magical powers were imparted to her by her father or whether she learned them through her own studies, the female rabbi was recognized as the wisest and holiest woman in Kurdistan. But this did not mean her life was in any way easy.

A School of Her Own

Asnat married her cousin Jacob ben Abraham. In the ancient custom of Mizrachi Jews, children were betrothed at an early age by their parents, and Asnat's marriage to Jacob most probably involved such a betrothal. Asnat's father, however, understood that once she assumed the role of wife, social pressure would force her out of her peculiar role of lone scholar into the more mundane life expected of women. To protect her status as *chachamah*, "wise woman," Rabbi Barzani specified in Asnat's *ketubah*, "wedding document," that Asnat "must never be troubled by housework." This was a radical proclamation, indeed, and must have sent reverberations through the entire community and shudders down the spine of her poor husband, who could not afford a maid!

As Asnat bore two children, first a son and then a daughter, and her husband took over her father's *yeshivah* in Mosul, we imagine that she, like many women, stretched herself to continue her sacred work and raise her children as well. Records show that Asnat was the lead teacher in her husband Jacob's school, allowing him to occupy himself with his own scholarly research. However, Jacob did not live long; he died, leaving Asnat with two young children.

Life had already been difficult. The *yeshivah* in Mosul, like others in Kurdistan, was dependent on help from neighboring Jewish communities. Documents show letters written by Jacob before his untimely death appealing for help in keeping the *yeshivah* afloat. His pleas, reminding his Jewish compatriots of their sacred duty to support their teachers and rabbis and promising them the rewards of the future world, apparently garnered little help. It seems that some donations were actually made but, owing to the dangers of the road, never arrived into the family's hands. Thereafter, donors were reticent to send more funds.

Asnat refused to close her husband's school. With Samuel, her son, still too young to act as dean, she stepped forward and took over the school herself, becoming the first female Rosh Yeshivah, dean and lead teacher of a men's Talmudic academy, in Jewish history. For a woman to be in this position is absolutely unheard of, even to this day.

Tragically, what little remains of Asnat's scholarly legacy is her letter of appeal to the community of her native town, Amidya, for support. In it she writes about the many troubles that beset her after Jacob's death. There seems to have been a debt due to Christians for one hundred piastres. The creditors obtained possession of her house and sold all of her clothes and those of her daughter.

As we read an excerpt from Asnat's only remaining words, we notice her ardent dedication to the path of study as the spiritual fire that illuminates and nourishes her people. Her Hebrew words are like the rich poetical laments of the prophets; her use of poetry and scriptural allusion underscores her erudition and her devotion to keeping the holy spark of sacred study alive at all costs:

> *I'll speak for the Learning and moan*
> *for its vanishing from my land,*
> *For the brilliant spark in a cloud of heaven*
> *has hidden from my people . . .*
> *You who are righteous have mercy—*
> *For the word of the Lord, my Rock, my Master,*
> *Not for my own well-being or glory*
> *Is my wailing and weeping before you;*
> *Not even for the needs of my household,*
> *Nor for my clothing and food—*
> *But for the house of study's survival*
> *That my strength not fail me there. . . .*
> *For this the fire within me burns. . . .*
> *If my students are forced to disperse,*
> *What would my nights and days mean?*
> *Therefore, O pious ones, listen,*
> *And your righteous men hear me out. . . .*[7]

Asnat's passionate lament, unfortunately, met with little response. However, her *yeshivah*, miraculously, did not fold. Under Asnat's guidance, the school continued, as did she and her children, struggling for several more years in the starkest poverty. When her son came of age, he took it over as its dean and fund-raiser.

A Father's Daughter

Like Hannah Rachel, Asnat was groomed by her father to be more like a son than a daughter. As in Beruriah's story, Asnat's mother is never mentioned in tales about her. We might call all three of these women sages "father's daughters," or women who derive their sense of self and purpose from their father and his values.

A father's daughter is a woman who identifies with masculine values, not necessarily in regard to gender issues, but in terms of the energetic or archetypal principle that the masculine connotes. Masculine energy runs straight like an arrow. It points to its goal and drives forward until it is achieved. In a woman, this masculine energy often expresses itself through forthrightness in speech and purposefulness in action. It is found in no-nonsense women who have charted a path for themselves and are determined to stay the course.

Feminine energy, on the other hand, is less oriented to the goal ahead and more to the moment at hand. Paying attention to the path itself rather than zeroing in on a bull's-eye, the feminine flows in a more meandering style. When we are oriented to the feminine compass, we are less likely to be dashing around with an eye on the clock, getting through our list of tasks, and more attentive to the relationships with people and things along the way. For this reason, the feminine is known to be relational and, because of this, more oriented to the here-and-now feelings and needs of the present moment than to visions of the future.

Both masculine and feminine sensibilities materialize their vision, but in very different tempos and styles. Although a woman who is oriented to the feminine might also be highly successful in the world, the woman we are calling the "father's daughter" is one who most easily finds her place in the world of goal setting and accomplishment. Because she identifies herself with the values of the father, that is, fulfilling the goal—whether in the world of academia, commerce, or, as in Asnat's case, the study of the sacred—the father's daughter sets her goals high and shoots for them with everything she has.

Throughout the generations, women have taken—arguably, been given—a life route that required constant attention to the home fires, to the sick child at one's side, to the food that needed stirring. The women's path has, on the whole, required more immediate, peripheral vision. In exchange, it has provided its riches in the form of deeply textured days and the accumulation of those days.

Because feminine values have been so greatly discounted through the centuries and seen through the eyes of men as lacking in wisdom and importance, it has most often been the girls or women who aligned themselves with masculine values, the fathers' daughters, who are seen and remembered as special. This is one of our dilemmas as modern women. We are left with so few recorded legacies of women, and what remains for us are most often the lives that have bypassed feminine norms in favor of the preferred kind of excellence, that of the father.

Asnat is an example of this, but with an interesting twist, as we shall soon see. She was decidedly a father's daughter who stepped away from the outward values of the women of her culture to take on another set of goals. Yet she used her stalwart masculine determination to bring into the world the fruit of her deep study, arguably a feminine endeavor.

The Feminine Path of Wisdom

Asnat succeeded in breaking away from the traditionally accepted feminine norms in order to live a different kind of feminine life. But if you examine her story carefully, it becomes clear that Asnat employed distinctly masculine values in order to attain goals that were actually deeply feminine. Her deepest love was to immerse herself in the world of ideas, knowledge, and philosophy. This is the feminine world of Wisdom, known from ancient times by the Jews as *Chochmah* and by the Greeks as *Sophia*. These names point to a living principle, a feminine spirit who was considered by the ancients to have special allure: When we are captivated by wisdom, our minds and hearts are engaged as one entity.

The path of wisdom is very different from the sensuous path arising in Malkhut. Unlike Malkah, Asnat was not attuned to the gifts of the natural world. She did not cook, bake, or engage in the colorful handiwork of the Kurdistani women. What fed Asnat was the interior life and the pursuit of wisdom. Asnat was nourished by her penchant for study and her unusual good fortune to be raised as a scholar.

Asnat's life exemplified total immersion in the world of ideas for the sheer love of wisdom. This is a distinctly feminine way of relating to knowledge. Surrendering to a text is very different from mastering it. Losing oneself in discovery is very different from tearing through books for data. Gathering information is purposeful; it is an act commissioned by a goal. Diving into an ocean of knowledge, however, is less self-conscious. In this mode, we are more focused on the sheer pleasure of discovery.

Study for the love of study is one of the highest values in Judaism. The Talmud lauds this type of study as *lishmah,* which literally means "for her sake." Who is *her*? The Torah, the *neshama* ("soul"), and the Shechinah are all feminine principles in Judaism. Note that none of these are quantifiable or attainable entities. Studying "for her sake" means studying because of a pure love of wisdom. This was Asnat's way.[8]

The Wisdom Triangle

Asnat's approach to the Divine Feminine through the path of Wisdom was vastly different, for example, from that of Malkah of Belz, whose more sensual path was equally strong and direct. But both approaches are found in the Tree of Life because it is a system that includes all possible spiritual pathways.

Malkah's connection was through Malkhut, an earthly, grounded place, but Asnat reached to an area of the Tree that I term the Wisdom Triangle. It is composed of Keter/Oneness, Chochmah/Wisdom, and Binah/Discernment (see Appendix). In the last chapter we learned that Tipheret serves as a gateway to the upper branches of the Tree, the ineffable realms of our spiritual nature, symbolized by these upper three *sephirot*. It is this upper triangle (or diamond, if you figure in the mercurial flash called Da'at) that we must address to find the place of Asnat's contemplations. But this transpersonal dimension is not an easy place to reach.

This is because the Wisdom Triangle is not the abode of a warm and protective God or of a wrathful God. Nor do any images or adjectives belong there at all. Nor do these three *sephirot*, Keter, Chochmah, and Binah, have biblical characters, names, and attributes associated with them as do the lower seven. This is because they represent aspects of God's mind, which includes us, but goes far beyond us. Only when we have been trained through meditation or other spiritual disciplines to temporarily loosen our grip on our personal selves can we begin to comprehend this upper segment of the Tree.

The lower seven *sephirot* are where the more concrete particulars come back in, as we shall see. They are filled with personality and the affairs of life, while the upper three *sephirot* are about the ineffable essence of God.

Ayin: The Experience of Nothingness

In a beautiful section of the *Zohar* called "Ra'aya Mehemna" ("The Faithful Shepherd") there is a poetic rendering of the idea of Ayin:

God is like the ocean
For the waters of the ocean
Cannot be grasped and have no shape
Except when they are channeled into a vessel,
Such as the land,
And take on a shape;
Then we are able to measure them.
The source, the waters of the ocean are one.[9]

The Source of the waters is the primordial *sephirah*, Keter, the uppermost *sephirah*, which was discussed in the last chapter. We saw how Keter, like an infinite ocean of light, is difficult to grasp. Whatever words we use to describe this formless infinity automatically limit it. It is almost humorous, therefore, to discover how many names are used to point to that which is ineffable! A few of the many names are: Flame of Darkness, Cause of All Causes, Ayn Sof ("Limitlessness"), Keter ("Crown"), and Ayin ("Nothingness").

Ayin, Nothingness, is the most enigmatic of these. Because our human minds are fixed on conceptualizing in order to make sense of our reality, the word Ayin, Nothingness, continually reminds us to let go of our mental concepts. It says to our egos, No, there is something that is beyond you: God. God is like *no thing* in the world—not like physical objects or any of the concepts, ideas, theories, and labels we use either.

But this realm beyond humanity and all its divisions is certainly not a purely Jewish concept. The world's greatest mystics, from East and West, point to the paradox in their own way. Hindus use the term *neti neti;* to Taoists it is *wu;* and for Buddhists, *sunyata.* To Zen practitioners musing over koans it is *mu;* to Meister Eckhart it was *Nichts;* and St. John of the Cross termed it *nada.*

So powerful is this idea of cosmic emptiness that the term Ayin has been appropriated for use in the psychological realm. Ayin used in the psychological sense is a state in which one experiences a sense of personal formlessness and lack of identity. This usually occurs when we are in transition between one state of affairs—a career, marriage, or set of beliefs—and another. As difficult as this experience of emptiness is for the ego, it is a necessary one if we are to grow in life and be transformed into something beyond our limited self-images. As we shall see, the experience of Ayin can lead a person to her soul's deepest wisdom.

As a psychotherapist, I see numerous people who have reached a psychological Ayin state, most often without knowing what is happening to them. It is not uncommon for a person who may never have considered psychological support before to seek help when she encounters the nebulous feelings associated with this condition.

Maureen was one such person. She had been a workhorse all her adult life, putting her career as a social worker above all else. When she turned thirty-five, she suddenly felt an enormous urge to create a nest. She and her husband, Hank, sold their tiny studio apartment, bought a run-down Victorian house, and spent a year fixing it up.

Maureen got pregnant shortly thereafter. She was elated. But suddenly her perceptions of the world she lived in began to change. She started to daydream at work, thinking of nothing else but preparing for the arrival of her baby. In the spring, Maureen gave notice at her agency and left her job the next month. She was overwhelmed with relief and excitement and relished her free time to prepare for motherhood.

But then tragedy struck. Deep into her fifth month of pregnancy, Maureen suddenly began to hemorrhage, and within hours her baby was lost. Maureen sustained an emotional shock: the child around whom her entire world now revolved no longer existed.

By the time Maureen's body had healed, she was suffering from a deep depression. Pacing aimlessly through her new house, feeling its emptiness, she knew she could never go back to her previous work-centered life. Despite Hank's tenderness and attempts to distract her, Maureen could not recover a sense of life's meaning.

Maureen came to me in this Ayin state. Her tears and repeated iterations of her story began to loosen her depression, but there were no quick fixes to be considered. When one is in a psychological Ayin state, it is critical to surrender to it to allow the wisdom of the unconscious to heal us from the inside.

For several months, Maureen stayed in bed in an agonizing state of emptiness, not knowing who she was or what purpose she had in being alive. Others worried that she was losing her will to live. But during that time, Maureen watched her dreams and journaled every day. Unlike the old Maureen, who had kept to a regimented personal schedule, she began to give herself permission to follow her own impulses and rhythms—how much to eat, when to sleep, and what kind of movement felt right for her body. Maureen was learning that some deep inner wisdom was indeed guiding her back to health.

It was only after a full year that Maureen began to emerge—like a gorgeous butterfly from a thick and gummy cocoon—into an entirely new chapter of life. Her Ayin experience had put her in touch with her interior life and her own voice of wisdom. In two years time, Maureen began an entirely new career in the field of women's philanthropy, in which she has the freedom to create her own schedule. She is now the mother of a healthy little girl.

Many of us come to an experience of Ayin through the death of a dream. What follows such a death has been called a night sea voyage, a time in which we must navigate through total darkness without moorings or vision. Arriving at the far shore after such an experience, one is radically changed. For Maureen and others I have worked with, the state of Ayin leaves one with a sense of "nothing left to lose." They have been stripped of all hopes and illusions about life. But in disillusionment there is also an enormous power and a sense of liberation that brooks no excuses, compromises, or shortcuts with regard to one's inner truth. The great Hassidic master Rabbi Dov Baer put it this way:

> Nothing can change from one thing to another without first losing its original identity. Before an egg can grow into a chicken, it must completely cease to be an egg. Each thing must lose its original

identity before it can be something else. Before a thing is transformed into something else, it must come to the level of Ayin.[10]

Ayin, to be sure, is not the goal, but the necessary moment of transformation into new life. Sometimes we are graceful and bow to it with
appropriate humility; sometimes we rail against it, our egos inflamed by
the thought that we must let go one more time and begin anew. Much
as we resist, there can be no new beginnings, and as we are about to
see, no Wisdom, without first submitting to the empty void that is Ayin.

Moving into Somethingness

The Kabbalists knew that the transition between nothingness and
somethingness, or Ayin and Yesh, did not happen once and for all
time when the great primordial essence of God contracted into a point
of somethingness. What happens on a cosmic plane, they knew, also
takes place within each one of us because we are each microcosms of
the Whole.

Just as at the cosmic levels the unity of Ayin makes a space for
creation, by which it can be known, so we too, after having been "Ayin-
ized," that is, having come through a state of nothingness into new
being, are open to entirely new levels of re-creation. Likewise, in
order for our Yesh—what we have made of ourselves and of our
lives—to be reinvigorated with new life and new awareness, it must
be touched by the great power of emptiness, Ayin.

It is important to seek the Ayin state on our own. We can do this
through quiet walks, meditation, reading poetry, or going on silent
retreats. When we do not seek Ayin of our own accord, we are sometimes pulled there against our will.

Sarah was a client of mine who experienced this pull. She had been
a professor of sociology at a local college for over two decades. Bright,
funny, and committed to her students, Sarah would invariably come
into my office fired up about some public issue, whether it was a jus-

tice violation on campus or female genital mutilation in Muslim Africa. Sarah was never without a cause and never idle.

Sometime after her fiftieth birthday, Sarah's energy began to wane. She went through the motions of her active life, but now in a lackluster way. She complained of sleeplessness, and when she was able to recall her dreams they were often violent. Macabre images such as blood-stained fields and the bones of decaying animals crowded her nights. At first it seemed that these images were symbols of the death and destruction from the external world that Sarah frequented in her social action work. But as her lethargy gave way to depression, it became clear that there was an inner violence that Sarah needed to attend to.

Self-violence was an almost impossible concept for Sarah to comprehend, until she stood back from her life and tabulated how many years she had been working and how long it had been since she had taken a break to nourish her own self. She was deeply tired, not just physically, but spiritually.

The way Sarah had configured her world, Yesh, her substantive life, was not getting fed; it had no relationship with Ayin at all. Sarah had been so intensely focused on the ills of the world that her inner self had to verge on violence to get her attention, tugging her energy down like an undertow in the ocean. The obliteration of energy that Sarah experienced (she feared it to be chronic fatigue syndrome) was actually Ayin imposing itself to balance her inability to restore herself naturally with vacations, meditation, and other means of recreating.

Sarah and I discussed how she might respond to her situation. She would take a sabbatical, she decided, and go to a devastated region of Central America as a volunteer worker. But Sarah soon realized that her plan was part of the same troubled pattern. Yes, she needed to get away from her familiar routines, but she did not need to fill her days with more work, however good the cause.

Sarah was being invited to reinvent herself, to enter a new level of Yesh in which her own life could be integrated into her work for peace and justice. In order to do this, she needed to exit all the activities that kept her wheels spinning and give herself enough empty, unstructured time to relearn herself. Without dropping into a deep enough emptiness, what I call a state of personal Ayin, there was no way that Sarah could make a fresh start.

In the end, Sarah did take a year's sabbatical, spending some of that time rebuilding schools in Honduras. But before that, she took four months to be footloose and travel on her own. This was a revolution for Sarah, for she was extremely afraid of wasting time.

Sarah called this time off her "been nowhere, done nothing" break. It was during this time, spent in a fishing village in Mexico and wandering the outlying hills, that Sarah regained her life on the inside. When she returned to teach, she was calmer and more vital than ever. Knowing that her new state would evaporate in time, she took up yoga and scheduled for herself one hour each day of unstructured time. Sarah had found a way to tap into the vast open spaces, the Ayin, within her, and thus to claim a new Yesh.

Life renews itself continually. Each time we allow ourselves to dip into our own emptiness we are recreated with fresh vigor. And each time we navigate our way to a new level of being, new consciousness is born. This consciousness—the ability to reimagine ourselves—is part of the Divine Wisdom called Chochmah.

Chochmah: Divine Wisdom

The first *sephirah,* that astonishing Oneness we called Ayin or Keter, is so all-encompassing that it is completely hidden from sight, something like water might be to a fish in the ocean. The mystery is that from within this Totality there was a first glint, an impulse of desire to be discovered and known. But in order for this Unity to see Itself, it had to contract and create what looks like an *other* in which to be mirrored.

Imagine a person who has lived alone with no contact with any human or animal creature for fifty years. This person has no ability to understand him- or herself or evolve a self-concept because there is no reflection or feedback; there is simply no *other*. As soon as we come into relationship with an other we have the opportunity to know ourselves. If we could anthropomorphize God and imagine God's yearning to be known within the infinite expanse of Ayin, we would have an idea of the impulse behind creation.

The imagination to create is Chochmah, or Divine Wisdom. The Kabbalists knew that true Wisdom comes from the immense spaciousness of Ayin.[11] It is Chochmah that stands at the beginning of manifest creation, spoken about in the first words of Genesis.[12] What kind of Wisdom is this? The second *sephirah* is not wisdom in the traditional sense of accumulated knowledge about life. It is, rather, the fertile field of imagination from which all thoughts and creative images flow.

Chochmah is the bridge that leads from the infinite Source into manifestation. It is here in the *sephirah* of Wisdom that Nothingness becomes Somethingness.[13] The first *sephirah*, we learned, is known as Ayin, Nothingness; the second *sephirah*, Chochmah/Wisdom, is Divine Somethingness, also known as Yesh. We are not yet talking about physical somethingness, though, rather that first spark of the *desire* to manifest. Chochmah is pregnant with the potential to create. For this reason it is sometimes considered to be feminine and, as we shall see, the partner and helpmate of God.

But what, after all, does this really mean to us? Traditional teachers of Jewish Kabbalah sometimes ground these lofty ideas by saying that the Divine Unity came through Wisdom in the form of the Torah. The Torah was created before the world, the Midrash teaches. God looked into the Torah, the cosmic blueprint of creation, to see how to create the world.[14] But taking this literally seems slightly absurd. How can we possibly accept that the architecture of all of creation came through the sacred book of one people?

It is more likely that the Torah, in this allegory, stands for the embodiment of the divine intellect, what Christians call Logos and the Greeks once entitled the divine pleroma. All of these terms are names for the second *sephirah*, Wisdom, for they all point to the fullness of God's mind, where every idea, invention, thought, and solution lie in pregnant potential, waiting to be birthed. It is through human imagination that we can enter the divine intellect, for Wisdom is not just the accumulation of ideas. Wisdom is the ability to access the endless reservoir of possibilities, poetically termed God's mind, by using our imagination and ingenuity.

The idea that God's mind is available for humans to access through imagination is an ancient idea, but it is an idea that has been concealed. One reason that it may have been considered too dangerous to divulge is that it may have given rise to great hubris. To think that we humans could tap the mind of God was surely a heresy. Nevertheless, the world's greatest minds—Galileo and Michelangelo, Beethoven and Einstein—knew that they were doing exactly that.

God's Feminine Companion

There was yet another reason that the idea of God's accessibility may have been hidden. This was the fact that Divine Wisdom was portrayed by the ancients as a feminine companion of God. Long before Wisdom was considered the second *sephirah* on the Tree of Life, She was known as a powerful female character, God's own partner and intermediary between God and human beings.

> *When God established the foundations of the earth,*
> *I was by God's side,*
> *A master craftswoman,*
> *Delighting God day after day,*
> *Ever at play at God's side,*
> *At play everywhere in God's domain,*
> *Delighting to be with the children of humanity.*[15]

Although Wisdom has long been forgotten as a feminine figure, reminders of Her importance as God's creative function and as an ally to humanity are found throughout Hebrew scriptures, both in the

Hebrew canon and in the Apocrypha, books that were excluded from the official scriptures. These latter writings were saved and are still considered sacred to many communities.[16] Throughout the ancient texts, Wisdom is personified as a beautiful, caring, and extremely savvy feminine figure who, like mortal women, has many roles. She is portrayed as the beloved consort of God, a mother, an agent of justice, the architect of creation, chef and hostess, preacher and judge. Consistently female, Wisdom pervades the world and interacts with us all to call us into righteous living and to remind us of our highest potential.

Beginning with the ancient book of Job,[17] Wisdom makes a brief debut as a hidden treasure whose whereabouts are known only to God. About three hundred years later, She shows up again, this time striding onto the stage with unabashed bravado in the book of Proverbs. Here Wisdom's feminine voice comes across with unmistakable clarity. First she is a street preacher who speaks in first person; her message is like cold water on the faces of spiritual sleepers:

> *How long, you simple ones, will you love being simple?*
> *And how long will scorners delight in their scorning?*
> *And fools hate knowledge?*
> *Turn at my reproof; behold, I will pour out my spirit to you,*
> *I will make known my words to you.*[18]

Wisdom is depicted as a giver of life, a tree of life, as our very life itself.[19] In fact, She is so intrinsically associated with the divine blessing of physical life and spiritual awakening that She can rightfully proclaim, "Whosoever finds me finds life."[20]

Wisdom calls us to leave behind shallow living, in which we are tricked by appearances and fleeting pleasures, to remember that we are here on earth with a mission born of our eternal nature. She begs us to walk in Her ways, which are the ways of insight, right action, and peace.

Yet Her voice has been masked. For example, if you visit any synagogue or temple during a Torah service, you will most likely hear the famous song "*Eytz Chayim hee lamachazikim bah:* She is a tree of life to all who hold fast to her; all of her supporters are happy. Her ways are pleasant and all of her paths are peace."[21] This beautiful passage is sung just after the Torah scrolls have been replaced in the ark. Most people do not know that these words were meant as a description of Chochmah, Woman Wisdom, the personification of depth, learning, and insight. They were reappropriated by the rabbis, who were uncomfortable with a divine feminine figure, and came to mean the Torah instead.

There is little wonder why Jewish scriptures portraying Wisdom as a feminine entity were disguised, ignored, or excluded from Jewish sources. The male leadership believed that the figure of Wisdom might threaten the foundation of Jewish belief, the Oneness of God.[22] The fact that She was female also ran counter to the established role of YHVH, who was understood to be the solo male Creator, as discussed earlier.

Moreover, even if She were not somehow associated with God, Wisdom as a female personage was far from a decent model of womanly behavior. Like Asnat, She defied most all of the feminine norms prescribed for Jewish women by their society. Just look: Wisdom is portrayed as proud, assertive, highly energetic, sometimes angry, often threatening, and persistently loud—not the kind of woman a Jewish man of the day (or perhaps any day) would want the females in his home to take after!

Although She has been overlooked, Wisdom is, in fact, the most highly developed feminine personification of God's presence and activity in Hebrew scriptures.[23] As biblical personages go, Wisdom is far from being a minor figure in Hebrew sacred writings. Including apocryphal writings, there is quantitatively more material on Wisdom than almost any other figure, including Abraham, Isaac, Jacob, and Joseph.[24] Yet how many schoolchildren or even biblically erudite adults have ever heard of Her? Apart from the theological problems that Wisdom brings to light, this feminine personage—who is not God, yet somehow divine, and who flies in the face of Jewish societal norms—is so ambiguous and difficult to categorize that She was, either consciously or unconsciously, dropped out from the accepted body of knowledge of the ancient tradition.

Why is this strange and forgotten feminine figure important to us today? Could she have any bearing on our modern lives?[25] Remember that ours is a Christian society, and Christianity, whose central figure was a revolutionary rabbi, grew out of Judaism. This is why, to understand where we are as a society now and where we might be, we must hark back to the early teachings and writings of the Jews.

Imagine that from ancient times all Jews had read and integrated their own scriptures, free of censorship and political pressure from the dominant male leadership. Imagine a people who deeply understood that there was a Divine Feminine Principle at work in their lives. They knew that She not only was involved in the creation of the world but served as the matrix from which all creation emerges. Imagine that men and women taught their children to know that this wise and loving force called Wisdom was the bridge to the unknowable divine mystery, and that She was there to guide them as a living presence in the world, accessible within their own hearts. How different would our worldview be today?

The world was designed to have children who grew up with a deep respect for nature and for their own inner world. Rather than learning to override the laws of nature and the interior realm of feelings, dreams, and inner signals, children would grow up cultivating a relationship with these territories, which are ultimately greater than us, but of which we are a part. Gratitude, reverence, and co-partnership would be the goal. And rather than competition, the prevalent value would be relating to each other as children of the same Divine Parents.

And because the feminine represents the interior world where new life, ideas, and creativity of all kinds gestate in darkness and come forth in their own time, people might have a different, more tolerant, relationship to darkness and what it brings forth, might relate more gracefully to the timely unfolding of events, as opposed to the control of those events. Our addiction to flawless perfection would then not be so compelling.

It is vital that we reclaim the undisguised truth of the Judaic texts, for they contain glimpses of a balanced and therefore healing model of the archetypal forces within us and within our world. The ancients who scribed the words of Proverbs, for example, had profound insight into the nature of reality. When they saw Wisdom as the bridge between the unknowable Ayin and creation, between God and us, and, further, portrayed this bridge as a living feminine principle, they were describing the unifying power inherent in the universe through a partnership of masculine and feminine, heaven and earth. They knew instinctively that without a deep and abiding respect for the feminine there could be no relationship to the world of spirit. By overlooking Wisdom or reducing the term to mean a body of scriptures, we are missing the potential power and guidance that is always available to us.

If we in the West were to allow ourselves to modify our creation story, which is so integral to our cultural belief system, to include a feminine partner as a central part of the divine infrastructure, our thinking might change drastically. With a cosmology that included the Divine Masculine and Feminine as loving copartners, men would not be so afraid of women's creative powers and would not have had to objectify women, reducing them, at best, to subordinates and, at worst, to mere flesh to be taken and consumed.

The sacred texts that describe Wisdom as God's creative partner and a loving intermediary between the human and the Divine present us with a radical reworking of the rudiments of Jewish theology. If they could be understood as symbolic of universal truths, the psychological ramifications of these principles might be revolutionary.

If only people revisited these scriptures today, not taking them literally, but as symbols of the intrinsic balance between masculine and feminine energies within our psyches, much good could come from them at last. Feminine strength and forthrightness would never again be chided, nor would women's insight and the uniquely feminine approach to seeing the truth be discounted. The feminine approach to life, which is naturally round and encompasses all aspects of life like a great wheel, might at last be valued along with the straight ladder that connects heaven and earth. With a reverence for the divine partnership of Ayin and Wisdom, there might at last be a harmonious and respectful partnership between men and women.

However you choose to see it, as a misunderstanding or as a cover-up, the absence of Wisdom as a Divine Feminine Principle from the Jewish tradition is but one more example illustrating the devolution of the feminine face of God in the collective mind. But, although the neglect of Wisdom as a divine figure is a painful fact to face, especially given the dearth of feminine images in the Jewish tradition, it is impossible to completely submerge that which is part of the true nature of the Divine Psyche. The truth will keep popping up again and again as our own psychic health reasserts itself. Wisdom's voice is as loud and clear as it was five thousand years ago.

What Asnat Knew

We know that Asnat was well versed in Kabbalah and therefore in the teachings of the Tree of Life. We also know that Asnat's chief oeuvre was a commentary on the book of Proverbs. As we have just seen, the voice of Wisdom weaves throughout Proverbs, the one book of Hebrew scriptures filled with the teachings of Wisdom as a divine feminine personage, calling its readers to penetrate the surface of life and live a life of insight.

Because her intellectual writings have been lost, we will never know how Asnat actually related to Wisdom, whether she found personal strength and guidance from this spirit of truth telling that helped her tell her truth to the public or whether she related to Wisdom as an intellectual principle. We do know, however, that the Kabbalah that Asnat studied transcends narrow cultural standards and sexual definitions. Even though it uses the language and idioms of its day and expresses itself as a Jewish opus, its deepest teachings go beyond any particular cultural attitude because it is based upon universal spiritual and psychological principles. Perhaps Asnat, who lived on the fringe of her culture and was in touch with this transcendent point of view, can help women today by pointing the way toward the intellectual freedom that she enjoyed.

Bringing forth a new idea in any field—from physics to fashion design, gourmet cooking to public policy—requires the unique ability to let go of the limitations of our previous learning and push past the world as we know it in order to invite in a new arrangement of possibilities. Whenever you birth an idea from the *sephirah* of Wisdom, you are using a distinctive kind of thinking, one that is markedly different from your normal waking consciousness. The consciousness that does not grab for answers but is curious and open to them, not focused on a goal but inviting discovery, is closely related to the kind of immersive study Asnat engaged in. We have discussed it as a feminine quality because it is more likely to be soft and receptive than fixed and penetrating.

This kind of open awareness is by nature intuitive, predominantly calling on the right hemisphere of the brain. Clearly, this is not the primary mode of cognition in our Western culture; in fact, it is far less used than in so-called primitive societies that garner their knowing in a more intuitive fashion.[26] Both the intuitive and the analytical modes are critical to being a whole person, two parts of one whole. The ability to tap into the field of mind is tantamount to penetrating the second *sephirah*, Chochmah or Wisdom, the Divine Imagination. To bring it through, though, to dress it in concepts and words that can carry the true essence of the inspiration, requires Binah, the third *sephirah*.

Binah: Discernment

Binah is most often translated "understanding." But the word Binah itself hints at its deeper meaning. It has within it two root words that give that meaning away. First, the word *beyn*, "between," points to the human function of differentiation or making distinctions between one thing and another. Binah also has within it the word *boneh*, "build."

Binah is the kind of understanding that builds one idea upon another to help organize reality. The energy and skill to build a life plan stem from the realm of Binah.

Both discernment and building are qualities of understanding found in the *sephirah* called Binah. They carry us from the diffuse awareness of Wisdom, the intuitive experience that is beyond words, to a more functional mode that gathers, classifies, and articulates information so that the experience of Wisdom might be used in a worldly fashion.

Chochmah and Binah: Two Halves of a Whole

Binah is the function within us that places formless concepts into the words and categories that allow for communication and, ultimately, for actualization. Sometimes it is necessary to use critical thinking first, which is the realm of Binah, and only later to explore the source and deeper meaning of the experience, which is Chochmah.

Joseph, an author friend of mine who is a diabetic, was under a great deal of stress working toward a book deadline. His wife and children were away on vacation for two weeks, and during this time Joseph neglected his diet, letting his health run down. On the verge of diabetic shock but not realizing how sick he was, he picked up the phone to find a friend. Fortunately, Jonathan, an emergency medical technician, was alert enough to recognize the danger signs and quickly sized up the situation.

Jonathan rushed Joseph to the emergency room. Once there, he pushed his way past Admissions, insisting on immediate medical intervention. This was not the time for asking questions or holding hands. As they learned later, Joseph had been just minutes away from falling into a diabetic coma.

In one sense, the distinction between the Chochmah and Binah is completely arbitrary. There is no definitive line that distinguishes them, just as there is no boundary between Ayin and Chochmah, the first two *sephirot.* Chochmah and Binah may be seen as two halves of one whole, naturally flowing into one another.

Turning Enthusiasm into a Plan

With regard to the part of the human body that each *sephirah* on the Tree of Life correlates to, Chochmah and Binah signify the right and left hemispheres of the brain, respectively. We experience them whenever we attune ourselves to the inner workings of our minds. When we are guided by a strong yet diffuse sense of inspiration, Chochmah is at play; when the mind seeks to translate inspiration into the reality of our lives, we have activated Binah.

One remarkable experience I had in the Rocky Mountains stands out as an example. I was hiking one autumn morning, transfixed by the gold shimmer of the aspen trees above me and overcome with an almost palpable sense of the wild presence of God. At the top of the pass, I nestled into a soft hollow in the earth to eat lunch and read in the sunshine. My book was *The Legend of the Ba'al Shem,* a collection of stories about the Hassidic mystic. Suddenly I felt a warm surge of excitement pour through me. This feeling had no words, but I knew it had something to do with God's wilderness, my joy in nature, and my ardent desire to pass on these sensations to others.

I had been reading a tale about the mystic as a young man. He had begun his career by leading children through the woods to their village classroom, teaching them to attune themselves to the animals' voices and to feel God's protective presence all around them. I began to make a connection. I too had a love of children. My own childhood had felt devoid of the freedom and natural beauty that I now had access to. I shared the Ba'al Shem's passion: I wanted to bring my teaching into nature, to work with pure minds and hearts and remind them of God's presence.

Now it began to come together. I had just been asked to consider taking on a group of Jewish youngsters to teach them about Judaism.

The children were fresh and enthusiastic, but I was uncertain about what I had to offer them. Suddenly I knew that my answer would be yes. This was a Chochmah experience. It had neither words nor plan, just an abundance of energy in the form of enthusiasm. Because entering Wisdom is by nature nonconceptual, we know we know something, but not yet *what* we know. Binah translates our enthusiasm into viable ideas, bringing this experience into a form that we can understand.

That evening I felt moved to write down words that matched my experience, building a conceptual vision and formulating a schedule, fees, and curriculum. Throughout this task, I referred back to my experience in the mountains. When Binah follows Chochmah in this way, it is important that our plan stays true to our first passionate impulse.

Too often we divorce Binah from Chochmah and try to put a structure in place without passion, attempting Discernment without Wisdom. In this example, had I handed the parents a well-researched curriculum that had not stemmed from inspiration, it would have rung hollow. Conversely, all that momentum and sense of possibility would not have gone far on enthusiasm alone; without bringing Chochmah into Binah, our inspiration stays in the realm of private reverie, beautiful but ineffectual. I could easily have gone home leaving my ecstatic experience behind in an undocumented haze. As many women know, our worldly lives have their own powerful current. All too often our greatest inspirations and dreams get lost in the ceaseless turbulence of daily life.

The Divine Couple

Whatever moves us, our greatest need is to bring our inspiration into the world in a realized form. In the language of the Tree of Life, Chochmah and Binah need one another; Divine Wisdom needs Discernment to be realized. It is for this reason that these two *sephirot* are portrayed in the *Zohar* and throughout the Kabbalah as the archetypal Divine Couple. Chochmah is known as Abba, the Great Father, and Binah as Ima, the Great Mother.

But isn't Chochmah feminine, you may be asking? Wasn't She the feminine personage who spoke as the beautiful preacher in Proverbs? How did She suddenly become the Father? And Binah's need to delineate and cut a plan sounds more like father than mother.

Here we taste the rich paradoxical stew of Kabbalah. Lest we get caught in our own gender categories, Kabbalah comes to remind us that masculine and feminine are always fluid and changing and that gender definitions are eminently dynamic. Most important, they are only real when we are in relationship with one another. Each relationship has its own chemistry. In other words, in relationship to Ayin, the first *sephirah*, Chochmah becomes the Divine Feminine, for She receives and carries the divine impulse of the great Oneness to know Itself. As feminine, Chochmah takes the form of the pregnant imagination that contains all creative possibilities. However, in relationship to Binah, Chochmah changes. Next to Binah, Chochmah becomes the one who carries inspiration, the one who plants the seed. Although Binah is analytical and plan oriented, She is the one who receives the seed and carries it into form, the Mother. Facing each other, Chochmah and Binah become Father and Mother, respectively.

As the Divine Couple, Chochmah and Binah, Wisdom and Discernment, are linked together throughout the Hebrew scriptures.[27] They work together, an unbroken unity of masculine and feminine forces. The *Zohar* teaches us time and again "The Father and the Mother never separate."[28] They are lovers interlocked in divine harmony. The loving interaction between these two archetypal powers gives the world in which we live a potent imaginative power.

Whether we see Chochmah/Wisdom as a Divine Feminine Presence, our own inspiration, or as the Torah prior to the birth of words and letters, it is the reservoir of Divine Imagination that works in tandem with its mate, Binah/Discernment. Refracting the endless light of Ayin, these three form the inscrutable Wisdom Triangle, which reverberates in our minds as the process of creative thought.

We can look to Asnat as an example of a woman who experienced spiritual inspiration and then translated that inspiration into a form that could hold the original impulse. In Asnat's case this form was sacred study, writing, and teaching. But each of us has our own way of opening to the Divine Imagination and bringing forth the life messages that are the truest to us. We must deliver these messages into the world in the form of our ideas, words, and actions. How we do this is the topic of the next two chapters.

CHAPTER 5

SEEING WHOLLY— DARKNESS AND LIGHT

Dulcie of Worms (ca. 1170–1196)

Dulcie was a young woman who lived in the walled town of Worms in the Rhineland area of Germany. To begin to encounter Dulcie, we must prepare ourselves to confront a haunting tale of two ageless extremes: the powers of pure goodness and the basest evil. Dulcie's is a story of a dedicated young mother and sage whose life was abruptly terminated in savage murder. Ironically, it was her brutal end, which occurred just before Chanukah in 1196,[1] that immortalized Dulcie. Like that of so many women whose lives were illuminated with the sacred but were ignored by historians, Dulcie's life would probably never have been chronicled had it not been for her husband's anguish and the eulogy he was moved to write after losing her.[2] How sad that it is only because of her harsh end that we have a glimpse at the life of such a holy woman as Dulcie.

Dulcie's story—a life of extreme goodness that culminated in a macabre death—will serve as a springboard for our exploration into the difficult terrain of good and evil, light and shadow. We shall see how, once again, the mystical impulse in Judaism advocates a marriage of polarities rather then a one-sided leap toward the light. Ever the model of wholeness, the kabbalistic Tree of Life will illustrate how we can achieve a healthy integration of opposites through the *sephirot* of the Integrity Triangle and draw out the lessons of Dulcie's life for our own application.

Dulcie was a woman who was accomplished in both the material and the spiritual worlds. Her husband, Rabbi Eleazar of Worms, one of the great scholars of medieval German Jewry, tells us that Dulcie independently supported her entire family as well as his students by means of her successful moneylending business.[3] Like so many Jewish couples throughout the ages, Dulcie and Eleazar divided the family's labors along gender lines. As boys went off to Hebrew school at the age of five, girls were trained to spin, weave, sew, and cook, in preparation for a life of domestic duties.[4] Like many traditional Jewish women to this day, Dulcie took on the material responsibilities of the household (raising the children, running the house, and earning the money), freeing her husband to engross himself for long hours in sacred study. Immersing oneself in Torah study as one's primary occupation was—and still is in many Orthodox sectors—seen as the highest occupation available to a Jew. Women earned their merit by making this path possible.

Although it sounds unfeasible, Dulcie did not stop there. In addition to taking care of her business, her household, and her three children, Dulcie somehow managed to be a scholar too. Unlike most Jewish women of her day, Dulcie was learned in the sacred texts. She gave public discourses about the Torah portion on Sabbath afternoons to the townspeople of Worms, and, completely fluent in the Hebrew prayers, also found time to mentor the women of Worms and neighboring communities in their prayer lives.

In fact, Dulcie was one of the first women in a movement called the *firzogerins* (literally, "foresayers"), or female prayer leaders, who led the women's section in synagogues throughout the towns, help-ing women to understand and recite prayers.[5] Her husband extolled her as a singer of "praise, prayers, and petitions" who went to the prayer house morning and night.[6] Had there been women rabbis in the Middle Ages, Dulcie would have been one of the finest, for she uplifted the women with her translations, teachings, and ability to pray from the heart.

In addition to her public life as women's prayer leader and com-munity teacher, Dulcie specialized in other sacred practices such as escorting brides;[7] weaving gut string for *tefillin* (phylacteries), sacred books, and scrolls; sewing Torah scrolls;[8] weaving shrouds; washing the dead before burial; and making candles by which to pray.

Most women today would find the level of responsibility that Dul-cie took for granted quite overwhelming. Yet Dulcie mastered these tasks as a very young woman. Although we have no documentation of Dulcie's birth date, we do know that Jewish girls in her day were often betrothed before the age of thirteen.[9] This means that Dulcie, who was married for about fourteen years, was probably in her late twenties at the time of her death. Dulcie's numerous accomplishments, in this light, are all the more astonishing.

Dulcie's Lineage and Circle

In order to understand the mystical themes that Dulcie's life and death illustrate, it is important to examine the assumptions of the society in which she took her place. Dulcie descended from a promi-nent family of Franco-German scholars that, not surprisingly, had a reputation for unusually learned women. Many people have heard of Dulcie's grandmother and great-aunts, the daughters of the renowned French Torah commentator Rashi. It is a well-known fact that Rashi's three daughters, Yocheved, Miriam, and Rachel, donned prayer shawls and phylacteries every morning, praying and studying as completely as their roles as wives and mothers allowed. Few, however, have heard that, at the end of his life, Rashi dictated his writings to his daughters, who, it is believed by some, actually wrote many of his *halakhic* responsa (the answers to religious queries put to him).[10]

To some modern readers, these facts may sound insignificant. But in the Jewish world of medieval times (and in many Jewish sectors to this day) such a lineage dictated the outcome of one's life. Dulcie's outstanding pedigree, or *yichus*, guaranteed several things: that she would likely be of remarkable intelligence, that she would be extremely well educated due to her family's unusually high standard of education for girls, and that she would be betrothed to one of the most exceptional scholars of her day.

All of these were true. Dulcie was indeed brilliant. She was highly educated in her parents' home, and she was matched to the most promising young scholar in the Rhineland, Eleazar ben Judah. Dulcie's husband himself came from a family of leaders known as Kalonymous, who were central in establishing the Jewish community of Mainz, where Reb Eleazar was born. Eleazar was a close relative and disciple of the famous rabbi Judah HaChasid, the fiery and outspoken protagonist of the Pietist movement. Their elite circle of ascetic Jews, called Hassidei Ashkenaz, or Ashkenazic Pietists,[11] warrants our study because Dulcie not only supported these men financially, she was herself steeped in their unusual philosophy.

The early Hassidim, or Pietists, were, in a sense, the forerunners of the more famous movement founded by the Ba'al Shem Tov more than five centuries later. Like its later incarnation, Rabbi Eleazar of Worms's circle of Hassidim were on fire for God. Not satisfied with the learning and practice of Jewish law alone, they sought to cultivate an even more impeccable life based upon their passionate love for God.

But, unlike the later movement, which was characterized by joy and simple goodness of heart, the earlier Pietists aspired to a perfect love of God through a stringent reduction of worldly pleasure. Their focus was inward, their senses were bridled, and their sights were on the next world, not this one. Later on, we will look at the historical context that contributed to such a philosophy. For now, it is important to realize that what looked like a society built on hair-shirt austerities on the outside was, upon closer examination, a circle of ardent Jewish mystics who expressed their love of God through effusive love poetry, rich treatises about angels and the spirit world, the sacred magic of amulets, and the study of the soul's journey after death.[12]

This mysterious circle that surrounded Dulcie believed that God never entirely revealed His divine will at Mount Sinai, but, rather, withheld it so that people might search for it and discover it on their own. They were preoccupied, therefore, with seeking the complete will of the Creator (*ratzon haBorey*), believing that it was only through perfect love that the will of God could be discovered. This perfect love was a result of the highest state of fear (*yi'rah*), the fear of God.[13] Continually searching for the implications of the hidden divine will, the Pietists would infer prohibitions not found in the Torah and design new safeguards to keep themselves focused on God's will, rather than on their own needs and wants.

Life as a Balancing Act

Much of the philosophy of Dulcie and Eleazar's sacred society might be boiled down to a pithy rabbinic dictum that states, *L'fum tza'ara 'agra:* "One's reward is proportional to one's suffering."[14] The world, they believed, had been made by God in the form of an endless series of trials and obstacles. Every human act was weighed on the divine scales of judgment, a symbol that characterized the nature of life itself. On one side was personal enjoyment; on the other, weighed against pleasure, were the rewards of the next world.

Through an elaborate theory of sin and atonement, self-imposed penances and prohibitions that exceeded the 613 commandments of the Torah were enacted.[15] These personalized austerities were understood to cancel out the inevitable punishment for one's sins in the world to come. Every day was seen as a path fraught with divine trials and temptations imposed by the evil impulse. For the Pietists, life took the form of a carefully executed balancing act between the forces of good and the forces of evil.

Eleazar succeeded in creating a practical, personal version of Pietism and bringing it to the public. It has been speculated that Dulcie's approach to spirituality, which we know was grounded in long hours of hands-on service, influenced her husband's philosophy by bringing it down to earth.[16]

The Divorce from Earthly Life

To Dulcie's husband and his followers, the love of God had little to do with the material world, except insofar as it required restraint, avoidance, and, of course, the physical performance of *mitzvot*. If you asked a Pietist how to go about serving God, the answer would be clear: by withstanding the temptation of the evil world around us; by living among the "wicked" and not yielding to their influence; and by subduing the *yetzer hara,* one's own inclination to do evil.

How did the religious philosophy of Dulcie's community become so disconnected from God's creation, that is, from earthly life? In the period in which Dulcie lived, poverty, plague, and social injustice were rampant. Belief in magic, spells, demons, spirits, and all manner of dark charms and enchantments was the collective standard.

Imagine living in a dark and overcrowded city where rats, disease, and violence were the norm, where life's physical pleasures were so few and fleeting that they came to be mistrusted in favor of a higher, more consistent ideal. That higher ideal was a God removed to another sphere of reality, accessible only to those who could successfully remove themselves from the distractions of this world and ascend to that same hidden sphere.

In this context, it is not difficult to understand that to Dulcie's circle, the highest of values was *kiddush Hashem,* to give up one's life in martyrdom. The ultimate prayer on the lips of a Pietist was for one's life to be taken by God as an offering, received like the burnt offering

(*olah*) that was sacrificed during Temple times: *utterly consumed.* Given
the destruction that befell Rabbi Eleazar's family, this private prayer
takes on a macabre tone.

Terror in the Night

Worms was encircled, as many medieval European towns were, by
a great stone wall. In the shadow of its wall ran the narrow, sinuous
streets and alleys in which the Jews were confined. Much hatred was
directed here; the insults and abuse that Jews suffered in these dark
streets during and after the Crusades are famous. Dulcie and her fel-
low Jews must have lived in a constant state of terror and dread that
at any moment a new form of abuse or violence would break out. It
is no wonder that she and her people turned their gaze inward to
another, more "godly," reality, far from the relentless oppression of
the world around them.

But it is doubtful that any spiritual practice could sufficiently prepare one for the kind of terror that befell Dulcie and her family. Her
murder occurred at the advent of the Third Crusade, when the Warriors of the Cross began to force their way, once again, across Europe
on their mission to liberate Jerusalem.

Although the Crusades have been romanticized as the height of
Christian ideals and nobility, they were, in truth, tainted by appalling
violence and greed. Many of the soldiers who held high the standard
of the Cross failed to uphold its truest values of justice and humanity, falling prey to the basest of human impulses. If you were not
bowing low to their frenzied troops, pledging fealty to the Church
that commissioned them, then you were against them, and this spelled
a savage death or, more beneficently, forced baptism. For much of
Europe's Jewry, the Crusades were a time of stark terror, when their
villages were plundered and their communities decimated.

There is little information about the two knights of the Cross
who stormed Dulcie's home on that winter night. It was a common

enough incident during that barbaric period when countless acts of wanton violence such as this one took place. To the two soldiers, the crime may have been as arbitrary as any other night of drunken sport in the Jewish quarter, as meaningless as a child's game of crunching leaves or smashing beetles.

Two extant texts[17] tell of the events that befell Dulcie and her family that night. Eleazar was studying Torah with his students in the adjacent quarters of their house while Dulcie prepared food for the Sabbath. Swinging their great axes, the soldiers flew into their home, running after the family, splitting open the heads of Dulcie's two daughters, who died in front of their mother's eyes, and then striking Jacob, the young son, who was knocked unconscious.

Then they came for Dulcie. She was hit in the head yet managed to escape and run out of the house crying for help. None came. The soldiers pursued her and finished their work in the street, "splitting her head down to the windpipe and shoulder, and from the shoulder to the girdle."

Little Jacob did not die until the following week. Dulcie's husband's head and hand were injured; why he and his students were not killed or injured more seriously is unclear.

After the soldiers had departed, Rabbi Eleazar closed the door, cried out for help from heaven, and wept over the remains of his wife. "It is my great sin that she and my daughters were killed," he wrote later. "Judgment is truly upon me…and woe unto me on their accounts! So much of their blood was spilled, and they were dying in my sight.… Let there be mercy on their souls and mercy upon the remnant which remains.… Amen."

Dulcie and the Powers of Good and Evil

The story of Dulcie's death gives rise to many difficult questions. Why did Dulcie and her children suffer such a monstrous fate while her husband and his students survived? How are we to make sense of a life of such goodness succumbing to such unbridled evil? Why is there such evil in the world? Where is God in this story? Could evil be part of God's plan?

Although we grapple with these questions on Dulcie's behalf, we know all too well that Dulcie does not stand alone, that history is filled with stories like hers in which ugliness and evil triumph over good and pure-heartedness. What is evil and how does the Jewish tradition make sense of it?

The power of evil is understood in Judaism to be part and parcel of creation, built into the very fabric and design of the world. God tells us this directly: "I form light, and create darkness; I make peace, and create evil; I the Lord do all these things."[18] The tension between the polarities of light and darkness, good and evil, is planted into the very nature of all created things. And because human beings are seen as an *olam katan*, a microcosm or a fractal of the whole, each of us enters life with all of the same polarities found in the universe latent within us.

This means that each one of us is born with an inclination toward the dark side of life, the *yetzer hara*, balanced by an equal nature, the *yetzer hatov*, which leads us to develop our inherent goodness. Judaism teaches that the tension between these two opposing natures never leaves us. In fact, it is by virtue of the inevitable struggle between them that we continue to grow as individuals, the moral tension serving as grist for the mill of our evolution into whole human beings.

We will never know what went on in Dulcie's heart as she struggled with the darkness that consumed her physical form. Was her soul wounded or did she emerge on the other side of this life with a shining new identity? Did she lose her faith or was she confirmed in it? Did she feel betrayed by God as she was quartered like an animal in the streets, or did she die saying the Shema Yisrael, ascending to God with greater wholeness?

We know only that Dulcie's entire life was a struggle between light and darkness. And we wish for her that in her death she achieved the wholeness that comes from marrying these two seeming enemies, a task she was not allowed to accomplish in her life.

Finishing God's Work

As we have been seeing throughout this book, the Jewish mystical tradition is, at its core, an expression of the oneness that comes from the marriage of opposite energies, the masculine and the feminine, the dark and the light. But one more fundamental belief helps us to understand what we are doing here in the world. Creation has been left incomplete, and human beings, that is, *all of us*, are needed by creation—and the Creator—to do the ongoing work of completing it.

If this sounds paradoxical, it is! The work of completing creation is never done. We are asked to take creation further by holding a dynamic balance with the archetypal forces that are beyond us, such as evil. Why humans? Because it is we who have within us all of the elements of creation *and* the capacity to recognize them, wrestle with them, lose our balance, and regain it through the work of consciousness. It is through us, mystical Judaism says, that creation can be made whole.

Judaism is about wholeness, not perfection. Perfection implies the highest attainable standards, a final superlative state. But in the Jewish way of thinking, there is no final state of perfection, no final enlightenment or spiritual end of the road. As long as we are alive we are in a state of flux and growth, to our last day, balancing the different inclinations within us, not just the good and the shining, but the parts of ourselves that we would prefer remained in the shadows. There can be no wholeness without ethical conflict, and the wholeness espoused by mystical Judaism is the result of embracing our opposing parts, the light and the dark, our highest aspirations and our basest instincts.

Although Dulcie's circle aimed for perfection in its service to God by restraining their impulses and practicing austerities, the deeper truth in Judaism says that such a one-sided approach is actually dangerous. It tells us that those things that we consistently deny and withdraw our attention from—for example, our sexual longings, the desire for power, the need to express our passions—will not shrink, but instead grow, pushing back into visibility with a vengeance, ultimately emerging against our volition as fate.

It would be far too simplistic and irresponsible to posit that Dulcie's fate was a result of any lack or imbalance on her part whatsoever. It would be hubris to imagine that we could begin to understand the mechanisms of fate or the workings of evil. Suffice it to say that it is important for those of us who seek spiritual wholeness to explore the depths of our own dark or shadowy side, which, when suppressed, gains potency and, when claimed, can reveal hidden gifts. The struggle for wholeness requires that rather than submerge our dark side, we hold it in tension, acknowledge and understand it but not be dominated by it, and, ultimately, incorporate it to serve our life's purpose. For only when we are aware of what lies within us can we know what lies beyond us.

But is evil really needed in the world? Perhaps it is a mistake that snuck in through the cracks of God's plan, wreaking havoc on a beautiful and loving design.[19] No, says Jewish mysticism. Evil is God's agent, and each of us has the capacity to hold it in tension or play host to its insidious power.

Darkness Uncovered

In its most powerful form, evil is an archetypal, or universal, power. It is possible, although rare, for an individual to totally give herself over to the dark forces and become evil, that is, eager to create pain and destruction. More relevant for most of us is the negativity that arises from an individual who is unconscious of herself. I call this form of negativity an aspect of our dark, or "shadow," side, our unexamined self.

Whenever we push out of awareness some aspect of our personalities, it enters our shadow. Examples of the shadow at work are all around us: assuaging our unhappiness with alcohol and then getting behind the wheel, stereotyping and judging others whom we don't understand, indulging our needs at the expense of others. We cannot be aware of everything within ourselves, but sometimes our unconsciousness can create consequences of real pain, even though they were not the result of ill intent. It is my belief that we are nevertheless responsible for the pain we cause.

Another category of personal "evil" is the ego's drives for power and gratification. The rabbis called these drives our "evil inclination," that seed within us bent on feeding and pleasing itself to the exclusion of others and our Divine Source. The grasping nature within us, when taken to the extreme, can lead to the destruction of self and others. Nevertheless, the rabbis explained, without it there would not be enough passion, selfishness, or ambition in the world to make life move forward. They explain that our ego's drive to progress, do business, build ourselves up, and even get married would not have the necessary fuel without this aspect of our nature![20] This is because our progress toward wholeness can only exist in a system of polarities. Only when we have the tension of opposing forces in our lives do we feel the fire to move ahead, to struggle against complacency and keep growing.

It is for the sake of wholeness, says the *Zohar*, that we were created with two hearts. "One is called the good heart and the other, the bad heart."[21] The mystic's path is to love God with *both* hearts. But how do we manage to love God with our dark side, the very force that is hostile to our growth and tries to prevent us from serving God? Amazingly, Judaism tells us not to deny, suppress, or even transcend the force of darkness, but to work with it, know it, and harness it so that it can be turned toward serving that which is the highest in our lives. A beautiful prayer said by traditional Jews at the beginning of each day asks God to help us take in hand our evil inclination so that it may be put into the service of that which is holy.[22]

Claiming Our Darkness

Living with both of our hearts means that we must claim our own darkness. It is easy to feel overwhelmed by the darkness in the world. Kabbalah asks us to go farther, into a much more difficult terrain. The path to wholeness is found when we can claim a part in the workings of the evil in the world and say, "I have that within me too," rather than just seeing it as a terrible force outside of ourselves. When we can own our capacity for darkness, we are living life in a wholehearted way.

Brigitte was a woman I met years ago in a childcare co-op. She was a small, muscular woman with intense blue eyes and a body that seemed to say, "Don't mess with me!" Brigitte lived alone with her two daughters, lovely little girls of nine and five, who were always coming around for hugs and affection. Whenever I encountered them, their eyes seemed to be pleading, but I couldn't tell for what, and, frankly, I held back a little bit around them, given their mother's intimidating effect.

One day Brigitte approached me and furtively asked if we could talk. She had heard that I was a therapist and thought I might be able to help her. When she came to my office later that week, Brigitte sat opposite me with her eyes averted. She told me that her sleep was troubled and that she felt increasing impatience and even rage toward her girls. When I asked what that meant, she admitted that she punished them harshly. This meant putting them into dark closets when they misbehaved and refusing to feed them when they annoyed her. "But I never hit them," she said. "Physical contact just ain't my thing." Her comment helped me understand her girls' need for warmth from outsiders.

The next time we met, Brigitte told me a recurring dream. It took place in a dark basement that smelled of stale beer and sewage. Each time she dreamed about this place something bad was happening there. One night she found a cat with its belly sliced open, and in another dream there was a crowd of drunken men jeering at women. It was becoming clear that Brigitte had come to me to help her uncover some dark and terrible secret that lay in the "basement" of her subconscious mind, and this secret was somehow related to her treatment of her daughters and her inability to love them.

At our sixth meeting, Brigitte came in crying. I had never seen her look so fragile and so young. With her head bowed and her face in her sleeve, she told me that she had been out walking the alleys the night before and that, when the words came to her, she had said them over and over again, all night long until dawn, when she finally went home.

"What words, Brigitte?" I asked.

"I need to say it again and again so I won't forget it no more."

"What are the words you said, Brigitte?" I persisted

"But now I am *so angry!* Do you hear me? *So angry!*"

"Tell me the words, Brigitte."

Finally, she threw her head back and through great sobs yelled, "I was gang raped! I was gang raped! I was just sixteen...and gang raped!"

Although Brigitte did not know it, I cried with her that day. Her story of having naively walked into a bar in Denver to ask for directions broke my heart. She could not say how she found her way home the next morning, but she had managed to wash her face, change her shirt, and get herself to work as if nothing had happened. She had been too frightened and ashamed to go to the police or tell her own mother. I was the first person she had ever told.

For eighteen years, this atrocity had lain submerged in Brigitte's memory awaiting healing. That time had finally come. Brigitte was now ready to work with her pain and the price she had paid to conceal it.

Over the course of several months, Brigitte did the hard work of recollecting her feminine side, which, as she put it, "had been sliced up like a cat that night and left for dead." Brigitte began to see how her hateful attitude and her tough, "Don't touch me," stance had taken the place of her femininity, her softer side, which she had believed "got me into all that trouble" in the first place. In time,

Brigitte understood why she had become callous and hard-nosed, disregarding not only her own vulnerable side but that of her little girls. Although it was hard to admit it, she came to realize that she had become more like the men who had abused her and whom she had never forgiven than like the girl she once was.

"That which we cannot forgive we are doomed to become," the old adage says. Our first instinct is to seek shelter from the pain and ugliness of what haunts us. But ultimately we must descend into the darkness where we can face these hateful things and reclaim ourselves. The greatest work we can do as humans is to look at those events that have broken us and at the characters who have demoralized us and wrestle with them, understand them, and, if possible, forgive them. If we don't, we are bound to internalize them, unconsciously acting out the very elements that brought us pain, and unconsciously passing on the pain to others.

I do not know if Brigitte ever came to forgive the perpetrators of her shame, but she was ultimately able to say of their cruelty, "I have some of that nastiness in me too." She recognized that the way she had treated her daughters was a facet of the same abuse that she herself had experienced. All of the hard work that Brigitte did to come to terms with her wound expressed itself in a happier, more feminine appearance. But even more telling was the slow and steadily growing affection she now shows for her two young daughters.

Tolerating Ambiguities

I have always appreciated Judaism's commitment to life and how it celebrates all aspects of it. In its portrayal of reality, all sides of human nature are included, the light and the dark, the proud and the shameful. Judaism gives us neither an overly rosy perspective on life nor one that is utterly cheerless. I believe this commitment to wholeness has made the religion psychologically sound and therefore enduring.

When we examine the Hebrew scriptures, we see how the Torah, with ever competing themes of light and shadow, holiness and corruption, unabashedly portrays the personal and spiritual failures of the patriarchs, a priesthood given to the exploitation of its power, a first king who loses his mind, and a body of commandments that includes the noblest universal truths alongside tribal laws that border on xenophobia!

In the same way, Jewish heroes are rarely just good guys. In many cases, they are depicted as complex women and men who lived righteous yet flawed lives, struggling with their own dark tendencies just as we do. Even God is a paradoxical character who wears many opposing faces, patient and hot-tempered, compassionate and ruthless, universally loving and one who plays favorites. As above, so below.

I remember one student named Nancy who railed at these contradictions, unable to tolerate a tradition so riddled with inconsistencies. She needed a God who could be depended upon to be just and even tempered; she needed ancestors who were models of goodness and did not fall prey to such rash acts as Rebecca's deception of her husband or King David's adultery. I explained to Nancy that she might look at these inconsistencies, not as contradictions, but as a celebration of the full spectrum of life's experience. It took her years to understand this. Interestingly, it was only after she had done a great deal of work to bring to light her own dark history that she was able to appreciate the multifaceted nature of the Torah and its depiction of life.

The display of opposites in the Torah may be seen as a mandate to its readers. It says to us, "Here is the raw material of life. All of these elements are available to you; all are within your reach. Now what will you do with them?" It is ours to find our way, balancing among all these elements, to acknowledge, for example, that the power of evil is alive in the world and to take great care to hold it in tension, to neither turn away from it and deny it nor add to its power by falling prey to it.

For evil too is part of God's plan. Respect for the dark side of life has from ancient times been a pronounced element within Judaism.

This respect—often turning to fear—is reflected in the rich demonology seen throughout Talmudic literature and was greatly elaborated upon during the medieval era in which Dulcie lived.

Demons as a Projection of Our Dark Side

In Dulcie's day and long after, Jews were greatly preoccupied with the nature and pursuits of evil spirits (*shedim*), angels of destruction (*malachei chabbalah*), and night demons (*liliot*), and the magical sciences that taught one how to protect oneself from their insidious offshoot, the evil eye (*ayin hara*).[23] One might see the intricate lore about demons, angels, and everything in between as a means by which people could externalize and give faces to the negative and positive energies that they experienced within themselves and the world around them.

Liliot, for example, were the league of female night demons that were headed up by Lilith, the notorious evil spirit who was, according to folklore, the first wife of Adam, considered to be a seductress, child killer, and all-around menace.[24] The Talmud and later the *Zohar* richly illustrate Lilith's antics. Beginning with her refusal to submit to the missionary position when consorting with Adam, Lilith, being the free and instinctual female spirit that she was, uttered God's magical name, rose into the air, and left Adam. Summoned by God to return, Lilith refused. Instead, she chose to wander above the earth, tempting men to spill their seed, creating demons from it, and taking for her own newborn babies.

It is not difficult to imagine that the mythological character of Lilith may have originated as a projection of men's fears of women's wild and instinctual feminine powers. Because when we don't integrate the strong unconscious powers within ourselves (such as our sexuality, creativity, anger, and so forth), we tend to externalize them and see them play themselves out through others. This is called projection.

Projection is when we unconsciously ascribe our inner thoughts, feelings, or qualities to others because we cannot see them within ourselves. For centuries, non-Jews projected their own dark side upon the wandering Jews who seemed so strange and different from them. This kind of scapegoating was found within Jewish ranks too. Men's ambivalence and even disgust for their own bodies was often projected upon women, who were excluded from the "holier" aspects of life. Likewise, the Jewish tradition as a whole may have been said to have projected its ambivalence toward and fear of the feminine side of life onto a she-demon personality called Lilith.[25]

Throughout the Middle Ages, Lilith served men and women by giving an external face, form, and story to their own dark passions and the fearful, unpredictable powers in the world. Lilith played the role of the feminine shadow beautifully; neither demur nor patronizing, she wouldn't even listen to God Himself! Instead, she willfully demanded her way. She insisted upon taking power over men's sexuality and took into her clutches the most precious thing on earth, new life.

Both men and women feared Lilith, especially at night,[26] when men are susceptible to their libidinous passions and new babies are vulnerable to the dark and angry forces that are not grounded on God's earth but act of their own agency in the nefarious realms. Lilith, like the hundreds of other evil spirits in the Jewish mystical imagination, was an outward face given to the fearful and unpredictable darkness in the world known as evil.

How did this negative projection affect women? As we have said, Jewish women too subscribed to Lilith's negative powers. They protected their babies from her with magical circles and wore amulets against her destructive powers. But what did it mean that they were trained to believe that the very first woman was evil because she talked back to her husband and would not submit to his assumed superiority?

One way to understand Lilith's dark success is to look at her historical context. Throughout their history in exile, Jewish men were rendered relatively powerless by the rulers and governments of the day. Continuously at the mercy of more dominant forces, Jewish men needed to know that there was at least one arena in which they had full control. This area of dominance was, of course, their homes. Jewish women, subject to the same capricious powers, fell in line with the men's thinking. After all, the image of women as secondary, inferior, and the root of man's troubles was endemic throughout the Christian world too. The myth of Lilith further strengthened the deeply inculcated notion that feminine power was evil. Colluding with Jewish women's negative self-image, the fear of Lilith's wild and insurrectionary nature helped to suppress the impulse in Jewish women to rebel against the gender imbalance in their society.

Most Jews have little awareness of Lilith in our day, and most no longer subscribe to the existence of demons and evil spirits at all. Yet there remains a widespread acknowledgment in Judaism of unseen negative entities in the world that seem to have an autonomous power and will of their own. For this reason, protective phrases and customs against these dark entities are still in use, harking back to Dulcie's day. These include the common practice of saying *Bli ayin hara* ("May there be no evil eye!") or *Al tiftach peh l'Satan* ("Don't open your mouth for Satan to enter!") upon expressing a compliment or fact worthy of pride. Some of us may remember our grandmothers spitting lightly to the right and to the left as a way of clearing the field of negative spirits who might prey on the good fortune of their families. Perhaps unwittingly, some Jews still take part in the originally Christian custom of "knocking on wood," which calls upon the protective power of the wooden crucifix.

Our discussion of projection would not be complete without considering the perpetrators of Dulcie's murder. Although it is tempting to dismiss them as subhuman thugs, we run the risk of falling into the same sort of projection of which her murderers were themselves no doubt guilty. It may be assumed that the two knights of the Cross, like their compatriots, were subject to the collective hatred of the day that projected upon the Jews all the ills of society. Sucked into the furor of the Crusade's holy war, they rendered their souls to its power just as Dulcie was forced to render her body. This is not to absolve the men of their guilt; in sacrificing conscience, they became powerless before the sweep of collective evil and sacrificed their own humanity.

How Evil Takes Hold

We have discussed evil as an autonomous force, bigger than life and dangerous to humankind, and personal evil, or "shadow," the result of our own unconsciousness, as those parts of ourselves that we cannot bear to deal with and that have, by virtue of our neglect, grown beyond our control. The personal and the archetypal are certainly related. Our own ignorance and unconsciousness feed the absolute power, which, Kabbalah tells us, is indeed an autonomous entity.

Some people think that the way to avoid the darkness in the world is "to stay in the light" and focus on positive attitude. Although there is merit to this notion, we run into danger when we become so one-sided as to deny the existence of darkness. A psychotherapist colleague of mine relates the story of her own initiation into the world of the shadow side. Not surprisingly, it occurred in a spiritual community, one that espoused the power of positive thinking.

Trudy had dropped out of college at twenty. Like many young Jewish adults, she was hungry to explore the world and seek the spiritual wisdom of other traditions. To allay their fears, Trudy told her parents that she was going to investigate college programs out West. But, in fact, Trudy was on her way to receiving a different kind of education, spiritual lessons that would change the course of her life.

The "healing community" Trudy joined seemed to be a dream-come-true. In exchange for her work in the community's perfectly organized kitchen, Trudy got room and board, meditation training, and a cheerful spiritual community. The leader of this community, Gerta, a Swiss woman in her late sixties, was a healer of some renown who had written books on the power of positive thinking.

Although Trudy rarely saw Gerta, it was understood in the community that she was a "holy woman" and a "seer" who could diagnose illness by reading a person's negative thoughts. Gerta had married Eduardo, her premiere student, a South American man fifteen years her junior. Over the years, Gerta had withdrawn into a more reclusive life, and Eduardo had taken over as the director of the spiritual community.

For the first several months, Trudy felt that a new world had opened for her. Every day she participated in community meetings, where she learned how to eliminate the negative thought patterns that mentally limit one's human potential. By reciting healing affirmations and limiting her speech to words that engendered goodness and positive energy, Trudy believed that she was retraining her mind to open to its fullest capacity. If something displeased her, she was directed to explore her inner obstacle to finding the good in the situation. If she did not feel well, she was asked to examine her thoughts to discover any negativity that she may be harboring.

It did not take Trudy long to discover that there was a shadow lurking in this positive-minded community. One day as she walked by the office, Trudy overheard strained voices talking about failing operations. After many inquiries, she learned that the family money with which Gerta had founded the community was running out. Surely by using their spiritual principles, Trudy thought, the community would pool its human resources to create a new business, grow its own vegetables, market its teachings. She had learned that no problem was too big if you thought about it right. Trudy waited for announcements to this effect, for a rallying of positive energy, but none came.

Instead, she noticed that, behind his poised façade, Eduardo was becoming increasingly frazzled and gruff. The people closest to him looked scared and miserable. Piece by piece, Trudy's perfect picture of a spiritual community began to crumble. As the full story came to light, she realized the fallacy in Gerta's doctrine of positive mental power.

Trudy learned that, over the years, the famous female "seer" had somehow turned a blind eye to her husband's exploits, which consisted of trafficking (and losing) her money in illicit deals he thought would be "lucrative" for the community. But the trouble did not stop there. Eduardo had been involved sexually with both female and male community members under the guise of healing treatments. Now it came to light that Eduardo was HIV positive. Priding himself on his superlative outward health and vigor, he had chosen to ignore this fact and keep it from his lovers. Ever faithful to the power of his own infallible mind, Eduardo saw himself to be above the laws of nature and, in the process, exposed numerous men and women to the HIV virus.

While all this was going on, another kind of denial was affecting Gerta. Trudy finally learned the true reason for Gerta's withdrawal from the community. She had advanced-stage cancer. Like her husband, Gerta had refused to admit the deadly truth to herself and others. Instead of submitting to medical treatment, she prolonged her own suffering by choosing to treat herself with her mental healing techniques, which were, of course, inadequate.

A young woman who nursed her had told of Gerta's agony. It was not only physical pain that she suffered at the end but the pain caused by berating herself daily for not being able to cure her own disease. In her eyes, her entire life's work had been tested through this illness and had failed. Gerta died shortly after Trudy left the community. By then, Eduardo had fled criminal charges and returned to his homeland. The community, in financial ruins, had disbanded.

To believe in a world that is all good is to hide in a dangerous fantasy. And although individuals indeed have enormous power to create goodness with positive thoughts and actions, there is also an equal and opposite force of negativity that is invited in when we deny the capacity for darkness within ourselves and others. This kind of negativity, generated by human denial and unconsciousness, is not in itself evil, but it can certainly lead to it.

Evil is not simply the absence of good, as many people think, but a force that must be acknowledged as real, and that, once acknowledged, must be held in check. Because humans were created with both tendencies, toward the good and the evil sides of nature, we have a powerful hand in the course of the world's outcome. We can fuel the force of evil or we can hold it in moderation by means of building upon that which is good. Kabbalah says that every human action and interaction, no matter how seemingly trivial, has the power to tip the delicate balance of goodness in the world.

Most of us have experienced extreme negativity in some form and seen how, once out of control, it takes on a life of its own. Even as children we taste a form of evil in the cliques and gangs that split off from the whole, when nastiness builds into cruelty and peer pressure overrides the empathy we would have felt on our own. Evil starts small and builds in power, sweeping us off course with its fervor and swallowing our more reasoned sensibilities. Like a hurricane that sucks in the air around it, creating a vacuum, evil feeds on our fear and on our intolerance for uncertainty. When we cannot tolerate the feeling of being out of control that comes with the tension of opposites, when we need security in the form of perfection and black-and-white clarity, we are most vulnerable to evil's insidious advances.

Just look at the film clips documenting the rise of the Third Reich in the late 1930s. The ideological furor of the party that swept over the crowds of German citizens built like an emotional typhoon, ultimately overriding their humanity with a colossal excitement and national zeal. The same righteous frenzy was experienced during the witch-hunts in Europe, the lynching of African Americans in the Southern states, among fundamentalist Muslims proclaiming *jihad*, and fundamentalists everywhere who are willing to endanger their own lives and the lives of their children for a principle they believe to be higher than life itself.

The hallmark of evil is the quest for perfection. Its doctrines are recognizable by their predilection for absolutes: the ideal race, the perfect ruler, the final solution. Evil cares not for the sacred nature of the individual; it does not tolerate the many hues of ambiguity or paradox; wholeness is its antithesis.

In the personal realm, too, the notion of perfection is an insidious one that invariably leads into dark territory. One of the most common struggles shared by women and girls in the West is the critical inner voice that demands perfection. For many females, this demand expects to be met in the area of physical appearance; perfection is achieved through a static norm of beauty. But even if we succeed in making our bodies look like the models and the stars, how hard it is, alas, to stay that way! One meal, one bite, one pound causes a rupture in our image, a fluctuation that is intolerable to a woman given over to this inner tyranny.

Nor is it only a perfect body that is demanded; the inner tyrant is wont to focus on many other aspects of our "imperfect" selves and finds innumerable ways in which we are inferior, inadequate, and at fault. As we shall see shortly, the addiction to perfection comes from an excess of inner rigor, which is an overabundance of the *sephirah* of Judgment. The medicine for this common ailment is found in the ability to tolerate our own ambiguities and forgive our fatally imperfect selves. As the kabbalistic Tree of Life will show us, the dynamic opposite of our judgmental inner ruler is, of course, Love.

Dulcie and the Tree of Life

The dark and fearful world in which Dulcie lived had its share of both kinds of evil: the evil of unconscious projection as well as the ruthlessness of archetypal evil. In such a coarse world, Dulcie managed to bridge heaven and earth in the most elegant of ways.

In the language of Kabbalah, we might say that Dulcie was deeply rooted in Malkhut, that is, grounded in the physical world, while also being an adept of the upper reaches of the Tree of Life. The list of Dulcie's activities, which included study, prayer, and the articulation of spiritual principles to others, reflect her ease in the areas of Chochmah, intuitive wisdom, and Binah, bringing that wisdom into conceptual form.

Everyone has areas of mastery and areas of challenge on the Tree of Life. Dulcie was a master of the vertical axis of the Tree, a rare spiritual ability and one that is found only in the most highly evolved souls. Given what we know about Dulcie's dedication to uplifting others during this dark time, we can assume she had mastery in *raising up* the spiritual state of her community and *bringing down* spiritual understanding by means of her words, encouragement, and service.

More challenging in Dulcie's life, however, was the area of the Tree of Life that is the home of good and evil, kindness and malice, light and shadow. This is the area I call the Integrity Triangle because it allows us to move out of one-sided viewpoints and see the world *wholly.* The Integrity Triangle is found in the area of our arms and hands, breasts and heart. It encompasses our unconditionally giving nature, the *sephirah* of Chesed/Love, on the right; our ability for restraint and boundaries, the *sephirah* called Din (Gevurah)/Judgment, on the left; and the true and discerning heart, which is the balance and synthesis of these two, the *sephirah* of Tipheret, in the center.

The Integrity Triangle

The Integrity Triangle is a critical area for women because it is our locus of connection to others. This is where women, whose tendency is to nurture others, must learn to balance all that we give with all that we might receive, care of others with care of ourselves. It is here that we learn about protecting our boundaries—and transcending them. And it is here that we learn that wholeness lies in recognizing and integrating the power of opposites.

Chesed/Love and Din/Judgment are the *sephirot* in which women most often lose their balance, either giving themselves away through overloving, on the one side, or getting caught in a quagmire of self-protection, cynicism, and anger, on the other. This area relates to a multitude of women's issues, from our behaviors with men to parenting our children, from how and why we diet to fluctuating mood disorders. Knowing about the expansion and contraction that naturally goes on in this triangle and the still point of balance that lies in the aware heart gives us insight into finding our own balance and integrity. It helps us to relate to our own goodness and shadowy elements so that we can see the world more wholly.

And, yes, evil is part of the Integrity Triangle, and knowing about it is integral to the work of finding one's balance. In the most archetypal Tree of Life, which stands beyond individuals, the elemental ingredients that constitute evil are, in their proper measure, necessary to the structure of reality. Evil lives in the *sephirah* called Din/Judgment and occurs when there is an overabundance of this *sephirah*. In its correct measure, however—that is, when it is in balance with Chesed/Love—the powers of Judgment stand in their correct tension, expressed in the compassion of true justice.

Chesed/Love

Chesed/Love is that lovely part of us that instinctively reaches out to help, heal, teach, feed, and soothe those around us. This *sephirah* is personified by the biblical figures Abraham, the big-hearted father of Judaism, and the wise prophetess Miriam, who was followed through the desert by a well of endlessly flowing water.[27] In the same way, Chesed is likened to the surge that a nursing mother feels when her milk lets down. As any lactating mother knows, milk lets down when the baby's hunger hits, regardless of how far away Mama is, how many bottles Grandma has on hand, or how beautiful the chiffon evening dress she is wearing is when the call comes.

Just so, Chesed is the unmethodical profusion of nourishment that seems to be quite beyond our control. Is there any surprise that Chesed is often seen as a natural strong suit for many women? One might say that nature has built the nurturing quality of Chesed into our very molecules to make for successful childbearing and the continuation of the species. But beware! It is easy for women to fall into excess Chesed. When we continuously put out nurturing energy without recharging ourselves from the center of the Tree, we often end up getting depleted, burned out, and resentful.

Din/Judgment

When we go too far to one extreme, our system automatically brings us back into balance. Too much giving results in rigor, and that rigor is Din, the side of a woman that instinctively draws boundaries for self-protection. Din says, "Stop! I've given enough. I've spent too much time, money, and emotional energy to go any farther." Din is also warrior-like, the part of us that can cut to the bone with a laser-like analysis or lift a two-ton car with the ferocity of a mother bear—whatever it takes to protect what it precious.

In excess, however, Din can be downright cruel. When a woman's Din is not integrated, that is, when it remains unrecognized in the shadows of her unconscious, it can have her act in surprisingly unkind ways. Catty and often vicious behavior between females, cliques that are given to gossip, blackballing, and ganging up on others are all painful examples of the protective quality of Din gone haywire. One example is what happens to intimacy, a Chesed quality, when women get fearful of their boundaries. As women, we value intimacy because it allows us to get close and share the depths of our being. But when women become fearful, a prominent Din characteristic, intimacy can quickly flip to its polar opposite, and suddenly all that has been shared turns to ammunition.[28]

The work is to sanction, never to suppress, our warrior-like qualities. When we acknowledge the extreme power we have to hurt or to heal, our Din side can more easily be brought into its correct relationship with our capacity for self-compassion and empathy, Chesed. Like our two hands, these two *sephirot* are meant to work together to make a whole person. Like Chochmah and Binah above them on the Tree, they require each other.

Imagine for example that you or someone close to you has discovered a fast-growing cancer in your body. Naturally, you would do anything to stop its growth. But saving a life, itself an act of great Chesed/Love, requires Din/Judgment to accomplish it. The surgeon who cuts away the cancer and the surrounding lymph nodes is exercising the aggressive and severe nature of Din, but she performs her work in the name of Chesed/Love.

Cancer, like other destructive forces in our lives, cannot be treated without Din's clear message, "Stop!" In many cases, encountering cancer with an overabundance of Chesed—letting nature have its way—will lead to the ultimate Din state, death. The paradox of the Integrity Triangle is that there are times when the patience and tolerance of Chesed are inappropriate to the point of being cruel, while the ruthlessness of Din is far more loving.

Returning to Balance

With or without our help, life attempts to assert the natural balance of these forces. But without our conscious involvement, this can be an unpleasant affair. For example, women who are "natural givers" are perhaps blessed with a good share of Love, but must also be careful to know and guard their own limits, or Din/Judgment will do the job for them.

Take Marilyn, a naturally good-hearted, energetic woman of forty-five. Marilyn had an abundance of Chesed/Love, and the whole congregation knew it. Because "she didn't have to work," Marilyn devotedly volunteered her time and energy in every conceivable way, from her children's schools to her synagogue's sisterhood.

But Marilyn had a problem, and the whole congregation knew about this part of her too. There was an unpredictable beast that lived inside of her, a vicious temper that flew out whenever she hit the limits of her goodness, limits that she had not yet learned. At those times, whoever was near Marilyn became the unenviable target of a caustic verbal attack. She was like a volcano that had to blow, and there was no method to her outbursts and no benefit to be had in trying to reason with her. After a few minutes of raging, Marilyn would typically fold up shop, slip out of sight, and go to bed, sometimes for days, with an excruciating headache.

Whereas Chesed flows on forever, Din is all about boundaries. It yells "Stop!" when we have gone too far. Chesed was Marilyn's modus operandi, but it lacked Din/Judgment, the voice of discipline that tells us when to pull back. As Marilyn continued to extend and overextend herself, she was probably receiving but not hearing the voice that whispered to her to recharge her batteries before it was too late. Her explosions were actually her health, in the form of Din, asserting itself, saying, "You won't stop yourself, so I will stop you for you." When Chesed/Love goes too far, life's pendulum insists upon balance, swinging with a vengeance to the opposite extreme.

After years of suffering from this pattern, Marilyn learned the middle path of Tipheret. She began to pay more attention to her system's early signals, such as fatigue or lifelessness. She learned various ways to conserve her energy to restore and give to herself, like taking naps, curling up with a book, or receiving a massage. Most important, Marilyn learned that giving to others rarely warrants serious self-depletion, especially when such exhaustion threatens one's inner peace. Marilyn is now able to say no in good conscience when she has come to her limits of giving. She has learned that she need not sacrifice herself to be a valued part of her community.

The dynamic balance of the Integrity Triangle is found everywhere in a woman's life. Most of us have experienced some form of Marilyn's dilemma in our own lives and the price we pay for overextending at work, with friends, or in our communities. We strive for Tipheret's balance between generosity and boundaries. But the swings of Chesed and Din are not always easy to monitor, and we can get out of balance in many other arenas of our lives too. How we relate to our lovers and partners is another prime example.

Balancing Our Affairs

Diana is an extremely attractive woman who has spent years being miserable in her relationships with men. It took a dramatic experience to finally teach her the importance of balance. Diana was in love with a long-haired musician named Justin, and she held nothing back from him, including her money. Justin was exciting but self-absorbed and irresponsible. After a year, Diana finally realized that she was being used and that she was losing her self-esteem quickly. With the coaching of friends, she finally cut the relationship off.

Months after their breakup, Justin roared up Diana's driveway on a new Triumph motorcycle. "Now where did he get the money for *that*?" she wondered as she marched outside to tell him off. But Justin looked so good and behaved so lovingly that her resolve quickly melted. She hopped on back of the bike for a quick ride. Not far from her house, a car appeared out of nowhere, and, as Justin swerved to avoid it, the bike tipped over and fell. Luckily, they were unhurt and safe from traffic, but the bike had fallen on top of Justin. Diana reached out to lift it off him, grabbing the bike by its red-hot tailpipe! She was so caught up in Justin's well-being that she didn't notice until later that she had been badly burned.

Diana's housemate came home to find Diana with her hand on ice, crying from pain. For the next few weeks, her bandaged right hand, the hand of Chesed/Love, was a throbbing reminder that her tendency to "overlove" was dangerous. Diana learned the difficult lesson that when you give without balance, you get burned.

What does a love relationship balanced in Tipheret look like? The main characteristic is that both partners are nourished in a reciprocal relationship. A woman balanced in Tipheret is never *co-dependent,* dependent upon the other for her happiness. Rather, she seeks *interdependence,* that is, both she and her partner are responsive to each other's needs, while also being able to stand on their own two feet. In a Tipheret relationship, there is a conscious flow of energy that is never exactly fifty-fifty, but that nevertheless finds its own unique balance.

Creating Family Equilibrium

Understanding and keeping a balance between our giving nature and our limits is critical for most women. Another clear arena in which this need for balance plays itself out is in the realm of parenting. Most parents know the temptation to spoil their kids. We also know that an overly generous style of parenting, giving few limits and trying to be our children's best friend, is bound to boomerang on a family, if not before, then certainly during, the teen years. As we have been seeing, when the pendulum swings too far to the side of Chesed/Love, it returns with an equal and opposite force to reassert boundaries.

The result of over-Chesed/Love parenting comes in the form of disrespect, tantrums, or rude or dangerous behavior. This is the child pushing us for limits (Din). Acting out may be seen as the family system's health trying to reassert itself. It is a signal that we have lost that delicate balance between Chesed and Din.

In these cases, it is important to proceed with caution. We may be so angry that we overblame, overpunish, or set consequences that we cannot keep. Our reactions are simply the pendulum swinging to the opposite (Din) extreme. If we react to our children's antics in overly harsh ways, we will, sooner or later, find ourselves making up for our harshness with apologies, treats, and special attention to make them love us again. Back and forth we swing on that pendulum, from over-love to overharshness and back again.

Parents need to exercise caution *especially* when they feel an urgency to react to the child. Beware the impulse to lash out, to take a parental stand, to "put an end to this nonsense once and for all," and even to take away their pain. (When we overreact, we can be assured that our children will too.) A more temperate approach is to calmly inform the child that you are fully aware of the situation and are weighing things carefully. Without a storm of reaction, the children can rest, knowing that there is no one to be manipulated, and this security restores their own inner balance.

Arlene had to learn this the hard way. "After 'laying down the law' with my teenagers again and again, I realized that my word was beginning to mean nothing. So I changed my tactics. Instead of knee-jerking into a yelling match and calling out a tirade of threats that I couldn't keep, I now say something like, 'Please go to your room. A lot has happened today and I am considering all of it. We'll talk more in the morning.'"

This tempered response is the return of balance, or Tipheret. It is the point of equilibrium in a family system, the synthesis of love and warmth (Chesed) and firm limits (Din). Although no self-respecting child would ever admit it, having too few limits is scary. It means there is a lack of protection in the field. The Tipheret approach assures children that they will receive both love and boundaries.

Danger Signals

Living without or with too few boundaries can be scary for grown-ups too. It takes practice, but eventually we learn that the Integrity Triangle within us has a built-in intelligence that is always trying to bring us back to our point of balance. This intelligence is both loving and ruthless. It first gives us subtle indications that we are getting off track, then harsher warnings to wake up, and finally does whatever is necessary to pull us back into honoring our physical and emotional limits.

The signals that we are out of balance are unique to each of us. They come from our bodies, dreams, intuition, and others around us. Some women experience signs in the form of fatigue, headaches, or gut feelings ("I just can't cope with this anymore!"). For others, there are emotional indicators like irritability ("If one more person calls me, I'm going to scream!") or an inability to remember details ("Where did I put my keys this time?"). When we ignore and override these signals, we invite danger.

A female rabbinic colleague was on her way to a neurosurgeon for symptoms of blanking out in mid-thought when she called me. She told me that she would find herself at a board meeting or in a consultation with a grieving family, and in the middle of making an important point she would completely lose her train of thought. This frightened her greatly; she felt her own mind was becoming unreliable. "It feels like my mind is seizing up and refusing to work. How can a rabbi function with brain-freeze?" she joked with a tremor in her voice.

The neurosurgeon's tests proved negative, but my friend was still scared. When I probed her situation, asking her what part of her was really "seizing up" and "refusing to work," she admitted that, because of her inability to say no, she hadn't had a day off from her rabbinic duties for three straight weeks. Not surprisingly, she hadn't been sleeping either.

This was another case of overextended Chesed/Love. The pendulum had swung too far, and it was making its way back to balance (Tipheret) through some fearful symptoms. A two-week leave of absence helped to right this rabbi's mind, and her mental clarity returned. Her synagogue has since hired a full-time assistant to help with the workload.

Din/Judgment is often frightening. In fact, another name for it is Pachad, "fear." It is characterized by Isaac, who lay on the altar ready to be sacrificed, before the divine voice told Abraham to put down his knife.[29] Din is also characterized by the hard work and rigor of Leah, the mother of many of the Israelite tribes, as well as by other contractive experiences, such as anger, punishment, the constraints of time and health, and even war. All of these are necessary facets of life. It is only when they are sudden and uncontrollable, the slap-in-the-face reaction to an overly expansive attitude, that they are difficult to bear.

Redeeming Dulcie

The Integrity Triangle finds its balance in the heart. As we learned in Chapter 3, Tipheret/Compassion is not one-sided love, but the wise and seasoned response to life. It is born of deep caring and self-knowledge, a desire to serve others and a realistic understanding of what one has to give.

We are all striving for the integrity and balance of Tipheret, which speaks to us through our inner voice of truth. Remember, Tipheret is both ruthlessly honest and extremely loving. We can become more aware of our inner voice by asking How do I normally speak to myself; that is, what is my "self-talk"? Am I overly tolerant and lax? Am I judgmental and harsh with myself? Am I willing to look at the truth that is born of both evidence and self-compassion?

If Dulcie were positioned in the place of Tipheret, for example, she might be both flawlessly factual about what happened to her as well as earnestly forgiving. We can imagine her telling her story from all angles, not only through her own eyes, but also her children's, her husband's, and even her murderers'.

But in truth, we have no idea what Dulcie's inner life was like, nor what she would say to us if she could speak. Nonetheless, the pain of her horrific end, even after eight hundred years, is still fresh for us. We must ask What is the gift of Dulcie's life? How we can redeem her? Perhaps we can use Dulcie's story to raise our own awareness about the great swings of good and evil, both in the world at large and within our own selves. Through studying Dulcie's story, we can learn the lesson of light, shadow, and wholeness: that neither suppression, nor projection, nor taking refuge in a one-sided reality can bring about a whole life. Only balance holds the answer.

CHAPTER 6

BRINGING PURPOSE INTO ACTION

Leah Shar'abi (1919–1978)

Of the seven women mystics in this book, only Leah Shar'abi lived in modern times. For forty-five years,[1] Leah lived and worked in the slums of Jerusalem, feeding, clothing, teaching, and administering to the immigrants who had moved there from all over the Middle East. Leah fed the elderly, mopped their floors, and carried parcels of clothes to poor young mothers. Through these and countless other acts, Leah restored people's dignity and uplifted thousands of lives. This, she declared, was her life's purpose.

This chapter deals with the feminine approach to putting one's purpose into action. Leah Shar'abi exemplified the art of manifesting vision, which requires both energy and the art of implementation. For this reason, her story will lead us into the lowest triangle on the kabbalistic Tree of Life, the Energy Triangle: Yesod/Creativity, Netzach/Energy, and Hod/Method.

Leah Shar'abi is the one woman in this book whom I was privileged to know personally and from whom I received direct teachings and guidance. For this reason, this chapter is, in part, told as my own story. Because Leah's greatest teachings to me were about the soul's journey and evolution, this chapter will also address the multilayered fabric of the human soul and the work each of us must do to refine ourselves and live out our ultimate purpose.

I met Leah Shar'abi in May of my eighteenth year and spent the summer working at her side. Throughout Jerusalem this robust Yemenite woman was known as the Rabanit (literally, the "Rabbi's wife"). I addressed her simply as Leah.

Leah's elderly husband, Rabbi Mordechai Shar'abi, still recognized as one of Jerusalem's greatest Kabbalists, was treated with deferential awe by most.[2] But I never saw Leah so much as walk out of her house without the needy rushing up to kiss her hands, ask for a blessing, or tell her the latest installment in a sad or miraculous tale. When I walked with her through the streets and alleyways of Jerusalem, people would invariably call out their blessings to her or stop what they were doing to run after her, following for blocks if necessary to submit their appeal or simply have a word with her.

The Shar'abis took me into their household as if I were a grown daughter who had come home to help. Each noon the shutter doors looking out onto the polished stone courtyard were closed and the lingering recipients of help and blessings left to wait outside. In the cool front room, barely bigger than the foyer of my parents' home in America, the three of us sat down to rest and enjoy the meal that Leah had prepared earlier that morning. These meals were made up of simple foods such as stuffed peppers with rice, okra simmered with tomatoes, cucumbers and herbs, and pita bread.

The rabbi spoke little. Even when we ate he would pore over a holy book, chanting quietly to himself. He was a tiny man, and his dark skin was strangely exotic, especially against his white kaftan, cap, and billowing white beard. Every so often, in response to something that had been said, the rabbi would look up at me and his eyes would sparkle. I do not believe that Rav Shar'abi ever once addressed me in words. Yet his face radiated an unmistakable amusement at my presence and a kind of recognition that I took to be a personal blessing.

It was Leah who spoke. Her throaty voice poured out like music, punctuated here and there with a great sigh or a cascade of laughter. At lunch she would regale us with stories of her cases, the people she worried over and pondered the most, the ones beyond the reach or capacity of the Department of Welfare. Leah's cases were the poorest and most destitute people of all ages, from Iraq, Kurdistan, Yemen, and Morocco—Mizrachi Jews who had left their homes in the Arab countries to settle in the Holy Land. In those days, many of the emigrants from around the Middle East and northern Africa were extremely poor and underprivileged.

On any given day, Leah's stories were shocking. There was the blind mother of nine whose husband had just been diagnosed with cancer, the schizophrenic shut-in who had been denied welfare help because his grown children refused to visit, and the family of thirteen who lived in one room and was still sleeping on the earthen floor spread with cardboard and rags. And there were the ubiquitous orphan girls who had come of age and were anxious for the Rabanit to match them to their future husbands, collect their dowries, and help prepare them for marriage. The year before, Leah had married off seventeen girls.

My fateful path to the Shar'abi house was forged by my father. He had first read about Leah Shar'abi in 1971, when she won the title "Mother of the People," an award for good citizenship to the unfortunate on behalf of the Jerusalem municipality. Leah hated having a fuss made over her and avoided the press whenever possible. But in this case, she put up with the fanfare because it came with a prize of 1,000 lirah (about $250), which Leah immediately spent on her neediest cases.

Born in 1919 to wealthy Yemenite parents, Leah had been betrothed at the age of ten to "a religious schoolteacher who later became a rabbi."[3] Leah and her new husband immigrated to Israel in 1933, when she was fourteen. The couple could not have children, a tragic fate for a woman, according to the Mizrachi worldview.

As her husband established his *yeshivah*,[4] Leah worked as a menial servant in wealthy Israeli homes. But God clearly had other plans for her. Very soon she became a different kind of servant, a servant of souls, one might say, first in her Yemenite neighborhood, then in her district, Nachalot Zion, and with time in the seven districts around hers, called Nachla'ot.

With my father's prompting, I began accompanying Leah on her rounds through the impoverished sections of Mizrachi Jerusalem, doing what I could to help. Each day as I scrubbed floors, cooked food, washed aged bottoms, and sat at bedsides to listen to marvelous and sordid end-of-life tales, my neatly packaged American worldview came apart a little more.

Nothing in my middle-class Jewish upbringing had prepared me for the phenomenon I was encountering. It was more than being exposed to physical squalor, although the scarcity and stench found in these alleyway dwellings was truly staggering. Impressive too was the near absence of complaining that I would have expected from such unfortunate people.

Most remarkable, though, was an unnamed experience that these new immigrants were sharing en masse. They were living a miracle— the long awaited return of the exiles to the Holy Land after centuries of being outcast minorities throughout the Middle East. Yet could such impoverished lives really be called miraculous? To me it looked more like these people's centuries-old idealism was plummeting from sky to slum, silent and sudden, in one short generation.

Leah, of course, did not agree. Yes, there was a lot of work to be done to improve conditions, but to Leah, the State of Israel was nothing short of a miracle and the emigration of Jews from around the world the fulfillment of God's prophecies. I took refuge in Leah's stalwart confidence that God's will was unfolding perfectly and according to schedule.

Nevertheless, as we got to know one another, I often found myself reeling. Leah's grasp of the universe struck me as utterly foreign; even her Jewish outlook differed radically from my own. I was learning the great disparity between the pragmatic Ashkenazic worldview in which I had been steeped, and the more "primitive," mystically inclined, Mizrachi understanding of life.

A few days into my new job, I stood at Leah's cutting board chopping vegetables for our lunch when she looked over my shoulder and said glibly, "*Tizharee al haneshamot!* (Be mindful of the souls, eh?)" When she repeated herself, I stopped what I was doing and turned around.

"What did you say?"

"The *neshamot* (souls). Be careful."

"I don't understand. What *souls* are you talking about?"

"In the food, of course. The more aware you are, the more you can raise them." Leah must have seen the stark incomprehension on my face, and she started to laugh at me.

"I'm talking about *gilgulim* (the chain of incarnation), silly one. What did they teach you over there in America, eh?" I still had no idea what we were talking about and felt the blood rising to my face.

"You told me you went to a religious Hebrew school, didn't you? Rabbi, come hear this. She does not know about *gilgulim*!" she called to her husband.

After she had chided me for a while, Leah proceeded to explain that there are souls in everything. "Everything you see has a spark of holiness in it that is waiting to rise up. It wants to be free, like a person in prison who longs to be rescued. It waits and waits until someone like you or me comes along to free it."

The mystical reason Jews recite blessings before they eat a fruit or smell a flower, Leah explained, is that as soon as they mention God's name, they awaken the hidden spark buried inside it, by which it was created. This spark is a thing's inner life. Whenever we use God's name with a desire to help, we literally raise the soul up to its next station. This is also why people bless each other.

"*Everything* has a soul waiting to be raised up. You think you are the only one? Every creature yearns! And we are bridges. Whenever we help another, we carry their soul to its next level, with God's help. And also when we eat, if we cook and cut and then bless what we eat, we raise up the souls of that fruit or meat. So *now* you finally know why you make a blessing!" she chortled loudly.

As I struggled to understand what she was teaching me, I had the strange image of Leah bending down in a big arch, the souls of many people but also those of lettuce, chickens, asparagus, and fish climbing over her on their way to the next stop in their evolution. Leah had given her life to being a bridge for others. And she was telling me that all people could and should do the same.

"*Gilgulim,*" Leah went on, "are the many rounds of life we must live on our way to God. You didn't think you lived just this once, did you?" Again she threw her head back and laughed heartily. "No, no, you've been here many times, I promise you!" Then her look turned solemn. "Listen to me now. Each time there are both dangers on the way and opportunities to rise up. This is why the company we keep is so important. Remember, holy people will help you in a world that is interested in burying your spark."

"Even when it looks like we are making a descent into darkness or, God forbid, unholy states," Leah told me as we walked through the marketplace one day, "in the final analysis, our fall is for the purpose of raising ourselves or someone else up. This may not be clear right away, but eventually it will be. That's why it's a sin to become hopeless. And it is a sin to hold back from helping another soul, God forbid. Anyone who asks or needs, do whatever you can do."

Leah, like Malkah of Belz and myriad unchronicled women throughout history, knew that nothing, not even the most seemingly menial act, is devoid of God. Every action and interaction is an opportunity for holiness and the raising of life's sparks.

From that point forward, Leah felt free to talk to me about reincarnation. It was clear to her that I had not come by accident to her home; there were no accidents. To Leah, every event, even the greatest misfortune, had its purpose—to help us ascend. And every life had its special task of repair, called *tikkun,* which, when accomplished, created a fulfillment for the whole world and caused God the greatest of delight. Leah's *tikkun* was to raise up the lives of others. I believe that it was due to her clarity about this sacred purpose that she was able to tap an inexhaustible wellspring of energy that allowed her to accomplish her work.

Every day I studied Leah as she talked, listened, blessed, and distributed clothes, food, and comfort. Even when she was bone-tired from being on her feet all day long, her eyes flashed with *nitzutzim,* the sparks of her exuberant soul. And I saw the eyes of the people she helped also sparkling, mostly with love of her and the hope that she brought to them.

On our way home from our rounds that day, a weathered-looking Moroccan man approached Leah in her courtyard. He was crying and wringing his hands, his voice high pitched, almost wailing. His fourteen-year-old daughter was pregnant again, he cried to Leah. The first time they had gotten the girl an abortion. Now her boyfriend said he would marry her, but the family had ten children and there was no money for a ring, a wedding, and a room to rent.

I felt embarrassed to hear words like "boyfriend" and "abortion" in front of my holy friend. What did she know about such things? But Leah did not bat an eye. She consoled the father with calm words, agreed to raise funds for the new family, and told him not to worry because she would see to it that all would be made holy again, with sacred blessings under the wedding canopy. There was not a hint of judgment in Leah's voice. I wondered to myself if she knew the soul of the baby from another *gilgul.* At any rate, Leah had already raised up the entire situation from its shame and woe, and the new baby would have a chance at life.

How Leah found the money to solve so many problems was a never-ending mystery to me. She certainly had no connections to philanthropic organizations or big donors.

One afternoon when I returned to Leah's house from my rounds, I found her in tears. She had been walking down the street toward the marketplace when she discovered her handbag open and her money gone. Someone had undoubtedly opened it at the street corner and made off with her wallet.

"But it's not my shopping money that I care about," she cried. "The thief snatched my charity envelopes too." Leah's collections had been ready for distribution, one envelope for marrying off orphans, one for Sabbath allocations, and one for general charity. In despair, Leah had gone to the police, knowing that they would be unable to help her. When I left that evening, she was chanting Psalms, the one book she turned to most.

The next morning, I found Leah dancing about like a happy child, her mourning of the night before gone like a bad dream. She had woken up to find all three of her envelopes at her bedside! She did not seem to care how this miracle had occurred. She was anxious to tell me that next to the restored money was a note reading, "Please forgive me for my awful misdeed. I hadn't realized I had stolen charity money. Please find enclosed an extra 50 lirah to put toward the orphans' fund, and again, forgive me. Destroy this note at once." Leah happily obeyed the order and the incident was never mentioned again.

Money, like all worldly things, was holy in the Shar'abi home. It was there to be raised up to its highest purpose. Although I did not understand this fully at the time, I eventually learned.

One day I needed to catch a bus back to my apartment and had no change. Overhearing my need, Rabbi Shar'abi dug beneath his robe and wordlessly held out a 10 pound note for me to take. I took the rabbi's gift nonchalantly, thanked him, walked out the door, and promptly bought a falafel with the money before catching my bus.

A few weeks later I overheard mention among Rabbi Shar'abi's followers that the rabbi had himself handed me a *segulah*, an auspicious gift. There seemed to be a lot of excitement about this fact. What had I had done with it? I was asked. I turned away, ashamed that I had so cavalierly used it to sate my own hunger. The tension between my customary self-service and the new worldview shrieked inside of me.

I watched closely the choices Leah and her husband had made. They had elected to live simply—some might call it in poverty—in a one-and-a-half-room apartment in one of the poorest neighborhoods of Jerusalem. The Shar'abis clearly had a talent for finding the necessary funds for others, yet this facility to draw down blessings was rarely used for their own benefit—and never to have something that others did not share.

Everything that Leah and her husband received—money, food, clothing—was immediately distributed to those who were in danger of losing their dignity. As for the Shar'abis dignity, it was never at risk. Their standing in the world came from their connection to the Divine and their life of service. They could afford to be poor. Others could not.

A Shared Purpose

Although Leah and her husband each had their own domain, their respective work was not separate; nor were their lives. Rav Shar'abi spent the night awake studying at the front room table. It was widely rumored among his followers that he was visited by angels at night and that it was from them that he received his Torah innovations. Leah confirmed to me that this was true. She understood her husband's divine purpose. His *yeshivah* and synagogue stood just across the stone courtyard, and he prayed and studied there daily.

Leah rarely set foot in her husband's place. Yet it was clear for all to see that she was the physical backbone of his work and was inextricably united with it. By means of her work in the physical world, Leah anchored Rav Shar'abi's work in the upper worlds. This took many forms. Along with the hundreds of people she tended, she also cared for his students. Leah looked after their health, matched them up, married them off, and then secured loans, housing, and jobs for them.

Equally, Rav Shar'abi's holy work, although far less visible than Leah's, complemented her life. Even as a teenager, I could see that Leah's accomplishments were due, at least in part, to her mysterious husband and what he and she stood for together. The prolific and inexplicable funds that circulated through her hands, the boxes of clothes that arrived in scores at the post office and at their front door, the healings and miracles that occurred regularly in their home, like that of the stolen purse, were the result of a field charged with holiness.

As in the holy partnership of Malkah and Shalom of Belz, a kind of sacred magic was created in the Shar'abi home. How did they create such a powerful field between them? They had a shared purpose in life, a mission that they served devotedly. Their devotion to serving others was so clear and unimpeded that every thought and action became, in effect, a means to that end.

Devotion to the Shared "Third"

Years later and far from their world, Leah and her husband still stand imprinted in my mind as models of a healthy partnership given to a shared ideal. As a psychotherapist, I have worked with many couples who struggle to find a common meaning. I remember one client in particular, a man named Roy, who learned the lesson of surrender through a string of failed marriages. He came to me for counseling while in the throes of his third divorce. Although Roy claimed to want nothing more in life than a successful marriage, now, at the age of fifty-three, he had given up his dream.

"I always thought women wanted to be adored and put first," Roy claimed, "but each time I tried a little harder and each time it got a little worse." His was a path of devotion and surrender, he told me, and as proof he enumerated the gifts, the financial support, even the alimony he paid these women! He had approached each one of his wives as an object of worship, and in each case the women eventually lost respect for him.

I told Roy that although his intentions were admirable, I believed he had spent years surrendering to the wrong thing. A woman or man who needs to be worshiped is not a fully mature individual, and the individual who serves another person in order to keep the partner happy will eventually lose his or her own dignity and, therefore, the relationship.

Roy took a lucrative sales job in the Middle East to get away from his broken life. Several years after he left the States, I received a letter from him. Roy "had made a killing" at his new career, with enough money to retire and do what he had always wanted to do. He was now the assistant director of medical distribution for the American Red Cross in Istanbul, a position that put him in the thick of post-earthquake disaster sites.

Roy was never happier. He had finally discovered how to focus his natural impulse to surrender himself to a higher cause. Roy ended up remarrying, despite having sworn off women forever. His fourth wife was the Red Cross volunteer coordinator, who had committed herself to a life of service. I suspect that their marriage will last a long time.

For a marriage, or any meaningful partnership, to thrive, it must be built on some ideal greater than either of its partners. A shared sense of devotion to a mutually meaningful "third" element is necessary to feed a couple spiritually, or the relationship risks becoming a closed system that will eventually die. Leah and her husband modeled this shared devotion to a higher principle.

With this "third" element in mind, I ask the couples who come to be married by me to put into writing a "mission statement" for their marriage, a sentence or more that expresses their highest aspirations for being together, a shared purpose that goes beyond simply caring for and loving one another. Writing a statement of this kind is useful because even when we cannot see ahead to what our destiny will bring or what our eventual purpose might be, the exercise opens the way to understanding that we are brought together to grow beyond ourselves and to make a difference in the world around us. In order to be fed, we must feed the world around us, or our system collapses.

Every marriage has its own unique synergy based on the talents of both parties. But when a couple brings their spiritual visions together and commits to putting them into action, their partnership shifts from the utilitarian to the sacred.

This leap can happen whether or not we are materially blessed. One partner loses a beloved pet and is moved to foster animals at risk. Her partner, a builder, joins her to design a wildlife sanctuary, an idea that is adopted and funded by the rural county in which they live. One partner believes ardently in women's empowerment in under-privileged countries. Her partner has a wealth of experience in the non-profit business sector. They pool their interests and together create a string of successful women's micro-loan businesses throughout West Africa. Whatever our spiritual purpose, it can be made more fruitful by the power of two.

The Power of Surrender

But how do we discover our spiritual purpose? One way is to watch over time what moves us most deeply. This may be anything from teenagers at risk to decorating houses. When we discover what it is that stirs our soul, it is wise to adopt an attitude of surrender, to ask to be "deployed" in the service of a greater good.[5]

The idea of dedication to principles such as goodness, justice, and beauty belongs to people of all traditions. For many Christians the prayer "Not my will, but Thine be done" is a watchword that helps one remember there is a larger design at work. As Leah taught, each of us is here with a purpose and that purpose is part of God's plan. This is why many people feel that their greatest fulfillment comes when they have surrendered to their life's purpose. A maxim made famous by the popular Twelve-Step Program, "Turning one's life over to a Higher Power," is another poignant message for our age, underscoring the freedom found in surrendering our personal control to a Power greater than ourselves.

In Judaism, this Power is known by many names—Yah, Adonai, Elohim, Shadai, to name but a few—the unifying Source behind all life. Most prayers in Judaism reflect the assumption that we are here on earth, not as free agents, but to carry out the will of this unifying Source. This is "done" by means of performing the commandments in the Torah.

Although much of Judaism is expressed in terms of holy action, a Jewish approach to life does not exclude the nondoing side of life: feeling, receiving, and contemplation. Although these more feminine approaches—inclusion of one's body and passions in one's religious life, and surrender to a greater Will—have been less emphasized in the Jewish tradition, they are just as effective a path to God.

One of the more reflective scriptures in the Torah is the book of Psalms, the book of devotional prayers from which Leah recited daily. Throughout the Psalms, one finds passages that refer to this receptive orientation. Leah used the book of Psalms as an oracle. She would meditate on a question or problem with the book in her hands. Then she would open it three times in quick succession, each time allowing her eye to fall on one verse. By sewing the verses' meanings together, Leah received an answer to her question.

Leah's husband also relied on the Psalms for sacred assistance. He used to recite the same passage from Psalms daily. Long before I understood the power of these verses, I actually experienced Rabbi Shar'abi's mantra, the last line from Psalm 90, transforming the energy around him. He would chant this three-part prayer three times throughout the day, and every time he did, the words seemed to sweep the air of doubt, fear, and negativity and restore the home to its quiet, shining clarity.

> *May the grace of God be upon us.*
> *And may the work of our hands establish us.*
> *And may the work of our hands establish God.*

One might say that Rav Shar'abi's incantation had magical powers. But it was also the power of his faith and surrender. In my own life I have found that saying this passage before undertaking a project such as cooking, writing, or a community meeting can help to unify and uplift one's efforts to their highest purpose.

The Sealing of Our Soul

When the summer months waned, I took my leave of Leah and her husband, promising to return the following summer after my first year of university back in the United States. But it took me longer than that to return. By the time I finally showed up on Leah's doorstep again, over a year had passed and I was ensconced in a life of my own making in a culture that had taken me far from the purposeful life I had experienced in her home.[6]

I will never forget the look on Leah's face when she saw me again. For a long time she just stared at my forehead, rocking from side to side. Finally, her eyes dropped to mine, and she asked, "What have you done? Your letters are gone!"

That day I sat with Leah as she gave me the most difficult teaching of all. When we come to earth, she explained, our soul has a clear connection to its purpose, our *tikkun* for this life. We have made an agreement with the divine forces to do a piece of work specific to our soul's development. Upon birth, God's three-letter name, Shaddai, is engraved in light upon our foreheads, like a seal on our soul. As long as we are in clear view of our purpose and our source, the letters shine brightly. "It looks as if your letters have been smudged out. What have you been up to there in America, in your Land of the Free?"

I did not need to tell my holy friend about the frivolity, confusion, and loss of meaning I had experienced in my time away. I was transparent to her.

"Don't worry," she said with a sad smile. "You are simply making a *yeridah l'shem aliyah,* a descent in order to ascend. There is still time."

With that Leah excused herself to go off on her visits. She looked more tired than I had remembered seeing her. That was the last time I saw her.

Leah's final teaching had the most profound impact on me. Mirrored in her eyes that day I saw how far I had come from my first pure-hearted desire to help her in the raising up of sparks. Yet I knew with equal clarity that I could not simply jump over the darker path that now compelled me.

Finding the truth sometimes means descending into the dark world of freedom and learning the hard way, from our mistakes and failures, how to return to the light of our soul's purpose. The path of free choice is a difficult one and often fraught with danger, but in my case my soul chafed at any other prospect. In time, I hoped, I would naturally recover my connection to my holiness and recover those letters on my forehead, emblazoned in light.

Returning to the Tree

Leah Shar'abi had inner vision. I am convinced that she could see the soul of a person in all its dimensions and discern a person's deepest longing just by looking at her. Leah's gift of seeing was doubtless strengthened by her own clarity of purpose, which was to uplift the lives of others.

Leah stands out among women because she brought her vision into the world and turned it into action. I imagine her as a great tree, drawing down her spiritual purpose through her uppermost branches, using all of the spheres to assist her: Wisdom to imagine it and Discernment to conceptualize it. Tempered by the powerful forces of Love and Judgment, she held her vision in her compassionate Heart.

But her purpose still had to find its way into action, to be rooted in the world so it could be of actual benefit to others. Otherwise, it was doomed to remain in the realm of intention, high-minded and beautiful perhaps, but not yet *real.*

The Energy Triangle

How do our spiritual visions find their way to the earth? The way Leah served was with hands on, feet marching, tongue talking, and brow sweating. Her vision was carried all the way down into action by means of the lowest triangle on the Tree of Life called the Energy Triangle. This downward facing triangle helps finish the job of rooting vision into action. You can find it just above Malkhut, the root system of the Tree. It is composed of Netzach/Energy, Hod/Method, and Yesod/Creativity.

The Energy Triangle is an area on the Tree of Life that is often misunderstood. What is important to remember is that its right and left components, Netzach/Energy and Hod/Method, cannot function without one another. In fact, they represent a person's right and left hips and legs. We cannot move ahead in life unless we have both legs. Nor can we effectively take a stand for what we believe unless both hips work together. Together with Yesod/Creativity in the place of the low belly, the spheres of Netzach and Hod make up the pelvis, hips, and legs, arguably the most dynamic center of action in a woman's body.

Netzach/Energy and Hod/Method

Netzach/Energy is the sphere in which an idea is made manifest. It most often arises as an impulse to do, make, or give. This impulse says, "Let's go!" It has enthusiasm, spontaneity, and a beautiful glow that, like fire, warms and excites. To be around people whose soul root is in Netzach/Energy can be exhilarating. Often elegant in appearance, they are full of pizzazz, personality, and high ideals. You may have guessed that Netzach is the domain of the politicians, community leaders, spiritual teachers, and visionaries among us.

But this firecracker called Netzach may lack the focus and perseverance to carry out all her ideas. She may be gorgeous, but she needs Hod/Method to follow close behind to channel all her vigor into productivity. Without the organizing principles, steady work habits, and savvy of Hod/Method, this energetic pacesetter can easily burn out.

Netzach/Energy is like a glowing fire, but it requires oil to burn. Like Moses (the male representative for this *sephirah*), whose vision of the burning bush ignited an entire people to transformation, Netzach/Energy blazes the way, illuminating the path for many to follow.

But Moses required his brother, a demure pacifist named Aaron, to articulate his vision. A less-famous and less outwardly thrilling character, Aaron (representing Hod) quietly created a context for the revelation that Moses would bring, setting the stage for a holy society with the sacred oil of the priesthood. Without Aaron's oil, Moses' fiery vision could not have lasted. Aaron was, in fact, the high priest. His gift was the sacred technology of the sanctuary with all its rituals, routines, and procedures. With his oil, he anointed the priestly tribe, lit the seven-branched menorah, mixed fragrant herbs for incense, and brought offerings to God. He enabled the people to put into practice their enthusiasm and devotion. He created the vehicle by which to serve God.

When visionary energy exists and there is a practical method by which to apply it, success is at hand. These two spheres, Netzach/Energy and Hod/Method, need one other, and when they find their harmonious balance, anything is possible. One might say that Leah Shar'abi and her husband personified these two spheres, the rabbi providing the mystical fire of Netzach and Leah providing the means of bringing it into the world.

Look at any highly functioning institution, business, school, or marriage. If it is truly flourishing, both the spark of inspiration and the practical arrangements—the income, housing, and operations—are interacting together. Both Netzach and Hod are necessary for success. Together they provide the essential ingredients for new life, which are then nurtured in the container of Yesod, the sphere of personal creativity.

Remember that all the spheres on the Tree of Life are stations on the way to wholeness. Yesod is where we find our creativity and personhood. It is the sphere on the middle pillar where our will to fulfill our life's purpose is formed. But if Yesod is to bring our soul's desires to physical fruition (Malkhut), it will require both the spark of inspiration (Netzach) and the practical ability (Hod) with which to implement our dream.

The synagogue where I grew up had its share of rabbis. Some were great orators; some were great fund-raisers; some were learned sages. These men came and they went, staying for two to ten years at a stretch on their way to more prestigious congregations. Each one had his talents, as the Netzach personality must, at galvanizing the congregation. But the synagogue would never have lasted without the methodical, steady competence of Mona. Mona was called the synagogue administrator, but she did every job conceivable to keep the congregation together, from handling payroll to plunging toilets, from pinch-hitting for sick teachers to comforting mourners in the rabbi's waiting room.

Mona played the part of Hod/Method, and without her the leaders of the synagogue would have had no containing structure in which to do their work of religious leadership. Hod is about follow-through, carrying an idea from its inception to its final conclusion. It requires only the spark of purposeful enthusiasm, and it knows what to do to carry it out.

Most partners of long-term relationships, romantic or otherwise, know about the twin roles of Netzach/Energy and Hod/Method. It is common in many relationships for one partner to take over the job of generating the energy—in the form of money, enthusiasm, projects, to-do lists—while the other partner implements, spends, executes, and mops up.

Murray and Lex were clients who fit this profile in a very dramatic way. They had been married for twenty-six years, and I could tell at our first meeting that they had weathered many a rough storm together. Lex was a svelte, gray-haired woman with an elegant yet flat demeanor. For the entire hour she sat upright, all business, and would never smile unnecessarily. Murray, on the other hand, was almost puppy-like in energy. Ardently expressive, Murray gesticulated with his hands, his eyes moist with feeling as he discussed his love for Lex and his frustration.

"When I come to her with my ideas, she judges and evaluates them. I just want her to listen and let me know what she feels," Murray said.

"He's *full* of ideas, but he never thinks any of them through or does anything with them!" Lex replied. "He shoots from the hip without bullets. I don't take him seriously anymore."

"And by the time she shares *her* ideas, they're practically trademarked! Why won't she share herself with me?"

How can such extremely different styles work together? Murray, who plays out the energetic Netzach character in the couple, loves to bounce his ideas around for weeks, asking for feedback and advice. Lex, the methodical Hod-type, has a more interior, business-like process. She prefers to work on her own. She researches her ideas, thinks them through, and then systematically takes steps to make them happen.

Communication between these two types is essential or walls of judgment can quickly form. Once Murray and Lex could see that their respective styles were natively different but neither one better nor worse, they could relearn how to work with each other's styles respectfully. They adopted a weekly communication ritual that involved uninterrupted active listening to one another. After several weeks of this process, Lex learned to be a little less guarded about her personal plans and ruminations; Murray learned to think his ideas through and express them in more cogent form. Lex has helped Murray come down to earth by asking practical questions with real, not sarcastic, curiosity. And, as Murray becomes more grounded, he is helping Lex to recover some of her natural playfulness.

It is quite common for couples to complement one another by playing out the opposite characteristics of the Tree of Life's right and left pillars. For example, one partner is hospitable and ever available to friends. She pushes limits, shops on a whim, and forgives easily (Chesed). Her partner is the more disciplined one who thinks ahead, puts the brakes on at parties, asks when the houseguests are due to leave, and shops at sales (Din). Another combination, as we saw, comes into play with impulse and practicality. One partner generates energy, new ideas, and projects (Netzach), while the more methodical one pays bills, gets things done around the house, and is generally more of a practical character (Hod).

These sorts of complementary splits are very common. With all the bases covered between the two partners, the relationship can be highly functioning for years at a time. But it can also be extremely limiting, as many women who have unexpectedly lost their partners have found. When we are dependent on others for skills and functions that we are able to develop in ourselves, our wholeness as individuals is compromised. And if wholeness is the goal we are seeking, new ways—perhaps less comfortable, but more fulfilling—must be found. To develop these new ways, we need to extend ourselves beyond our own natural strengths and experiment with functions and roles that we normally leave to others.

Rotating functions, such as arranging social outings, doing the taxes, or setting limits with the kids, can help both partners grow. If a task feels foreign, so much the better! Doing well is not to be expected. Like exercising new areas of the physical body, we are bound to feel a bit odd when we exercise portions of our personality that are untried. But when we do, we increase our awareness and greatly expand our potential for wholeness.

Flash Fry or Slow Roast

In order to bring a spiritual vision into the world, we need to be able to understand both its timeless and its temporal needs. This understanding is especially feminine because women's nature is given to both the quick flashes of inspiration and intuition *and* the long, painstaking work—such as gestating and raising children—that requires patience. One way is beyond time; the other requires time. The first is Netzach; the second is Hod.

The word Netzach in Hebrew means "eternity." Its sparkling energy brings with it a vivacity that enlivens and gives hope. Moses is the masculine character that personifies Netzach, but Queen Esther, in all her gorgeous regalia, wins the role as heroine of Netzach. Esther, the Jewish queen of Persia, was not only stunning in appearance, her idealism and inner conviction made her put her majestic life on the line to save her people. Behind her charisma was her vision of longevity for her people, a true characteristic of Netzach timelessness.

Hod means "reverberation." Its power is never instant, but echoes over time. The Jewish matriarch Sarah holds the feminine place of Hod, for she was a priestess in her own right, long before there was ever a temple or laws to be enacted. For many decades she put into practice the vision of a new theological paradigm by feeding and teaching all who came her way. When she was well into old age Sarah experienced the miracle of conception. In Hod, the vision reverberates through time until it is actualized.

These two qualities of timeless vivacity and practical patience work together to bring about feminine nourishment. Since ancient times, women's wisdom has developed the art of cooking and nourishing: pickling, brewing, rising dough, baking, infusing, canning, drying, and storing; all of these arts require patience, know-how, and the passage of time. The impulse to delight and nourish, found in Netzach, combines with the patience and artfulness of Hod to create authentic nourishment. And although one may taste things along the way, these long creative processes require trust that the best results take time.

Successful action in the world calls for both energy and method. How do we know when to make our move and when to sit and allow a thing to evolve? This depends on the wisdom gleaned from the middle pillar. Yesod/Creativity, centered in the lower belly, is our instinctual sense of timing. The healthy animal in us, when unobstructed, has perfect reflexes. Tipheret, the heart center located just above it, holds the answer to the question What is most compassionate for all involved?

Leah's life exemplifies the beautiful dance of these two qualities, vivacity and patience, and the visionary wisdom of the middle pillar. Often Leah would calm people down in a panicky situation with the words "*Yesh zman!* (There's time!)" or "*Gam zeh ya'avor!* (This too shall pass!)." At other times, she would dash into a house and yell, "*YALA!* (LET'S GO!)" when there was no time to waste. She seemed to know instinctively which situations were cooking at God's time (for which rushing would not help at all) and which required *zrizut,* being light on one's feet.

Leah lived out her soul's vision and taught us to understand the importance of physically enacting what we believe in. The Energy Triangle is crucial in bringing our vision down to earth, because it is about wedding our personal energy to a practical method in order to be successful at creating our dreams.

Why is this especially important for women? Fulfillment is about making our visions real, not just floating our ideas or intending to do good things, but making things happen in physical form. Throughout history women have lacked the freedom, education, and means to fulfill their dreams. In our day, however, everything is available to us. We no longer need to sit by the sidelines wishing for a different, more balanced, just, or peaceful world. For the first time, the entire Tree of Life is ours to use as a way to bring into reality from the highest realms our souls' visions of wholeness.

The Summation of Wholeness

Leah was a rare soul who could see a person's soul with her inner eye. Her compassionate understanding of the elements that compose a soul, the difficult work it must do, and the many lifetimes that one must make on the journey to wholeness kept her from being dictatorial or judgmental. Over the past thirty years of my life, the lessons

Leah taught me about the soul's journey have been corroborated and expanded upon through my study of Jewish texts and work with individuals in depth-psychological counseling.[7]

I have learned that the soul is a magnificent fusion of five different bodies, each one lighter and more delicate as it spans out from the physical body. For this reason, in the Jewish esoteric tradition, there are five terms for "soul." Each term identifies a different facet or function that all people have, even those who do not consider themselves "spiritual people."

We call individuals great souls when they have mastered both their native talents and the weaker, more divisive, parts of themselves and combined them into a harmonious totality. A great soul is a whole soul, one who has integrated and unified all five of one's aspects, from the earthiest to the most lofty. This then, is the ultimate *yichud,* a unification that takes a lifetime, and perhaps more.

The Soul's Dress

At birth, we step into the five aspects of our soul as if we were stepping into layers of a gorgeous dress, the inner sheaths more vivid and thick and the outer ones as fine as light itself. Even the untrained person can sense the vivid energies of the denser levels of soul; the more gossamer tiers may be intuited by spiritual adepts but are rarely seen.

This five-tiered dress is our soul's new costume, in which we will live, learn, grow, and, hopefully, celebrate our next round of life's miracles. Slipping on this dress, we have said yes to another lifetime, another round of work and soul development, and a new constellation of genes, family, and the particulars of culture, religion, and environment that will help bring about our soul's desired fulfillment. Slipping into another lifetime also means choosing the challenges, losses, and ordeals that we will have to endure to grow as fully as we can.

In order to understand the journey the soul makes, we need to explore each of the five levels of soul in turn.

Nephesh: *The Vital Soul*

Our physical form and the vital force that runs through it are the first layer of our soul-dress, called *nephesh*. *Nephesh* is the densest level of soul and connects us to the earthly plane. It is at this level that our appetite for physical life and all its sensual gratification is found.

You may have guessed that *nephesh* abides in the sphere of Malkhut, the material world. *Nephesh* is the life force that flows within this very physical realm, enlivening and sustaining it. When we are healthy, our *nephesh* beams with vitality; we enjoy food, sex, and other sensual pleasures. It is the *nephesh* soul that gives us our sparkle, vigor, and appetite for life.

It is interesting to note that we share this aspect of soul with animals, and it is often our pets and the wildlife around us that bring us back into balance when our *nephesh* soul is ailing. The Torah teaches that the vital soul called *nephesh* flows in the blood of all living creatures, which is one reason that blood is considered holy and its ingestion therefore prohibited.

But *nephesh* has also been devalued in Judaism, as it has been in the larger culture. A woman's menstrual blood is one example. As we saw in Chapter 1, a bleeding woman is considered a *niddah,* one who is excluded from the community because her flow of blood renders her impure. Jewish law is extremely complex in regard to *niddah.*[8] In brief, contact with a bleeding woman causes contamination similar to that from a corpse, leprosy, seminal discharges, and certain kinds of insects. All of the laws concerning contamination have the same intent: to exclude the impure person from the "divine residence" of the Holy Temple and, later, from synagogue worship.

Although the menstruation taboo is certainly not exclusive to Jewish law but has been found throughout the Near East and the world at large, blood was not always feared or seen as a contaminant; often it was a sign of woman's mysterious power. Integrally related to a woman's ability to bring new life into the world, blood reminds us that the mystery of life, which is far beyond human understanding, needs a physical vehicle to carry it. That vehicle is woman and the fluids of her body.

Once, a woman's blood time was seen as a time of power, not filth or contamination. The Hebrew tribes shared in the widespread custom of the world's indigenous cultures in creating a segregated area for their menstruating women to rest, restore themselves, and deepen in their power.[9] In fact, this women's ritual lasted until the end of the twentieth century, as was discovered when Ethiopian Jews were brought en masse to Israel in the early 1990s.

But some things never change. Blood is still the carrier of the *nephesh* soul, and menstruation is still a perfect opportunity for a woman to access this aspect of herself regularly. This does not mean venerating the discharged blood itself; it does mean revering the cyclical wisdom of the body that provides the potential to create new life. During a woman's "moon time," the veil between the conscious and unconscious minds is extremely diaphanous. We are more apt to hear and receive inner wisdom in the form of our night dreams, daydreams, emotions, and the "felt sense" of life around us.

When we are too busy, stressed, or preoccupied to receive the inner wisdom that is coming to us at this time, we can easily become miserable and cranky instead. Paying careful attention to oneself at this time of the month is important. Taking quiet time to walk, rest, meditate, watch one's dreams, and express oneself in writing or other creative forms will put a woman in touch with the depths of her feminine wisdom. And, although our society is not set up to allow for women's monthly retreats together, it is important to remember that our women friends can provide us with a kind of sisterhood and wise counsel that, when tapped regularly, can deeply enrich our lives.[10] There are many other ways of nourishing the *nephesh* soul throughout the month: sunshine, digging in the garden, cooking, nondepleting aerobic sports, massage, and working with clay, wood, or stone. Many women find that physical rituals such as these serve as a spiritual practice. This is because the soul level of *nephesh* serves as an entryway into other, so-called higher, realms of soul.

The physical vitality of *nephesh* is, indeed, the necessary underpinning for the next layers of the soul. All of the other sheaths of our soul-dress rest upon it. If we are healthy at the *nephesh* level, the dress will fit us beautifully; if we are not comfortable at this level, our dress will be limp, lifeless, and borrowed looking. A weak *nephesh* makes us wan, restless, and decidedly unsexy.

But it is also possible to go overboard at the level of *nephesh*, as in any aspect of soul. This occurs when we become too rigidly attached to our physical cravings and their gratification—whether they are for drugs, sex, or chocolate. When this level of our soul is overfed, we are at the mercy of our senses, we cannot think or feel or intuit clearly, and we will lack the flexibility that life demands of us. *Nephesh* is the level of our being in which physical addictions take hold.

Having to have a physical outlet, substance, or fix means that our *nephesh* sheath has become inflexible and dominates us, often pulling us down in other areas of our lives. Having a *nephesh* imbalance, however, does *not* mean that we are not spiritually advanced people. It does mean that we need to focus on balancing this one area, lest our entire lives are pulled down with it.

Our *nephesh* attachments are often the most difficult ones to break. In freeing ourselves at this level we must often do as well as our parents' and even grandparents' our own work in confronting unhealthy family patterns. And physical addictions can be deceptive, at times disguising themselves as very real physiological needs. Most often, addictive physical behaviors are connected to deep emotional needs that are only temporarily assuaged by means of physical gratification.

How can women gauge the health of their *nephesh* soul? When we reflect on our own vitality, we can each ask ourselves, How vital is my appetite for life? Is my *nephesh* soul in need of strengthening or tempering? What are my needs in the areas of food, sex, sleep, and exercise to keep myself vital? Are there substances, foods, or activities that I enjoy so much that I cannot do without them?

One of the major themes in Kabbalah is the teaching that every aspect of life is to be enjoyed in its correct balance. The sensual pleasures of *nephesh* are here for our taking, but we must not indulge to the point of getting stuck.

Ruach: *The Emotional Soul*

The next tier of the soul-dress we wear is called *ruach*. This is our emotional nature. Just as the vital soul has an appetite for the physical side of life, *ruach* yearns for emotional connection, to be loved by and joined to others. *Ruach* is associated with the sphere of Yesod/Creativity, for it is the locus of our most personal feelings, creativity, and will.

Our emotional soul is nourished through our relationships; its food is love and belonging. Sitting around a harmonious Thanksgiving or Passover seder table with friends and family, the *nephesh* soul may be delighting in the food and wine, but it is our *ruach* nature that is filled by the connection to family, tribe, and world.

For many women, it is through the emotional soul that life has deep meaning, for here our deepest experiences of love and connection are felt, as well as our lofty yearnings for peace, self-dedication, and union with God. Indeed, *ruach* is the level that many women experience as their very essence. Women's spirituality, so distinctly different from the classical linear male model, is emotional, fluid, and given to devotion, nurturance, and relationship. All of these belong to the rich field of *ruach*.

Just as *nephesh* is the locus of action, *ruach* is the center of speech and self-expression. Speaking one's heart is critical for the health of this aspect of ourselves, whether we are sharing our truth in the context of friendship or expressing ourselves to the world at large. There are also numerous forms of counseling and spiritual direction that provide a safe setting in which a person can spiral down to her heart's deepest feelings.

And because the *ruach* soul is affected by beauty in all its forms, art, music, drama, and movement are also extremely healing at this level. Dance and movement therapy are known to be beneficial for emotional unevenness, helping trapped feelings to surface and express themselves. And music has been used since ancient times to harmonize internal discord found at the emotional level.

Ruach means "wind" or "spirit," a hint of our inner wind, which manifests as our breath. When we are out of balance at the *ruach* level, our breathing will give it away. It may be hot and heavy, or, more likely, we may have difficulty catching an easy breath. For this reason, activities that regulate or calm the breath, such as swimming, cross-country skiing, yoga, singing, and breath-related therapies all have a beneficial effect on the emotional soul.

When our *ruach* aspect is healthy, we are in touch with our feelings but not dominated by them; we have a feeling of being loved and connected to others without being needy or obsessed by our relationships; and we have some form of creative outlet by which to express ourselves with regularity. Other forms of nourishment for this soul level include moonlight, starlight, reading poetry, walking in gardens and woods, and swimming, especially in natural bodies of water. And, as we have said, music that uplifts and opens our hearts— whether it is Joan Baez, Brahms, or Tina Turner—feeds and heals us at this level of soul.

Ruach is the locus of our emotions and feelings, from the most lofty—empathy, spiritual longing, and rapture—to the storms of the ego's reactivity—fury, fear, and jealousy. Along with our yearnings for love, God, and the ecstasy of union, *ruach* is also the sheath of our soul in which baser feelings are harbored. These less attractive states of mind are completely normal human experiences and require regular "airings," as do our higher emotions. When not expressed freely, our emotional body can become blocked and stagnant, resulting in depression and an overall muting of our general health. It is important to note, however, that our "airings" need to be done in judicious ways, fully honest yet also responsible to those around us.

Those of us who are given to hot tempers, hypersensitivity, mood swings, and the wild rides of manic depression are suffering from an imbalance expressed in the *ruach* aspect of our soul. Depending on the severity of the imbalance, the best medicine may be at the physical level. However, treatment at the emotional, or *ruach*, level should also be considered.

And there is more to the shadow side of *ruach*. We have seen that at the *nephesh* level one can form attachments and addictions to physical substances and experiences. In much the same way, at the *ruach* level we can get hooked on relationships and ways of relating to others that keep us locked in unconscious patterns. Examples of such patterns include being dependent on others for one's meaning in life to the exclusion of our own ability to generate happiness. This is an insidious problem in the realm of the *ruach* soul that afflicts far too many women. Other familiar patterns include involving oneself in relationships that are abusive or demeaning and manipulating others with words or by means of withholding one's true feelings to the point of toxicity. We can also be out of balance at the level of *ruach* soul through excess. We have all met people who are hooked on self-expression and have no sense of appropriate boundaries for how and what they share of themselves.

It is useful to reflect on our own experience of the *ruach* dimension of our soul. We can ask ourselves, Which of my relationships nurture me and which drain me? How do I express my creative energy? Where am I on the emotional continuum between calm and upheaval? Am I presently involved in a relationship with another person that does not allow me the freedom to grow and express myself?

As we have said, the *ruach* aspect of our being is one in which women commonly find their greatest spiritual fulfillment. Our feelings of love and connection to others are often doorways to the most profound experiences of our lives. Yet these deep and rapturous feelings of *ruach* are often undervalued in a culture that elevates the rational mind above all other functions. It is important to remember that there are many ways to God, all of them good. Although it is more refined, the next level of soul, *neshama*, is but another door to apprehending the Divine, neither higher nor more direct than the others we have looked at.

Neshama: *The Mental Soul*

Every person has an eternal soul, and the next tier of our soul's garment, *neshama*, is said to be the one most similar to our eternal nature that we can directly experience. It is our ability to think, reason, imagine, and wonder. Like Tipheret, the sphere with which it is associated, *neshama* is a bridge between our personal selves and the very essence of our being, that which connects us to the Divine. It bridges well because it is made of both personal and impersonal capacities.

When it is functioning at its maximum capacity, *neshama* is the intellect engaged, stretching itself to encompass the mysteries of life, understand why we are here, and envision how creation might fulfill itself. The genius of Bach, who attuned himself to the music of the spheres and then translated it for human ears, lives at this dimension. Albert Einstein, Abraham Joshua Heschel, and the Dalai Lama are all examples of *neshama* souls who were or are able to attune themselves to universal truth and then systematize their ideas into useable principles.

In its more personal and basic nature, the *neshama* functions for all of us through our values, opinions, and attitudes. Our most deeply held beliefs on everything from child rearing to global politics to God all live at the *neshama* level. At *neshama* we have a great deal of choice: we can get stuck in tight mental boxes or open our lids to the wonders of the cosmos; we can clock in as Archie Bunker or we can spend our lives learning and stretching our minds.

A person who is alive in her *neshama* soul is a person who is curious. She questions, learns, and synthesizes ideas on any given matter.

Her natural interest draws her to new books, Web sites, and films, anything that will expand her grasp of life. Her niche might be literature, science, philosophy, or art history; all appeal to the *neshama* soul. So does a good game of chess, bridge, or a challenging crossword puzzle.

As we saw with Asnat Barzani, the feminine mind has the power to learn through enveloping a topic and becoming one with it. The thirst for knowledge as well as the intuitive and imaginative faculties all belong to *neshama*. These are necessarily cooler and less personal qualities than our *ruach* faculties, lighter and less physically attached than our *nephesh* faculties. Yet the *neshama* dimension can be just as exciting and provocative.

It is easy to sense when someone is vibrant in this realm because they are open-minded and eager to exchange news, reviews, or the latest political analysis. *Neshama* is healthiest when it is porous and flexible in regard to new ideas. But it is both easy and common to slip into the more fixed version of *neshama*, which comes in the form of our personal judgments, biases, and inability to listen.

It is no secret that many women lose confidence in the realm of *neshama*. I have known brilliant women who lost their nerve in a philosophical debate or slipped out the back when the conversation got too cosmic. This may be because the realm of the intellect is so often expressed in factual, linear, or competitive ways.

But the *neshama* of women is naturally grounded in present-tense reality and is sensitive to the emotional pulse of a given situation. Women are obviously no less quick-witted or capable than men intellectually, but they often express their *neshama* in a different way than a more linear thinking style dictates. A more natural feminine style may be to circumscribe a topic rather than to anatomize it, to include not only theoretical and factual data in one's thinking but also the "felt sense" of one's body and the relational wisdom of one's heart.

Women today are striding onto the public stage in every area from government to religion, bringing with them their *neshama*'s capacity to wed mental acuity with a feminine, grounded approach. But one need not be a professional aficionado to use one's *neshama* soul in meaningful ways. Writing a poem, organizing an event, playing an instrument, creating a blueprint for a house or a new recipe are all ways of utilizing the *neshama* faculty within us. Whether we are introverts by nature or very public people, the creativity of our *neshama* soul has myriad faces. The woman's way is to function at multiple levels. Whatever our enterprise, it is most satisfying when we utilize as many parts of our selves as possible, our physical energy and know-how, our emotional savvy, and our ability to think big.

Reflecting on the *neshama* layer of soul, we might ask ourselves, What book, idea, or teaching has inspired my thinking lately? How do I most naturally inform my opinions, with facts, feelings, or personal experiences? Where am I on the continuum of flexibly open-minded to staunchly fixed-minded? How do I nourish my *neshama* soul and make sure I am growing at this level?

In all of our questions, remember that we are constantly changing in this and all soul dimensions. Be open to the fact that we all go through periods when we have had enough (or too much) *neshama* stimulation, and we need to digest the latest feast of ideas. During these times, rather than picking up our book or newspaper, we might just sit on the couch with our cat in our lap and stare at the wall for a while.

Listening In

Remember your soul-dress. Notice that all the layers of this beautiful creation are interconnected, as if sewn together one on top of the other. This overlap between levels of soul means, for instance, that the music and art that stimulates you at *ruach* may, in turn, inspire you to think new thoughts or write a poem at the level of *neshama*. And as a lightbulb of new insight goes on at the *neshama* level, you might just feel an impulse of generosity toward that persnickety aunt of yours, or want to take some other action in the world like writing a letter or traveling to the Himalayas!

On the negative side, a soiled *ruach* slip will show through at the next layer, *neshama*. In other words, unaired and unresolved emotional issues will often find their way into one's beliefs. When they do, they rarely come across as wise and judicious. When an opinion is expressed in a caustic, hard-edged, or dogmatic way, it is often because it is tinged with unresolved *ruach* elements.

One way we can determine what level of soul is most dominant in our daily lives is to simply listen in. Most every conversation leans toward one level of soul or another. In your last conversation, if *nephesh* had its way, the topic likely concerned things and doings— what you ate, wore, bought, saw, or hung on your newly painted bedroom wall.

Ruach wants to talk about people and feelings. This conversation might take the form of sharing personal insights, feelings about world events or the challenges we experience in life. In a nastier version, the conversation might devolve into gossip, backbiting, or analyzing other people.

The *neshama* conversation is about ideas. Sharing our thinking, questions, and dreams is its highest form. Respectful listening and reflecting are its hallmarks; adding to what has been said is done in a synergistic style. At its lower end, *neshama* talk might turn into more hard-edged judgments, fixed opinions, and argumentation. Or if we surround ourselves with those who agree with us, it might sound like preaching to the choir.

The Tip of the Flame: The Imperceptible Soul

The first three levels of soul are relatively easy to identify—our physical, emotional, and mental selves. It is said that after we die, we let go of our *nephesh*, and with it all the preferences and cravings of the body. Likewise, our *ruach* soul must ultimately fall away and with it our personal emotions and ways of relating. That which is timeless remains: the love that we have shared and our capacity to love.

In the same way, Kabbalah teaches that the personal or lower side of the *neshama* falls away after death, meaning the content of our attitudes and our mental activity. The development of the higher *neshama*, however, remains our soul's indelible crown of light. It is composed of the truths that we have learned over lifetimes, born of our soul's labors, sacrifice, and good works. These travel with us across a mythological river of light into the realm of the eternal.

The Kabbalists of old used a candle flame to meditate on the soul.[11] The dark, grayish color closest to the wick is likened to the *nephesh*. Around and above it is a delicate circle of blue, the *ruach* soul. The bright yellow or gold part of the flame is the *neshama*. If one focuses on a flame with soft eyes, one may find that there is yet another layer of light, almost invisible, that surrounds the flame like a nimbus. This was likened to the next layers of the soul that are just beyond our perception, the *chaya* and *yechida*.

These last two tiers of our soul-dress might be described as the sheerest, most delicate, gossamers of light. Imperceptible to most, they envelop this beautiful gown that is us and expand out, merging with the rest of the world. It is said that these aspects of soul are our eternal dimension, unknowable to most people. What we know of ourselves is personal. The *chaya* and *yechida* are impersonal, divine, and eternal.

Chaya: *The Clear Self*

The *chaya* aspect of soul may be likened to what the Swiss psychiatrist Carl Jung called the Self. It is that paradoxical part of ourselves that is us and not yet us; it is already whole, yet we must grow into it over time.

Chaya is the part of us that said "Yes!" to coming into form. It might be called the soul's code, the essence that predates us and willed to come to earth. As Leah taught, at this etheric level the soul makes a divine contract to accomplish a specific task, develop in particular areas, or help effect changes in one's soul or in the world. The *chaya* might be likened to that part of us addressed in the Zen koan that asks "What is the look of your face before you were born?" Of course there is no firm answer to the question; it is designed to help us let go of our mental constructs.

I understood *chaya* personally after a dream I had while setting out to write this book. In the dream I had been called to heaven, and I was watching my death as if from above. I could see everything with a pristine clarity. I felt deep regret at having to leave my children behind and I supposed I would never finish my book, yet I was surprisingly calm. I knew I would continue to love and affect my children from the next dimension. As I passed from the physical world, I found myself standing before a full-length mirror one last time. I looked into the mirror but my form was no longer there. In fact, there was absolutely no image looking back at me, only emptiness. Yet I was undeniably there! And I was clearer and more present in consciousness than I had ever experienced myself to be.

This empty, formless consciousness is *chaya*. Behind the thoughts, opinions, and mental activity of *neshama;* beyond the feelings and heart connections of *ruach;* outside of the physical substance of *nephesh* is the clear and focused self who witnesses all. This is *chaya*.

Yechida: *Union*

There is yet another level of soul, known as *yechida*. *Yechida* is even more numinous and less knowable than *chaya*. It is unknowable to our finite personal minds because it is by nature infinite and impersonal. Like Keter, the limitless light at the crown of the Tree of Life, *yechida* is the One Source, beyond our consciousness and our individual program to live.

At *yechida* I am not me and you are not you. There is only one infinite Being. In this place, we are identical with the Divine. There is no other.

There are many ways to identify, understand, and strengthen the more personal aspects of our soul: *nephesh, ruach,* and *neshama*. But at the *chaya* and *yechida* levels, we are out of a job. They do not require our work or even our healing wishes, for they are already whole. If we are fortunate, we may be graced with a dream or a shiver of intuition that alludes to the silent presence and watchful wisdom of our divine selves called *chaya* and *yechida*. As we saw in the upper dimension of the Tree, with which *chaya* and *yechida* are associated, they are already balanced and complete.

Nevertheless, there is a transformative power in simply acknowledging that there is a part of us beyond our ability to grasp, a divine mystery that transcends our human minds. There is great healing potential in aligning ourselves mentally and emotionally with the Divine Source of our lives that is within and beyond us. After all, what is prayer if not placing ourselves within sight of that numinous wholeness that is both in and beyond us?

Gilgulim: *Reincarnation*

Leah taught that we continue to return to the world to work on ourselves and align all five aspects of ourselves until each one has been developed and our soul has been made whole. *Gilgulim,* or the rounds of life, is the great design that allows us many chances to develop each aspect of our soul.[12] The teachings of reincarnation in Judaism, I learned from Leah, were kept alive and in the mainstream more by the Mizrachi Jews than the Ashkenazic Jews, although many of the Hassidic masters, such as the Ba'al Shem Tov and the Alter Rebbe, who were given to the mystical view of life, were well aware of the bearing of past (and future) lives and drew upon their ability to see them when they counseled their constituents.

Individual souls, the Hassidic rabbis taught, descend to earth in groups, often for many *gilgulim*. These soul groups are sometimes called *shalshelet neshamot,* or "soul chains." Members of a soul chain may not be biologically related; they are more like a spiritual family who have come to earth together. Together, they have made a collective agreement to undertake some task or piece of work during their shared incarnations.

Incarnation is necessary, to the Jewish understanding, because it is only in the flesh that we have the power and opportunity to pull God's will all the way down the Tree of Life. Without being on earth in physical form, with full access to our emotions and intellect, we would not be able to bring to the world love, care, and intelligence in physical form.

Although Leah never used the word "wholeness," all of her teachings about the soul's journey pointed to that end. The levels of soul that require our work cannot be made whole in a single lifetime. That demands choice and the growth gleaned from our mistakes and failures. To arrive at the true wholeness of our souls, Leah would say in her matter-of-fact way, "Many lifetimes may be required, but, in the face of eternity, what's the rush?"

CHAPTER 7

RECEIVING
THE HOLY SPIRIT

*Francesca Sarah and the Female Visionaries of Safed
(Sixteenth Century)*

Nestled in the rocky hills of northern Israel lies the mystical
city of Safed (pronounced *tsfaht*), home of Francesca Sarah, the
sixteenth-century visionary who is our final teacher. We know little
about Francesca's personal life, not even the precise years of her birth
and death. However, we do know that she stood at the center of a
revolutionary group of mystics who forever changed the landscape
of Jewish spirituality. The teachings and innovations of this group,
and in particular the mystical practices of its women, are the topic of
this chapter.

Francesca and her female peers lived lives of deep mystical integration and, as such, model a quality of wholeness that helps us to
expand the scope of our own spiritual possibilities. In addition, our

own apprehension of the Divine can be enhanced by studying the mystical practices they employed: relationship to the *maggid,* dream interpretation, and truth telling.

Now that we have completed our study of the kabbalistic Tree of Life, we can use it to see how Francesca and the women of this chapter exemplify the wholeness and balance that it teaches. And we end our journey on a hopeful note, with a vision of what a balanced life might look like in our day.

Safed

Throughout the centuries, Jews had flocked to Safed, located northwest of the Sea of Galilee, from all over the diaspora. But in Francesca's day, the period just after the Spanish and Portuguese expulsions, Safed swelled to three times its normal population, becoming a cosmopolitan spiritual center.

Why did people come to this particular hill town? Word of Safed's pure air, favorable economic conditions, and otherworldly radiance had spread throughout the Jewish world. So had the folk legend that those who died here would sail more speedily to the entrance of the Garden of Eden. Scholars and mystics, *conversos* and plain pious Jews came to Safed to study and divine, to die and be buried. With intensified spiritual enthusiasm, the preeminent male scholars and mystics of the Jewish tradition congregated here,[1] as well as an enclave of lesser-known women visionaries, about whom we shall learn in this chapter.

Then as now, Safed had a mystical, if somewhat eerie, ambiance. Its stone houses and synagogues crowd its winding streets, and the entire town seems to slope toward the surrounding fields and hills, which are filled with the graves of Talmudic-era rabbis and mystics. These ancient burial sites radiate a timeless power, and for centuries people who were serious about their spiritual development were drawn to them to absorb their holiness and benefit their souls by planting themselves in the nearby town.[2] For those who had inner vision, the departed souls were apparent at and around their grave sites, their stories and wisdom available for the asking.[3]

To the people of sixteenth-century Safed, life and death were a continuum, and beyond the heavenly veil lay a world rich with information, power, and spiritual guidance. One can speculate that because the entire culture of Safed was so strongly inclined in this direction, the paranormal dimensions opened to them with a vigor that might never be experienced by a solitary person.

The inner vision was available to many of the denizens of Safed and served to illuminate their souls' journey. The broader panorama allowed one to see the larger meaning of life's challenges and to understand the implications that one's every action has on the development of the soul. For those who were mystically inclined, this inner vision, or clairvoyance, provided the keys necessary to see and uplift the departed souls that had fallen or become stuck along the way.

Francesca Sarah

Francesca Sarah had such inner vision. Not only was she a scholar who frequented the House of Study to learn with the men,[4] she also was a master in her own right, able to access her own internal authority. Francesca was a visionary, and the entire town of Safed knew about her gift. This was because Francesca's *maggid*, "angelic guide," requested that she publicly proclaim her visions.

Francesca's revelatory experiences were documented side by side with stories of the great Rabbi Isaac Luria, master of Kabbalah, whose work we shall discuss later in this chapter, as well as other mystical luminaries of Safed. She is described in the following manner:

> In those days there was a woman, wise and great in her deeds in the Upper Galilee, Safed.... Her name was Francesca. She had a *maggid* to speak to her and inform her of what was to be in the world. The sages of Safed tested her several times to discern if

there was substance to her words, and everything she said came to pass.[5]

The few stories about Francesca that have survived into modern times have much to teach us. In the first, having been informed from "behind the heavenly curtain" that a plague was decreed on the people of Safed, Francesca summoned the sages of the city and ordered them to decree a holy fast. The Jews of Safed, Francesca explained, needed to fight for their lives and repent for their wrongdoings. We are not told in what manner they had erred, but we surmise that the moral standards of the people had flagged seriously.

The rabbis, who were already familiar with Francesca's prophetic abilities, took her words seriously and immediately decreed a public fast for the entire population. Young and old, women and men alike, took the penitential practice to heart. During the community's prayer service on that day, Francesca sorrowfully foretold that the preacher, Rabbi Moses de Curiel, would die eight days later. By means of their earnest atonement, the people of Safed were saved from the heavenly decree. But exactly eight days after the fast, Rabbi Moses de Curiel died, just as Francesca has predicted. It was understood that de Curiel bore the sins of his community and that through his death, the people of Safed were absolved.

This remarkable story tells us about the extent of Francesca's spiritual prowess. Her abilities to attune herself to the Divine Wisdom and, more, to act effectively on her vision are exceptional. The story also demonstrates the degree of allegiance and respect that the male leaders accorded her.

One might remember Beruriah, who lived thirteen hundred years earlier, as another woman who frequented the House of Study. Yet we saw in Chapter 2 how deep the men's ambivalence toward Beruriah was, despite, or perhaps because of, the fact that she was a scholar of the highest rank. Beruriah's self-assured style simply flew in the face of the men's fixed notions of a woman's nature and place.

But something quite extraordinary was occurring in sixteenth-century Safed. The people responded in a completely different way to Francesca, who was both scholar and visionary. Francesca seemed to think nothing of summoning rabbis, decreeing fasts, and forestalling plagues. The people to whom she spoke—including the legion of rabbis—listened to her. Why? She, like Beruriah, was responding to an inner calling. But Francesca's inner voice addressed the spiritual needs of an entire community, which, unlike Beruriah's community, was open to her wisdom.

In contrast to the stories of either Beruriah or Hannah Rachel of Ludomir, in which the male dominant culture refused to find a place of honor for the feminine voice, Francesca flourished in a culture that revered feminine sensibilities such as spiritual surrender and nonrational perception. How fortunate she was to live in a society that was open to the truth of her words as well as to her method of divining.

Let's take note that in the same period (1550–1650) a very different phenomenon was occurring elsewhere. It was the "Burning Times," as they are now termed, on the European continent, during which European women who practiced country healing, herbalism, midwifery, and other "magic" arts were subjected to a grotesque inquisition directed by both church and secular courts that resulted in barbaric torture, human disgrace, and mass execution.

Lasting until the mid-eighteenth century and centered in central and western Europe, these witch-hunts were rooted in a deranged sort of misogyny. Linked to theological interpretations of Eve and Lilith, women were perceived as embodiments of inexhaustible negativity and considered "by nature instruments of the Satan...a structural defect rooted in the original creation."[6] Because 80 percent of those deemed corrupters of Christian society were female, the genocide that resulted from these beliefs has also been termed "gendercide."[7] The numbers of women who were tortured and burned to death are estimated in the millions.

Fortunately, Jewish history has no such outward misogynist violence to claim, despite the biblical injunction that states, "You shall not suffer a witch to live."[8] The only record of witch-hunting in

Judaism is found in roughly 1000 B.C.E., during the time of King Saul, who persecuted a coven of female soothsayers for political, not religious, reasons in the town of En-Dor. Ironically, at the end of his life when he was bereft of counsel, Saul actually returned to En-Dor to find the last remaining witch, whom he commanded to help him by conducting a séance![9]

To the medieval Christian clergy, any one of the women discussed in this chapter would have been considered a witch. But the rabbis of Safed did not consider divination to be witchery. They understood that consulting one's inner authority is nowhere prohibited by Jewish law. Most important, the rabbis, unlike their Christian counterparts, were not at all threatened by the women's wisdom or the means by which they accessed it. In fact, they revered it and sought it out.

Around the world, persecution of women has been men's way of denouncing women's natural attunement with the nonrational dimensions of reality. Greatly feared because such information has the potential to threaten male authority, such feminine skills were, in fact, most often used by women for the purpose of healing body and spirit. But all people have access to the timeless dimensions of their souls, in which healing and wisdom are harbored. If desired, these skills can be developed by anyone, female or male.

Francesca is an example of how far off the rabbis of the Talmud were in their stigmatization of women as light-minded and flighty. They categorized women as unable to disassociate themselves from the ordinary mundanities of life, which the rabbis believed they had to put down in order to receive the divine secrets.

But the woman's way is not to denigrate the material realm in order to receive from the higher dimensions. Women know that the physical world and all of its trappings are also manifestations of the Divine Presence. The woman's way to access divine secrets, rather, is to temporarily turn her psychic attention aside from her personal and physical realities without denouncing them. Then, freed to attune to the subtler dimensions, she is able to receive her information. Later she returns to the here and now with her full attention.

It is clear that Francesca had her own skillful means by which to clear herself of the biases and preoccupations that reside at the *nephesh, ruach,* and *neshama* soul levels. Stilling these parts of herself would have enabled Francesca to align herself with the upper dimensions of her soul, the *chaya* and *yechida,* to hear and then articulate her revelations. In this way she became a clear channel for the Divine Wisdom.

Francesca was able to see the workings of a person's soul from within as well as how to bring her insights into the world. Perhaps most inspiring, Francesca was absolutely faithful to her own revelations, even in the face of potential scorn. Many of us receive divine guidance in the form of our intuition or an inner voice, but we disregard it for fear of repercussions. How many times have we overridden our inner voice of wisdom for fear that we might upset someone or that our words might get us into trouble?

We may fear our intuition, but it is a gift that rarely deceives us. Francesca stood behind the power of her gift, understanding its potential for upheaval. We have no record of Francesca's struggles to convince others that her inner voices were authentic. But we know that she was tested by the rabbis many times and found to be reliable.

Francesca also understood that each one of us has the ability to turn inward to access the truth for ourselves. There are times in life when we are tempted to seek out the wisdom of "professional mystics" in the form of astrologers, psychics, tarot-card readers, and the like. Sometimes we need this external confirmation of what we sense or know already. But a responsible medium will always give information in such a way that empowers people to access their own font of wisdom.

Another story about Francesca is drawn from the famous mystical diaries of Rabbi Hayyim Vital.[10] Lead disciple and scribe to Rabbi Isaac Luria, the preeminent master of Kabbalah, Vital was one of the most famous sages of Safed. It is largely by means of Vital's writings that we have our in-depth picture of this mystical culture and know so much about its women.[11] Vital describes a meeting, of sorts, with Francesca in the year 1594. While he was in Safed to teach and preach, "a woman was there, Francesca Sarah, a pious woman who saw visions in a waking dream and heard a voice speaking to her, and most of her words were true."[12]

Other women seem to have been present at the House of Study as well. Vital describes a scene in which the (unnamed) daughter of Rabbi Solomon Alkabez turns to Francesca, most likely after hearing Vital's teaching, and asks, "Is it possible that such a holy mouth, someone so eloquent, should die?" Her question presumes the fact that the women have foreseen an untimely death for Vital. According to Vital, Francesca assured her friend not to worry, for great things would still happen in his lifetime.

Several years later, in 1604, Vital was indeed struck by a life-threatening illness and fell into a coma for twenty-one days, during which he saw numinous visions. He then awoke and lived for another sixteen years. Francesca and her friend had foreseen Vital's near-death experience years in advance, and Francesca had prophesied that he would live through it.

This story brings to light several significant points about Francesca and the women of this amazing era of Jewish history. First, women participated at the seminars and lectures in the House of Study, possibly in groups together.[13] Second, we learn that Francesca had other women friends who shared her proficiency at inner seeing. Finally, Francesca's remarkable ability to tap a source of inner wisdom seems to have been with her whether or not it was solicited by others, pointing to an ongoing relationship to that source of wisdom, possibly her inner angelic adviser, or *maggid*.

The Maggid

One little-known yet powerful mystical practice performed by rabbis and mystics throughout the ages is the accessing of the *maggid*. Because this practice of tapping the angelic realm for instruction and guidance is such a profound form of receiving, it is important to examine the *maggid* practice in the context of women's mystical wisdom, which is naturally receptive. The ability to bridge one's conscious mind to other dimensions of reality is also one more form of *yichud*, unifying one's personal mind, *mochin de katnut*, with a much vaster scope of consciousness, *mochin de gadlut*.

What is a *maggid*? From the Hebrew word meaning "to tell," the term *maggid* was traditionally understood to refer to a teller of the truth, that is, a heavenly or angelic being who comes to guide and teach us. The question arises whether this wise voice truly comes from *beyond* (heaven) or from *within* us, as a sort of verbal embodiment of our highest dimensions.

Although there may not be a definitive answer to this question, it may help to recall that each of us has a *yechida* soul, that which is eternal and connects us to the unlimited totality of consciousness. Because a part of each of us belongs to this Divine Oneness, we are able to attune ourselves to this infinite field to tap its wisdom. Of course, this attunement requires discipline, focus, and practice. But at the level of *yechida*, which is beyond individual consciousness, it no longer matters "who" the wisdom is coming through, whether it is "you" or another wise being.

Although the technique of accessing heavenly wisdom through a *maggid* is not well publicized within Judaism, Francesca was hardly alone among spiritual adepts in having an angelic companion. The *maggid* came to many serious Jewish practitioners throughout the ages who were desirous of a closer connection to the Divine.[14] It is not surprising to find that, according to most historical accounts, only very learned and devout rabbis (that is, men) had relationships with a *maggid*. Here is one more sad deletion from Jewish tradition, due to the absence of women's voices from historical records and ignorance on the part of male historians regarding women's spiritual lives. Francesca's story comes to correct this error.

Among published records of a *maggid* relationship, the first and most famous is that of Rabbi Joseph Karo, who lived in Safed at roughly the same time as Francesca (1488–1575).[15] Karo is most famous for his *Shulkhan Arukh*, "Code of Jewish Law," the four-volume sine qua non encyclopedia of Jewish law. Far less public is the fact that Karo communicated with a *maggid* later in life. His heavenly mentor called itself by the name Shechinah.

Karo's angelic companion came to him when Karo engaged in special meditative techniques, physical austerities, and intense study and recitation of the Mishnah. Karo received not only intellectual and spiritual instruction from his *maggid*, but personal guidance too. It was on the advice of his *maggid*, for instance, that Karo immigrated to Israel in 1537, where he established himself as a leading figure in Kabbalist circles.[16]

The origin of the *maggid* practice is understood to stem from the Talmud and its declaration that each time a person performs a *mitzvah*, an advocating angel is invoked.[17] The Talmud teaches that the angels called into being through our acts of goodness endure for a person's lifetime and accompany us after death, serving as our protectors and advocates in the next dimension.

Rabbi Isaac Luria, the Holy Ari, expounded upon this teaching at length. There are angels and holy spirits everywhere, he said, brought about by our actions. When we do a *mitzvah* with great intention and pure-heartedness, an angel of an equally true nature is elicited. That angel may choose to reveal itself to us, and its words are reliable. However, when our actions are half-hearted or we have ulterior motives, the angel created thereby consists of both goodness and falseness and its words cannot be completely relied upon.[18]

How does one know if the voice we assume is that of a *maggid* speaks the truth? Luria teaches that we can recognize the degree of truthfulness from its words. If it is a reliable voice, "it must continuously speak the truth, motivate one to do good deeds, and not err in a single prediction."[19] It was understood that there are many voices that speak to us from within and that the truly divine voice is sometimes difficult to distinguish.

When I lecture about Jewish mystical practices such as the *maggid*, I am often asked the same recurring questions: Are there really angelic presences around us? If so, how can we come in contact with them? Is it possible to elicit the voice of Divine Wisdom from within? How can we tell if it is a true and reliable voice?

These are the same concerns that the Holy Ari addressed almost five hundred years ago in his teachings on accessing *Ruach haKodesh,* the Holy Spirit. To understand the answers to these questions, it is important to know that Jewish tradition describes an invisible order in which every part of creation grows and evolves with the help of the angelic realm. Every blade of grass, the Talmud teaches, is assigned an angel to stand over it, encouraging it to keep growing. And if every blade of grass has that much love invested in it, how much more do human beings have?

The practice of invoking and communicating with an angelic adviser, or *maggid,* taps the belief that the world and all of its creatures are designed to be attuned to a harmonious divine order. In this design, all things grow and achieve wholeness, and angels are part of the plan, the heavenly assistance that helps us attune to this divine order and grow to our fullest extent.

Despite the fact that the *maggid* practice was originally an esoteric Jewish tradition associated with the devout Torah study and strict ritual practices of men, it is certainly not exclusive to men or orthodox observers, nor is calling upon Divine Wisdom a solely Jewish practice. Anyone who is pure-hearted and sincerely focused on receiving Divine Wisdom can access assistance from the invisible dimension.

Nevertheless, Luria's admonishment to be mindful of our intentions is psychologically sound and bears listening to. The purer we are in our intentions and behaviors, the purer the fruit of our intentions and behaviors. A person who is unclear about her spiritual purpose or one who has a mixed agenda (that is, sincerely wants to receive information or effect change in herself but does so for reasons that are selfish or ego-driven) will probably receive assistance that is likewise mixed in nature. A person who adheres to religious practices, is devoted to her spiritual calling, and fervently asks for help to prepare her life so that she can fulfill that calling will receive a more exacting response.

Once we know how to quiet our minds and focus ourselves on our soul's question, the *maggid* is not difficult to access. The tradition teaches that all of us have angelic guidance around us. In other words, we each have the capacity to tap the universal source of wisdom. Specific techniques and prayers can help focus our minds and hearts to allow us to hear the voice that speaks the truth directly to us.[20] Difficulty arises from the fact that we have so many other voices within, often discounting or contradicting that of the *maggid*. To discern the voice of divinity, as Francesca did, we must be exquisitely clear in our purpose. It also helps greatly when we know our inner voices well enough to be able to distinguish which ones are not reliable.

The *maggid* has many ways of making itself known. Sometimes the *maggid* first appears in a dream. But one can also invoke divine guidance and wait for it to come. Sometimes the *maggid* appears in the form of the soul of a wise and loving person who has departed, a sage, teacher, or beloved friend on the other side.

Jaimie was a young woman writer whose older sister, Megan, had died in a car accident when Jaimie was seven years old. Because she was so young when Megan died, Jaimie knew Megan more through stories than from her own experience. Nevertheless, Jaimie always honored her sister's memory. At her bat mitzvah she said a special prayer in her honor, and when she published her first collection of poems at sixteen, she dedicated it to the sister she barely knew.

The summer before Jaimie went away to college, she began dreaming about Megan. The dreams, Jaimie told me, were "realer than life," and Megan seemed fully alive. Yet these dreams disconcerted Jaimie. She felt as if something was being asked of her, but she did not know what. After the third dream of Megan in a month, Jaimie asked me for help.

Because Jaimie was a writer, I suggested that when her house was quiet that evening she sit down and begin a letter to Megan. I asked her to write from her heart whatever occurred to her to tell her sister, but to stop halfway and close her eyes. She was then to listen for

Megan's answer. If she felt like it, Jaimie should write down any words or message she received.

Jaimie did as I suggested. She called me the next day to tell me that although she hadn't slept much the night before, she felt so much better because she had finally heard from Megan after all these years. Their loving exchange had gone on for fourteen pages!

The sisters "corresponded" in the form of written dialogue throughout Jaimie's college years. Whenever she felt sad or troubled, Jaimie took out her journal and begin to write to Megan. She learned to rely on the voice of her sisterly ally to help her clarify all kinds of problems.

Had Megan truly reappeared to become a *maggid* for her sister? Or had Jaimie simply discovered a technique to access a wise and loving voice within herself? For years I was certain it was the latter, and I rejoiced that this lovely young woman, a child without any living siblings, had found solace in her imaginary pen pal.

Then, years later, when Jaimie was well into her twenties and newly married, she called me out of the blue. She was home visiting her mother, who had recently been diagnosed with breast cancer. We met at a café to talk.

"You know, I owe my mom's life to you," she said.

"What on earth are you talking about?" I asked, somewhat flabbergasted.

"I mean, you *and* Megan. If it hadn't been for you, I never would have started listening to Megan. I thought she was dead."

"Jaimie, she *is* dead,"

"Oh, yeah, I know that," she laughed. "But she's *anything* but dead in spirit. She's the one who told me Mom was in trouble and to get her to go right away to have a mammogram."

I was astounded to hear this. Jaimie's mother, who was in her late fifties, lived alone. Her breast cancer had been caught in its early stages, thanks to Jaimie's out-of-the-blue phone call in which she had not asked, but ordered, her mother to make an appointment with her doctor. It was her mother's first mammogram.

When I teach the practice of *maggid*, I often remind students to maintain a dynamic relationship with their inner figure. This means being their honest selves and never taking at face value any wisdom that doesn't sit right. It is fine to be direct and straightforward, to question or challenge the *maggid* as one would a friend or teacher, in one's own authentic way. For example, you might respond to a *maggid* by saying, "I don't understand what you mean. Could you please speak more plainly?" or "I'm not sure I can believe you. How do I know you are telling me the truth?" Then listen for the answer. If the *maggid*'s words, held to your heart, inspire you toward a more compassionate approach, then continue.

The truth of the *maggid*, Francesca and Rabbi Luria would likely tell us, lies in the outcome. We can ask ourselves, Does my *maggid* teach me a deeper level of wisdom, one that inspires me to be more whole? Does my contact with my *maggid* encourage me to be a better person? Am I being guided to discover a bigger view of myself and the world around me?

Rachel Aberlin

Rachel was another of Safed's female luminaries. She and her husband immigrated to northern Israel from Salonika in 1564. Rachel was a spiritual adept who "was used to seeing visions, demons, spirits, and angels…from the time of her youth through adulthood."[21] She shared her mystical pursuits with her brother, Rabbi Judah Mishan, one of Rabbi Isaac Luria's most devoted disciples. As we have seen, Luria had brought forth a mystical cosmology that revolutionized Jewish mystical thought. When he died in 1572, both Rachel and her brother Judah pledged fealty to Hayyim Vital, his top student and documenter.

Vital first met Rachel Aberlin in 1578 when he was preaching in Jerusalem. After Rachel's husband died around 1582, she became Vital's patroness, establishing a *hatzer,* a court, where Vital and his family could live and work. Rachel and Vital were close, but not romantically involved. They traveled together from Safed to Damascus and Jerusalem, and their shared wanderings demonstrate a deep mutual devotion. It has been speculated that Vital and Rachel may have been the great male and female mystic pair of their age.[22] Each one recognized the greatness of the other and each was nourished in this recognition.

But the two mystics had very different styles, and each is characteristic of a variance in spirituality often found between men and women. Because of the cultural focus on the sacred word, Jewish men typically excelled in and emphasized the importance of the text itself. Women, alternatively, who did not focalize their spirituality in the House of Study, could see the Divine Presence more readily around them without needing to refer to a textual source. The following story of Rachel's dream and its interpretation illustrates this difference.

In the dream Rachel enters a room and finds her friend Vital studying at a table piled high with books. As he studies, Vital eats a salad composed of radishes and lettuce.[23] Rachel asks Vital why he is eating these vegetables. He responds by saying, "Radishes and lettuce are never absent from my table. I always eat vegetables."

Then Rachel sees that behind him are piles of hay and straw on fire. The piles, however, are not being consumed. The blaze illuminates the house with a supernatural glow. Rachel is utterly astonished at the sight of such light.

Later, when Rachel asked her companion what he thought the dream meant, Vital quickly responded with a verse from the prophet Obadiah that says, "And the house of Jacob shall be fire and the house of Joseph a flame...."[24]

But Rachel was not content to dismiss the numinous blaze with a line from scripture. She had seen the very light to which the scriptures refer! To his interpretation, Rachel responded, "You quote me the words of the verse as they are written, but I *see* that it [the fire] is a literal reality."[25] Vital may have been the master of the mystical word, but Rachel was the mistress of the mystical experience. Like many women, Rachel knew that all the holy books in the world could not equal the true and manifest experience of the Divine Light itself. Sacred texts were guides and pointers to the light of spirit, not the light itself.

Unfortunately, what was true for Rabbi Vital is still true for many Jewish scholars: the words that were meant to point the way to a revelatory experience have become the way itself. The predominance of textual learning to the exclusion of other forms of religious discovery has affected all of us, narrowly restricting our experience of God to the definitions and stories that can be fit into words. This loss can be repaired by expanding our modes of religious learning to include less linear approaches, such as observing nature, artistic expression, and information from the unconscious mind such as dream imagery, intuition, and imagination. If wholeness is truly what we are after, we need to complement the dominant masculine approach that has emphasized text study and the power of the word with a more feminine approach as just described.

Rachel Aberlin, the mystical grande dame of Safed, was singularly unabashed about her feminine approach to wisdom. A wise woman who was consulted by both men and women, she divined through her dreams and waking visions, using them as faithful tools of spiritual revelation.

Listening to Our Dreams

Long before Freud and Jung revealed to the West the nature of the unconscious mind, Judaism taught that dreams come to us from dimensions beyond our conscious minds and that their interpretation is critical to the unfolding of one's life. Rabbi Hisda illustrated this understanding in the Talmud with the analogy "A dream that is not interpreted is like a letter that is not read."[26]

Mystical Judaism teaches that nothing is wasted. We spend our conscious time learning, growing, and testing our newfound knowledge. But while our physical bodies lie asleep in bed—roughly one-third of our lives—our soul's work continues. Every night, the *Zohar* explains, "the soul leaves its dwelling place and ascends on high, and only a tiny fraction of vitality remains in the body."[27] Connected by an etheric kite string to our slumbering bodies below, our souls fly freely in the upper dimensions. There, free of the ego's control, they are guided and taught at levels beyond our awareness.

The process of communication is twofold: a point of wisdom is first conveyed from the subtle dimensions to our souls and then translated into the symbolic language of dreams that our conscious minds might understand. "For no revelation comes to a human when his body is in full vigor, but an angel communicates things to the soul, and the soul transmits them to the person."[28]

Yet not all of us can remember our dreams, and when we do, they often remain like "unopened mail," messages from our soul that we cannot fully comprehend. The important thing to remember is that dreams are stimulated by our urge for wholeness. Even the most mundane dreams, the rabbis taught, have a revelatory power and provide us with a taste of true prophecy.[29] Every dream is sent to open one more door of understanding, illuminate one more corner of perception, so that over the course of a lifetime we will grow whole with awareness.

Kabbalists throughout the ages tried to accelerate the process, employing techniques by which to "compel" or gestate dreams. Summoning what was sometimes called the "Answering Angel" to resolve the dreamer's query, the dreamer would pose a question or problem for celestial guidance, using one of many available formulas. With a particular Divine Name written on a piece of parchment and slipped under one's pillow, the Angel of Dreams might be thus addressed: "I adjure you with the great, mighty, and awesome Name [of God] that you visit me this night and answer my question and request, whether by dream, by vision, by [indicating] verse from scripture, by speech...in a manner that I should not forget but remember [on waking up], my question and request [together with the answer]. Amen Selah."[30]

But divine grace cannot always be cajoled. Most dreams arrive when we least expect them, and with them come information, insight, and sometimes more questions! We would do well to find our own version of Rachel Aberlin, a friend or therapist skilled in the art of dream interpretation, to help us decipher our nocturnal messages. Even those of us who are adept with others' dreams may need a Rachel figure; our own dreams are often opaque to us.

We can learn to distinguish the meaning of a dream by first sensing its quality or feeling tone, asking ourselves when we awaken, what did this dream *feel* like? For example, experiencing great anxiety in a dream, say, at missing a plane or taking a test, might awaken us with an early morning shudder. Likewise, when we meet a spirit animal or speak to a numinous figure in a dream, we may also shudder upon awakening. But these are two distinctly different shudders! It is important to be able to discern the different feeling qualities in every dream. This will help us understand how to work with them.

From a Jewish mystical approach, dreams may be understood to be the symbolic language of the five levels of our soul. Dreams arising from the *nephesh* soul might be about our physical health and well-being or about our vital functions. In these dreams we might be sexually active, running a race, or getting advice from a doctor about a real physical problem. The dream may hold up a mirror for us, so we can recalibrate ourselves. When we see ourselves rushing about, showing up to dream events unprepared, not being fed properly, or not being able to find our shoes,[31] we know it is time for self-nourishment and care.

At the *ruach* level, our dreams can give us much information about where we are stuck in relationship to our feelings and to others. Without the self-conscious ego to censor it, the *ruach* dream can demonstrate our true feelings. In such dreams, we may find ourselves weeping deeply, yelling into someone's face, making heartfelt love, or telling off someone whom we fear to confront in waking life.

Ruach dreams can also give us information about parts of ourselves that reside beneath our surface, our shadow side. A glamorous realtor was horrified to find herself in one dream as an unkempt woman living in a trailer park. The dream had collided with her self-image as a well-groomed and resourceful individual. She admitted, however, that "even though she was overweight and poorly dressed," her dream self was remarkably happy. Like all shadow dreams, this dream had come as a message from her unconscious to help her become more aware of other, hidden, parts of herself, in this case, her more carefree, less self-conscious self.

At the *neshama* level, our dreams guide us and help us grow by making adjustments in our attitudes and beliefs about life. Here we may encounter figures that teach us, love us, or model for us new, more elevated approaches to life. One way to understand these figures is as higher dimensions of our selves. Another way is to see them as teachers and messengers who actually exist at other dimensions. Either way, we would not be able to experience these figures if we did not already have some aspect of their wise qualities within us.

Nevertheless, these dreams can sometimes be quite alarming because they come to rearrange our thinking. One striking example of this kind of attitude adjustment was the case of Sarah, a young rabbinic student who contacted me with an upsetting dream. I could tell that it was an important dream by how deeply it had disturbed Sarah. After a great deal of encouragement, she finally told me that she had dreamed about Jesus. She could not say how she knew, but she was sure it was Jesus. Why, she asked, did she have to dream about a Christian figure? Wouldn't Moses or Rachel have done the job?

In the dream, she and her husband were helping Jesus, who had just been removed from the cross, into their Honda Civic, trying to get him to the local hospital before he expired. Barely alive and bleeding profusely, he had looked at her with eyes that radiated compassion. "Even while he was dying, he had so much love. He was more concerned about us than about his own pain."

As Sarah told her dream, in which she and her husband failed to help this dying man, she began to weep. Despite the fact that her dream seemed to fly in the face of a lifetime of Jewish training and her forthcoming identity as a Jewish leader, Sarah had been genuinely moved by the loving figure she knew to be Jesus.

This dream required a great deal of work. It was important to remind Sarah to approach her dream as symbolic, not literal, guidance. It would have been a mistake, for instance, to interpret this dream as a message that Sarah was on the wrong religious path. It seemed clear, however, that Sarah's formerly strong beliefs and assertions as to the bogus nature of other religions now had to change, and what she began to understand as her "Jewish chauvinism" had to be abandoned. In time, Sarah was able to see that the suffering dream figure had come to teach her *neshama* a lesson that transcended even her most cherished religious beliefs. She finally concluded that Jesus was not a Christian symbol at all, but a universal symbol of unconditional love. His compassion went beyond religious labels or the politics of faith.

The deepest lessons that this dream brought Sarah remained wordless. Like many *neshama*-level dreams that have a radiant super-real quality, the learning is not conceptual. These are dreams that evoke the deepest level of understanding and feelings within us and, often, their impact is not translatable into words. Like many *neshama* dreams, this dream, which came at a crucial point in a young woman's training, was a dream of a lifetime. Sarah's entire spiritual journey was altered by it.

The rarest of all dreams are those that arise from the *chaya* and *yechida* levels of our soul. These have a unique and unmistakable quality to them. Like Rachel Aberlin's dream of the blazing fire, such dreams are often light-filled and numinous, awakening our minds to God's radical presence. When we awaken from such dreams, we may feel completely refreshed, our physical existence understood from a different, more forgiving, perspective. *Chaya* and *yechida* dreams may be in the form of a visitation with other souls or *aliyot neshama,* "soul ascents," in which we are shown the subtler dimensions and taught lessons that can potentially change our understanding of the meaning of life.

One final dream illustrates this kind of luminous nocturnal teaching. In it, the dreamer was shown a huge wheel in which all living things are included and have their rightful place. But the scene was extremely chaotic. Everything was out of its proper place and there was a terrible force at large that sparked like lethal lightning. The dreamer was frightened and rushed to find his own seat on the wheel. As soon as he slid into it, others all around the wheel magically settled into theirs. Just then, the sparking stopped and a numinous blue light shone over everything.

The dreamer was deeply affected by this dream. He learned that the most important thing each of us can do is to take our rightful seat in life. When we do, everything else is helped into its rightful place too. By knowing who we are and genuinely *being* ourselves, we have the power to affect the whole world and help to bring it back into its natural order.

Every dream tries in its own way to bring us back to "our rightful seat in life." And because the work of becoming whole requires actual, not only ideological, changes, each dream hints at some "homework" that we can undertake in the physical world to signify a further turn toward our wholeness. Dreams might signal us to make contact with a particular person, take our creativity more seriously, write a certain letter, or spend more loving time with our children. Whatever the message, it is important to do *something* that enacts the wisdom we have received from our dreams.

From whatever soul level they come, our dreams are a constant river of information that connects us to the wisdom of our souls, which are endlessly striving for growth and wholeness. All of us on the path of wholeness would do well to pay attention to the images and insights that arise from our nighttime journeys, bringing the revelations from our higher dimensions down the Tree, so to speak, into our everyday lives.

The Daughter of Raphael Anav

Among the accounts of women who sought out Rachel Aberlin for
help in interpreting their dreams and visions was one of the most
famous female visionaries of the day. This young girl, committed to
speaking the truth at all costs, met with Rachel upon discovering her
own unexpected talents as a medium. The daughter of a prominent
Damascus rabbi, she became a sensation among the rabbis of Safed
because she publicly accused the rabbinic leadership of corruption.[32]
Sadly, the talented young woman of whom we speak is nowhere
named by her male redactors, but simply called the daughter of
Raphael Anav.

The young Anav first came to renown when she became possessed
by the spirit of a wise elder named Hakham Piso. Although spirit
possession in Jewish tradition usually involves a *dybbuk*,[33] usually negative in nature, the daughter of Raphael Anav was the subject of *ibbur*,
a spirit pregnancy.[34] *Ibbur* is a phenomenon in which the spirit of a
saint or sage binds himself to a righteous individual in order to reveal
the mysteries of Torah from the other side. Although *ibbur* is a well-
known occurrence in Jewish mystical tradition, never had a woman
been known (or recorded) to host such a soul until the daughter of
Raphael Anav.

The Kabbalists of Damascus were shocked one Friday evening
when young Anav took ill and began to speak with the words of the
wise Piso. She summoned the rabbis to hear her proclamations to
repent their ways. To their credit, the rabbis immediately recognized
Piso's words to be words of divine truth. The spirit of Piso not only
spoke through the girl but took liberties to enact rituals traditionally reserved only for males (such as reciting the blessing over the
Sabbath wine), calling in other great departed souls such as Elijah the
Prophet, and chastising the rabbinic establishment for their secret
sinning. This episode lasted for one entire Sabbath.

But unlike most spirit possessions, which leave the "host" drained and debilitated, after Piso's spirit left the young woman she was spiritually transformed. No longer involuntarily possessed, Anav continued to speak her words of truth, becoming a powerful prophetess in her own right who traveled with ease in the heavenly realms, able to commune with the divine spirits and convey their messages to the community.[35] Ultimately, Anav was consulted for guidance by the rabbis of her day, as were Francesca and Rachel.

Perhaps most shocking was Anav's critique of the rabbinate. Although she never criticized the overall authority of the rabbinic establishment, she successfully exposed the ugly secrets of leading personalities in the Jewish community of her day, especially denouncing the hypocrisy and corruption among its rabbinic leaders.

Among the many she named, one particular scholar and rabbi stands out for his spiritual hypocrisy. Although this man was the greatest liturgical poet of the day, Anav could see that he was privately a foul-mouthed drunk who secretly engaged in hetero- and homosexual infidelities while being married. While publicly preaching piety and enjoying the reputation of a religious leader, this rabbi, claimed Anav, was a sodomist and a wife abuser, among other transgressions.

"Therefore," Anav proclaimed to the rabbis, "it is forbidden to act in any way that benefits him, and it is forbidden to give him marriage or divorce contracts to write; it is almost appropriate to invalidate those written [previously] by him."[36]

The community was shocked. The man whom Anav had accused was a prestigious rabbi, scribe, and preacher. But Anav was unimpressed by his worldly reputation. Rather, she saw his shadow side, that of a corrupt and hypocritical leader. The accused, who was not present during Anav's jeremiad, soon afterward confessed his sins when confronted by Rabbi Vital. Anav's words were true.

More vituperative in style than Francesca, Anav was similarly intent on raising the moral standards of the community. Anav was understandably revered (and feared) by her community. Her words were ultimately effective, and her impact was a positive one.

Telling the Truth

The daughter of Raphael Anav personifies the consummate truth teller. Because she was an unmarried young woman with no particular reputation to preserve (her father is said to have been one of her greatest supporters), she held back nothing.

Everything an individual does counts, Anav taught. Our every action sets in motion a set of repercussions, for positive and negative. Nothing in the world is hidden from God's eyes, so why would one bother to try? The first and last of all spiritual lessons is truth.

Truth is the only way to wholeness. And it is contagious. I will never forget a girl named Sophia in a class of sixth graders. She and her Hebrew-school buddies had run wild one day, doing some serious damage to a beautiful autumn garden, picking every rose they could find, littering, and climbing on a handmade trellis until it broke.

When I assembled the children and asked for the truth, no one budged; not a glimmer of confession was forthcoming. The children had resolved to keep the secret among themselves, and no one wanted to betray the group. As I looked from child to child, my glance fell on Sophia. Her eyes were riveted to mine and slowly they began to well up with tears. Still she maintained absolute silence. But even with tears streaming down her cheeks, she never turned away from me.

After a full minute of this, Sophia squeaked, "I did it." The children froze. They could sense how difficult this was for her and that she had no choice but to tell the truth. In that moment, their own sense of conscience was awakened. One by one, four other children stepped forward and confessed their part in the garden crime.

Sophia's moral compass was so strong that she was able to stir her entire class to truth. Rather than condemning her for her inability to hold the lie, she actually became a class hero after this incident, a spokesperson of sorts upon whom the other children relied to speak the truth and bring it forth from the group.

Not only children know the impact that one truth teller can have on a group. Ask anyone who has taken part in a women's support group, a Twelve-Step program, a Native American sweat lodge, a sacred council, a Quaker meeting, or any group designed to dive beneath the surface to the truth below. Once a single individual speaks the truth from her heart, the entire group is transformed. This is because truth has such a powerful resonance and naturally calls others to align with it.

Like all prophets, visionaries, and speakers of the truth, the daughter of Raphael Anav counted on the infectious power of the human conscience. She knew that her words were true and that they would ultimately call forth the integrity of her community. Anav's approach worked, and even those who seemed to have a great deal to lose were inspired to step forth and acknowledge their falseness, thereby inspiring others.

There can be no wholeness when we are double dealing. As women, our wisdom depends upon living in integrity with ourselves, and that means telling the truth. As many of us know, when we withhold the truth in one area of life, other parts of our lives begin to suffer.

Over the years I have known and counseled numerous women and men who were taking part in a marital infidelity, either cheating on their spouse by having an affair or having an affair with a married partner. Even though our society makes room for all manner of marital untruths, falling on the strength of numbers as a justification, I have never met a woman who did not suffer internally for engaging in this kind of lie.

Maggie, who was a sales rep and traveled nationally, had been sexually involved with Jim for three years before her life began to fly apart. While her husband, Mark, took care of the household and their young son, Maggie justified her romance by telling herself that she was the breadwinner and needed an outlet on her business trips.

But on a deeper level, Maggie was agonized. Try as she might to keep her love affair out of town, her life began to leak her untruth. First her husband reported that their four-year-old began waking up in the middle of the night while she was away, shrieking with bad dreams and calling for his mommy. Then Maggie came down with a strange digestive disorder that required special food and made eating on the road difficult. Then her wise unconscious, bent on getting beyond her lies, committed the final coup de grâce.

Rushing out of the house one morning to catch an early plane, Maggie left her journal on the floor near the bed. It lay open to her last entry, which alluded to an intimacy far greater than a business relationship with Jim. Cleaning up the bedroom that day, the open journal seemed to be inviting Mark toward it. In the end, he could not resist reading his wife's description of her last illicit encounter.

That night on the phone, Mark confronted Maggie. Sobbing, he asked her how long the betrayal had been going on. Maggie was mortified, but that night she confessed everything. She told me later that, although it was the "dumbest thing I have ever done," leaving her journal out for Mark to read was her conscience's way of demanding her integrity. She had been too fearful to come clean. She gave herself no choice but to tell the truth.

Whether we are truth tellers who walk with the angels like young Anav or more ordinary women on the path, all of us can benefit from the spiritual practice of telling the truth every day, at deeper and deeper levels. Beginning with ourselves, we can ask, What am I pretending not to know? What facts or feelings am I burying from my own conscious awareness? What am I trying to protect by not looking at the truth?

Because most of us are not mandated, like the visionary women of Safed, to reprove others, we may need to be especially cautious in our truth telling. Three simple questions to ask oneself in any discourse with others are, Is it true? Is it necessary? Is it kind?

Our spiritual wholeness depends on our ability to see clearly and express what we see truthfully. Given that every human being has blind spots (and an ego that is by nature self-serving), clear seeing and truthful speech are difficult tasks that require humility and the feedback of others. Women who are devoted to spiritual wholeness can serve each other by gently holding up a mirror for one another to see what they could not see on their own. This is one of the gifts that women give to one another.

A Sacred Circle of Women

There were many more women of vision during this magical period in Safed than have been enumerated,[37] and it is open to speculation how connected they were to each other. We might imagine that they indeed built on one another's strength and support, fully aware that their community was utterly unique to history. As one scholar put it, Safed in this era may be likened to an open monastery,[38] in which both men and women contributed to a tightly woven religious atmosphere. And although the male mystics and sages were prolific writers, giving us their picture of this period, there is clearly far more to be learned from the women's beliefs, practices, and spiritual support of one another.

None of the numerous accounts of Safed's dynamic women were their own firsthand reports. Although their individual stories may be sewn together to create an intriguing tapestry, much is left to our imagination. For example, given that diaries of people's mystical experiences were extremely popular during their day and that many of the women in Safed were highly educated, we wonder if women did not write their own spiritual records, which were perhaps not deemed important enough to be preserved.

Even though we have no diaries, letters, or books from the remarkable women of Safed, we nevertheless feel a distinct camaraderie with them. We can take inspiration and strength from the fact that they were so bold, expressive, and in tune with themselves. Finally, their stories tell of a society strangely lacking territoriality, built upon people helping one another and respectfully consulting one another for spiritual guidance.

Faith in Women

Many modern women know about the deep transformation that can occur in the company of women who are devoted to their wholeness. Where I live, women's groups abound, with themes ranging from poetry writing to political action, meditation to mountaineering. These are groups in which women can be fully themselves, share their inner lives, and also mirror for one another what they see to be their part of truth.

But women may also discover that they have been programmed to relate to other women by using masculine standards of our society such as competitiveness, superficial judgments, and mistrust of other women. If we can learn to put aside these adaptations of our male-dominant culture, there is a wealth of support, wisdom, and ingenuity waiting to be found among us.

Lilly was a young woman who struggled to shed her distrust of women. When she first came to see me, Lilly was twenty-five, but she spoke in a high-pitched voice that seemed remarkably girlish for her age. She described herself as a "daddy's girl," and, indeed, she was a classic "father's daughter," one who modeled herself on masculine values of action over feeling, hard work, and solitary living. She had many male friends from work but shied away from other women. When I asked her about this, Lilly told me she simply did not like many women. She was estranged from her mother, whom she felt had abandoned her early in life, and ever since middle school she had tended to associate with boys rather than girls, feeling that she could always depend on them, whereas girls and women were catty, overly dramatic, and competitive.

Lilly's suspicion of other females was fueled when Gregg, her husband of seven months, began having an affair. She told herself that he had been "seduced by a bitch" and was simply too weak to resist. She instantly filed for a divorce, but for the first time Lilly found no solace in fast action. She began to let in her feelings, and the fact that she had been betrayed by a man. Her worldview, built upon her faith in and solidarity with men, was falling apart.

Then Lilly received an odd letter in the mail. It was from the woman with whom Gregg had had the affair. The woman, named Marta, begged Lilly's forgiveness, saying that she had never suspected that Gregg was married. "As soon as I found out, I told him to leave. Please believe me, I am not that type of woman. I feel as horrible and betrayed as you must feel."

Lilly was astounded that this strange woman had reached out to her. And I too was amazed to hear that Marta had written Lilly, the second time asking her to get together to have coffee. As it turned out, neither woman returned to Gregg. But each of them found a friend in the other, in Lilly's case her first true woman friend. Over time, Marta introduced Lilly to other women with whom Lilly came to feel safe. Little by little, Lilly outgrew her distrust for women and, with the help of her new friends, softened into a wise and compassionate friend herself.

When women face each other and tell the truth, powerful things can happen. Sometimes it takes enormous courage to let go of our staunchly held beliefs about each other. But it is a deep relief to find that we can find shelter in each other's presence and freedom in each other's friendship.

Dialogue of Truths

Perhaps most important, the women of Safed teach us about wholeness. Their society was built upon the joining of opposites, seen in the mutual participation of both women and men in sacred community and in the religious practices that were both orthodox and mystical in nature. In addition, Francesca and her cohorts exemplify one more area of mastery, one that we must not overlook because it holds an important key for modern women. This is the dialogue between the inner and the outer authority.

From all that we have learned about the visionary women of Safed, it seems that they excelled at listening and receiving inwardly and were ever faithful to their inner truth, which came to them in the form of the *maggid*'s words, dreams, and revelations. With such an intense and rich inner life, it would not have been surprising if the women had felt spiritually self-sufficient and removed themselves from the more common Jewish practices led by the men. Yet it does not appear that the women of Safed cut themselves off from the outer, formal tradition or from their men. Rather, they were active participants in both the formal religious arena *and* their own private mystical domains. This is a very valuable lesson for us today.

For centuries women have been following the voices, traditions, and truths of others. Women have kept alive the laws and practices of the people, faithfully transmitting them to their children while observing them closely themselves. But in many cases, women have abdicated their own deepest wisdom to go along with the men's vision of the world. Especially in Judaism this has been the case, and historically women have not been served by this approach. Just the fact that we have barely any documentation of our feminine spiritual legacies from centuries of history is proof enough that women have lost and become disconnected from their own source of wisdom.

How we access and stay faithful to our internal sense of authority, the voice of our own spiritual wisdom, is the most critical key to women's wholeness today. Women need to listen inwardly in order to be whole. This is for two simple reasons. First, women are naturally built with an internal focus. Unlike men, women's bodies are constructed with their organs tucked inside. Even the simplest awareness of the cycles that govern so much of a woman's reality—her moods, energy, sexuality, and procreativity—requires that her attention be inwardly focused.

The second reason is sociological. Women have had to cultivate their inwardness because the outer legacy was appropriated in an exclusive manner by the men, who deemed themselves leaders of the people. Historically denied the possibilities of formal study, full ritual participation and leadership, women naturally took the inward path, mastering the inner landscape without the help of a formal, outer structure.

This interior focus yields a fertility of its own. The many voices of wisdom that generate wholeness arise from our dreams, reflections, signals, and the awareness of the wise interior dimension. The writer of the book of Psalms hints at women's special connection to the inner planes when he says, "The glory of the princess is found at the interior."[39] In modern parlance, we might say that the feminine side of life, symbolized by the princess, has its own special source of nourishment within.

But a serious problem arises from the fact that women have been trained by mainstream Jewish tradition to recognize and obey the outward authority of the textual Torah and the rabbis as the *exclusive* conveyers of God's word. This has created confusion and conflict for many women.

Every woman knows that there is an interior authority to which she must also answer. The Torah, which knows the balance of inner and outer truths, calls this inner authority the "Torah that is written in our innards,"[40] "the still small voice,"[41] and "that wisdom which was planted in the innermost recesses of our being."[42]

But if the "exclusive authority" is the tradition found in the books, what does one do with the inner voice, which may be telling us that we need to do or not do something very different than what is dictated by Jewish law? The answer is we cannot bow to an "exclusive external authority," and certainly not to a man's interpretation taken at face value, without a process of consulting our own inner wisdom.

The wise women of Safed, like the Torah itself, teach us that our inner voice must, at all costs, be discerned and listened to. And like the women of Safed, we also know that it would be foolhardy to ignore the ethics, laws, and practices of our ancient traditions, for they are based upon deep principles of truth that deserve our reverence and study. The ancient tradition must be brought into a conversation with what women know on the inside, for we can no longer forsake the clear and resounding voice of wisdom that arises from our bodies, our feelings, and our intuition.

Both voices are vital: the Torah understood by the outer tradition and the Torah received from within. To follow either one to the exclusion of the other is dangerous for men as well as women. But holding these two authorities in tension is not for everyone. It requires the hard work of listening and meditating and a taste for ambiguity. Nevertheless, when we listen to the inner feminine voice, we can hear more clearly how to open the doors of the tradition to our modern sensibilities and needs. The women of Safed model this approach for us.

The ancient traditions are begging for new life to be breathed into them, so that we can bring them into the world in fresh, relevant, and meaningful ways. This can only happen through those who are knowledgeable of the outer tradition, attuned to receiving their inner truth, and willing to grapple with the ambiguities of modern life.

At the Leading Edge

Exceptional though they are, there are individuals and spiritual communities throughout the world today that have taken upon themselves to live a radical form of Judaism, loyal to the principles of holiness rather than to fulfilling ritual solely for ritual's sake; faithful to the ethics involved in living holy lives rather than to the preservation of observances without connection to their living Source. These communities may be shunned or looked askance upon for their iconoclastic approach, but their rubric is ancient. They base their lives on three key principles: *Torah, Avodah,* and *Gemilut Chasadim:*[43] being faithful to the spirit of the ancient texts (learning, understanding, and grappling with Torah), being faithful to the work of becoming whole (receiving and applying the wisdom of the deeper self), and being faithful to the larger community (using both outer and inner voices of truth to dictate how to repair the world to bring about justice, peace, and a sustainable life for our children).

For the individuals and groups who choose this path, life is a complex balance of outward and inward attunement: receiving the external Torah of history and receiving the inner voice of its appropriate application. Both are critical; without its complement, each one alone becomes a mockery of the tradition.

This integrated approach has endless possibilities as we synthesize Judaism's powerful ethical system with the pressing needs of our world. This synthesis might show itself in a dedication to *eco-kashrut* (*eco* meaning "environment" and *kashrut* meaning "laws of clean living"),[44] or as social action for the homeless and poor in one's local community or as empowerment of young Jewish women. However it expresses itself, advocates of this approach listen to their conscience, taking the precepts of the outer tradition into the present events of the world, and seek to align their activities to match their guiding values.

Conclusion: A Life of Wholeness

The lives of Safed's women bespeak a wholeness that is born of marrying together sides of life that were traditionally separate, even exiled from one another, such as masculine and feminine modes of spirituality, orthodox religious observance and nontraditional mystical practices, outward and inner brands of truth. As we have posited throughout this book, wholeness is what we are seeking, and we arrive at wholeness by means of reconciling opposites, the mystical process known as *yichudim,* or unifications.

Our journey as modern seekers is also necessarily about *yichudim,* reconciling our opposites, both within ourselves and in the world around us: masculine and feminine, light and shadow, spiritual powers above with the physical aliveness of the earth below, the transcendent viewpoint with the wisdom of the present moment.

The Tree of Life, in all of its multidimensional complexity, teaches wholeness. We have learned that there can be no true and effective spiritual elevation, no authentic mastery in Wisdom or Discernment, for example, if we cannot root ourselves in the here and now. In other words, without grounding ourselves in the physical, action-oriented realm of Manifestation at the base of the Tree, we will never be able to aspire high and translate our revelations into the world.

The Tree of Life also shows us how our world of duality, symbolized in the Tree's right and left pillars, is reconciled into a balanced synthesis, giving full expression to each extreme. For example, we learned how the powerful opposites of Love and Judgment, and Energy and Method require each other in order to function well. We also saw that without the healthy integration of these opposites, our world becomes prone to rampant evil and chaos.

The middle pillar, core of synthesis and harmony of the Tree of Life, is the focal point for mastery. Every initiate can use it to learn about the balance and wholeness for which we all hunger. Focusing on Manifestation at our feet, Creativity at our belly, Harmony at our heart, and Oneness at our crown, we can root ourselves in both of our homes, the physical and the celestial, becoming a bridge between earth and heaven.

The five layers of the soul-dress also illustrate the principle of dynamic wholeness at work. This is because every tier of this beautiful gown is necessary for our overall health. We have seen how the most brilliant innovations and spiritual revelations require our bodily vitality and our personal voice to bring them through. Likewise, our mortal selves require the inspiration and divine purpose of our souls' highest dimensions to energize them.

Wholeness and balance are the ultimate goals of the Jewish mystical tradition. Each of the stories of the seven women mystics recounted in this book brings forth an element that has been lost and must be reclaimed for the tradition to be whole. Likewise, each of their lives can teach us about a specific *yichud*, a unification between severed opposites, such as eros and spirituality, shadow and light, earthiness and the transcendent life. And all of us are working, at many varying levels, both directly and indirectly, to create unifications in our own personal lives, to sew up the torn fabric of our own stories, and the pieces of our fragmented world. Herein lies the key to our healing.

Finally, the time has come for the Jewish tradition to receive the gifts that women's wisdom contributes in order to regain its wholeness and awaken Judaism's message to the world—a vision of oneness that is desperately needed in our fragmented times. The woman's way teaches that all of us have the capacity to receive Divine Wisdom, each of us in our own way. This wisdom will guide us toward the work we are each called to do to heal ourselves, our tradition, and the world. May we support one another in this holy work, and may the whole be bettered by the healing of its parts.

ACKNOWLEDGMENTS

I am indebted to all those who had faith in *The Receiving,* and in the idea of recovering the feminine wisdom within Judaism, so crucially needed now. First, my heartfelt thanks go to my Boulder editor and dear friend, Donna Zerner, who has supported me at every imaginable turn, from conception to birth of this work. Her skill, humor, and deep understanding of the mystical nature of this material made the work a joy. Deep thanks go to Liz Perle, editor at large at HarperSan-Francisco, who recognized the power of this material, and the public's need of it, long before I had brought it into its present form. Renee Sedliar, my interim editor at Harper, was extraordinarily helpful, thorough, and a delight to work with. My literary agent, Arielle Eckstut, of James Levine Communications has been an endless support to me, ever proficient, insightful, and optimistic.

Rabbinic colleagues around the country have been amazingly generous in their support and contributions to this project, offering me their own personal research to allow the seven women sages in this book to come to light. Special thanks to my teacher and friend, Rabbi Leah Novick, an expert on the topic of the feminine mystical lineage in Judaism, who pointed my way to Asnat Barsani and Malkah of Belz. Reb Leah's dedication to reclaiming women's mystical wisdom in our day is truly inspiring. Thanks to Rabbi Margot Stein, who was exceedingly gracious with her research and creative renderings of Dulcie's story. Gratitude to Yosi (Jeffrey Howard) Chajes, Rabbi Shohama Weiner, Rabbi Gershon Winkler, Rabbi Jonathan Omarman, Professor Art Green, Rabbi Rami Shapiro, Rabbi Mordechai Gafni, Ruth Kagan, Cindy Gabriel, Ginny Jordan, Dr. Jeffrey Raff, and my beloved rebbe,

Rabbi Zalman Schachter-Shalomi, whose life work and faith in me has allowed me to undertake all that I do.

At the conception and first stages of writing *The Receiving,* an inspired group known as the Bread, Blood, and Fire Women, came together to support this work, meditate on the women, and help bring them to life. Thanks to each of you. I am also grateful to the members of Sarah's Tent in Los Angeles for their loving support and ideas. Anne Marie Doherty, Judy Ford, and Kathi Rosenfeld were invaluable with much needed technical and research assistance. Special thanks to Cindy Bucks who did a brilliant job of copyediting, and to Lisa Zuniga for painstakingly and lovingly overseeing production. Thanks also to Laura Lindgren, who designed the interior of this book, and to Kimberly McCutcheon, for her meticulous eye for detail in proofreading. I am very grateful to Jim Warner of HarperSanFrancisco for the beautiful cover design, which so perfectly bespeaks the content of this book, and to Li Hertzi for designing the Tree of Life diagram.

David Friedman, my husband and best friend, I could not have done this without you. You are God's gift of love in the form of a generous and faithful companion, lover, and co-parent. I am blessed to have you by my side.

The Tree of Life

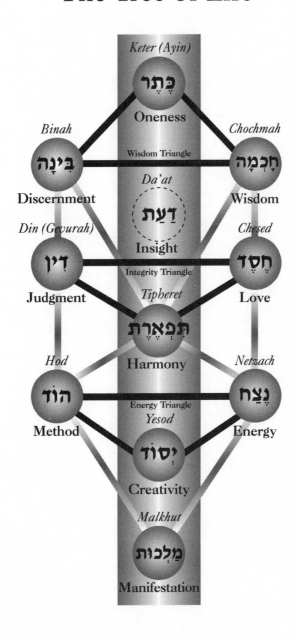

GLOSSARY

atzilut: The kabbalistic realm of divine nearness; emanation.

ayin: Nothingness, usually used in the archetypal sense.

Ba'al Shem Tov: Lit: Master of the Good Name. Rabbi Israel ben Eliezer (ca. 1700–1760), founder of Hassidic movement. Also known as the Besht (acronym).

challah: Braided bread eaten on the Sabbath.

ChaNaH: Acronym for the three commandments traditionally directed to women: the making of *challah,* the Sabbath loaf; *niddah,* keeping separate from one's husband during menstruation and for seven days thereafter; and *hadlakah,* the lighting of the Sabbath and holiday flames.

chaya: Level of soul that is formless consciousness.

conversos: Spanish Jews who converted to Christianity, usually under duress, during the Middle Ages.

Elohim: One of the names of God.

gilgulim: Life incarnations.

halakha: Jewish law as derived from Torah and Rabbinic texts, such as the Talmud.

Hassidism: Eastern European Jewish spiritual revival movement, begun in the eighteenth century.

hitlahavut: Ecstasy, rapture.

ibbur: Spirit pregnancy.

Kabbalah: Literally, "That which is received"; the Jewish mystical tradition.

Kaddish: A Jewish prayer declaring God's greatness, recited by those in mourning.

kedusha: Holiness, sanctification.

ketubah: Jewish marriage contract.

kiddush Hashem: Literally, "sanctifying God's name"; sacrificing one's life as a martyr.

maggid: Angelic guide.

mechitza: A dividing wall or curtain used to separate men and women during Jewish prayer.

minyan: Quorum of ten adults (traditionally men) needed to recite certain Hebrew prayers.

Mishnah: Third-century compilation of Jewish laws previously transmitted only orally; the basis of the Talmud.

mitzvah: Commandment; good deed; plural, *mitzvot.*

mochin de gadlut: Literally, "great mind"; expanded consciousness.

mochin de katnut: Literally, "small mind"; attention to personal detail, ego.

nephesh: Vital or physical soul, vital force.

neshama: Level of soul that connects the personal to the Divine; rules mental activity.

niddah: A menstruating woman; also laws pertaining to refraining from sex during and for seven days after menstruation.

olah: Literally, "that which rises up"; burnt offering.

phylacteries: See *tefillin.*

rebbe: Literally, "rabbi"; title given to a Hassidic teacher or master.

ruach: Emotional level of soul.

sephirah: One of ten vortexes of moving energy on the Tree of Life, each associated with a different divine attribute; plural, *sephirot.*

Shechinah: God's indwelling presence; the feminine face of the Divine.

Shema Yisrael: "Hear, O Israel"; a central prayer in Judaism that declares God's unity and totality.

shofar: The ritual ram's horn blown on Jewish New Year.

shul: Synagogue.

Talmud: Compendium of rabbinic law, stories, and wisdom, compiled from the second to the fifth centuries, which forms the basis of religious authority for traditional Judaism.

techinah: An informal woman's prayer, usually in Yiddish.

tefillin: Phylacteries; two small boxes containing the Shema Yisrael and other biblical verses that are bound by leather straps to the forehead and left arm.

tikkun: Repair, healing.

Torah: Literally, the "Five Books of Moses"; also the entire body of Jewish sacred literature.

tzaddik: A righteous person.

yarmulkah: Skullcap.

yechida: Level of soul that is unknowable, beyond consciousness.

yesh: Somethingness, the substantive quality of the ego and of this world.

yeshivah: School of higher learning for Jewish males.

yetzer hara: The instinct to fulfill personal passion.

yetzer hatov: The instinct toward altruism and selflessness.

YHVH: The four-letter unpronounceable name of God.

yichud: Unification, joining together of opposites to create a oneness; plural, *yichudim.*

Zohar: "The Book of Splendor," kabbalistic masterpiece from thirteenth-century Spain.

REFERENCES

Abrahams, Israel. *Jewish Life in the Middle Ages.* Philadelphia: Jewish Publication Society, 1911.

Adelman, Penina V. *Miriam's Well: Rituals for Jewish Women Around the Year.* Sunnyside, NY: Biblio Press, 1986.

Adler, Rachel. "The Virgin in the Brothel and Other Anomalies: Character and Context in the Legend of Beruriah." *Tikkun* 3, no. 6 (June 2001).

Angier, Natalie. *Woman: An Intimate Geography.* Boston: Houghton Mifflin, 1999.

Ariel, David S. *The Mystic Quest: An Introduction to Jewish Mysticism.* Northvale, NJ: Jason Aronson, 1988.

Baring, Anne, and Jules Cashford. *The Myth of the Goddess: Evolution of an Image.* London: Arkana/Penquin Books, 1993.

Baskin, Judith R., ed. *Jewish Women in Historical Perspective.* Detroit: Wayne State University Press, 1991.

———. "Some Parallels in the Education of Medieval Jewish and Christian Women." *Jewish History* 5, no. 1 (1991).

Ben-Jacob, Abraham. *Kehillot Yehude Kurdistan.* Jerusalem: n.p., 1961.

Biale, Rachel. *Women and Jewish Law: An Exploration of Women's Issues in Halakhic Sources.* New York: Schocken, 1984.

Bilu, Yoram. "*Dybbuk* and *Maggid:* Two Cultural Patterns of Altered Consciousness in Judaism." *Association for Jewish Studies Review* 21, no. 2 (1996).

Bloch, Ariel, and Chana Bloch. *The Song of Songs.* New York: Random House, 1995.

Buxbaum, Yitzkak. *Jewish Tales of Holy Women.* San Francisco: Jossey-Bass, 2002.

Cady, Susan, Marian Ronan, and Hal Taussig. *Wisdom's Feast: Sophia in Study and Celebration.* San Francisco: Harper & Row, 1989.

Chajes, Jeffrey H. "Spirit Possession and the Construction of Early Modern Jewish Religiosity." Ph.D. diss., Yale University, 1999. Ann Arbor, MI: UMI Dissertation Services, 2001.

Chesler, Phyllis. *Woman's Inhumanity to Woman.* New York: Avalon, 2001.

Cohen, Seymour J. *The Holy Letter: A Study in Jewish Sexual Morality.* Northvale, NJ: Jason Aronson, 1993.

Collins, John J., and Michael Fishbane, eds. *Death, Ecstasy and Other Worldly Journeys.* Albany: State University of New York Press, 1995.

Cordovero, Moses. *Palm Tree of Deborah.* Translated by Louis Jacobs. London: Mitchell Valentine, 1960.

Dallett, Janet O. *The Not-Yet Transformed God.* York Beach, ME: Nicolas-Hays, 1998.

Diamant, Anita. *The Red Tent.* New York: Picador USA/St. Martin's Press, 1997.

Edinger, Edward F. *Ego and Archetype.* Boston: Shambhala, 1992.

———. *The New God-Image: A Study of Jung's Key Letters Concerning the Evolution of the Western God-Image.* Edited by Dianne D. Cordic and Charles Yates, M.D. Wilmette, IL: Chiron Publications, 1996.

Eilberg-Schwartz, Howard, ed. *People of the Body: Jews and Judaism from an Embodied Perspective.* Albany: State University of New York Press, 1992.

Faierstein, Morris M., trans. *Jewish Mystical Autobiographies: Book of Visions and Book of Secrets.* New York: Paulist Press, 1999.

Fine, Lawrence, trans. *Safed Spirituality.* New York: Paulist Press, 1984.

Fink, Greta. *Great Jewish Women: Profiles of Courageous Women from the Maccabean Period to the Present.* New York: Menorah Publishing, 1978.

Ginzburg, Louis. *Legends of the Jews.* 7 vols. Philadelphia: Jewish Publication Society, 1909–38.

Gottlieb, Freema. *The Lamp of God: A Jewish Book of Light.* Northvale, NJ: Jason Aronson, 1989.

Green, Arthur, ed. *Jewish Spirituality.* Vol. 14, *World Spirituality from the Sixteenth Century Revised to the Present.* New York: Crossroad, 1992.

HaChasid, Judah. *The Book of the Pious.* Translated and condensed by Aryeh Finkel. Northvale, NJ: Jason Aronson, 1997.

Halevi, Z'ev ben Shimon. *Kabbalah and Psychology.* York Beach, ME: Samuel Weiser, 1986.

Hannah, Barbara. *Encounters with the Soul: Active Imagination as Developed by C. G. Jung.* Santa Monica: SIGO Press, 1981.

Hechasid, Yehudah. *Sefer Chasidim: The Book of the Pious.* Translated by Avraham Yaahov Finkel. Northvale, NJ: Jason Aronson, 1997.

Henry, Sondra, and Emily Taitz. *Written Out of History: Our Jewish Foremothers.* 3d ed. Sunnyside, NY: Biblio Press, 1988.

Heschel, Susannah, ed. *On Being a Jewish Feminist: A Reader.* New York: Schocken Books, 1983.

Jacobs, Louis. *A Tree of Life: Diversity, Flexibility, and Creativity in Jewish Law.* Oxford and New York: Oxford University Press for the Littman Library, 1984.

Johnson, Elizabeth A. *She Who Is: The Mystery of God in Feminist Theological Discourse.* New York: Crossroad, 1992.

Jung, Carl G. *The Structure and Dynamics of the Psyche. Collected Works.* Vol. 8. R. F. C. Hull, trans. Bollingen Series XX. Princeton, NJ: Princeton University Press, 1969.

———. *Memories, Dreams, and Reflections.* Rev. ed. Edited by Aniela Jaffé. New York: Vintage Books, 1989.

Jung, Carl G., M. L. von Franz, Joseph L. Henderson, Jolande Jacobi, and Aniela Jaffé, eds. *Man and His Symbols.* New York: Dell, 1964.

Kamelhar, Israel. *Rabbenu Eleazar me'Germaiza, HaRoKeach.* Rzeazow, Poland: n.p., 1930.

Kaplan, Aryeh. *The Light Beyond: Adventures in Hassidic Thought.* New York: Maznaim Press, 1981.

———. *Meditation and Kabbalah.* York Beach, ME: Samuel Weiser, 1982.

———. *Jewish Meditation: A Practical Guide.* New York: Schocken Books, 1985.

———, ed. and trans. *The Bahir: An Ancient Kabbalistic Text Attributed to R. Nehuniah ben HaKana.* York Beach, ME: Samuel Weiser, 1979.

Karpeles, Gustav. *Jewish Literature and Other Essays.* Philadelphia: Jewish Publication Society, 1895.

Katz, Stephen. *The Holocaust in Historical Context.* New York: Oxford University Press, 1993.

Kaufman, Shirley, Galit Hasan-Rokem, and Tamar S. Hess, eds. *The Defiant Muse: Hebrew Feminist Poems from Antiquity to the Present—A Bilingual Anthology.* New York: Feminist Press at the City University of New York, 1999.

Kien, Jenny. *Reinstating the Divine Woman in Judaism.* Parkland, FL: Universal, 2000.

Klirs, Tracy G., comp. *The Merit of Our Mothers: A Bilingual Anthology of Jewish Women's Prayers.* Translated by Tracy G. Klirs, Ida C. Selavan, and Gella S. Fishman. Cincinnati, OH: Hebrew Union College Press, 1992.

Kluger, Rivkah Schärf. *Psyche in Scripture: The Idea of the Chosen People and Other Essays.* Toronto: Inner City Books, 1995.

Koltun, Liz, ed. "The Jewish Woman: An Anthology." *Response,* 1973.

Koltuv, Barbara B. *The Book of Lilith.* York Beach, ME: Nicolas-Hays, 1986.

Kraemer, David, ed. *The Jewish Family: Metaphor and Memory.* New York: Oxford University Press, 1989.

Kraemer, Ross Shepard. *Her Share of the Blessings: Women's Religions Among Pagans, Jews and Christians in the Greco-Roman World.* New York: Oxford University Press, 1992.

Langer, Jiri. *Nine Gates to the Chasidic Mysteries.* Northvale, NJ: Jason Aronson, 1993.

Lowenthal, Marvin, trans. *The Memoirs of Glückel of Hameln.* New York: Schocken Books, 1977.

Mann, Jacob. *Texts and Studies in Jewish History and Literature.* Vol. 1. Cincinnati, OH: Hebrew Union College Press, 1931.

Marcus, Ivan. *Piety and Society: The Jewish Pietists of Medieval Germany.* Leiden: Brill, 1981.

———. "Mothers, Martyrs and Moneymakers: Some Jewish Women in Medieval Europe." *Conservative Judaism* 38, no. 3 (Spring 1986).

Matt, Daniel C. "*Ayin:* The Concept of Nothingness in Jewish Mysticism." *Tikkun* 3, no. 3 (1987): 43–47.

———. *The Essential Kabbalah: The Heart of Jewish Mysticism.* San Francisco: HarperSanFrancisco, 1995.

Nachman, ben-Yehudah. "The European Witch Craze of the Fourteenth–Seventeenth Centuries: A Sociologist's Perspective." *American Journal of Sociology* 86, no. 1 (July 1980).

Ner-David, Haviva. *Life on the Fringes: A Feminist Journey Toward Traditional Rabbinic Ordination.* Needham, MA: JFL Books, 2000.

Novick, Leah. "Rebbetzin Malka, Queen of Belz." In *The Fifty-Eighth Century: A Jewish Renewal Sourcebook.* Edited by Shohama Wiener. Northvale, NJ: Jason Aronson, 1996.

———. "Remembering Rebbetzin Dulcie of Worms: An Addition to 'Eylah Ezkerah.'" *New Menorah* (Autumn 1998).

———. "The Peaceful Maccabee: A Ceremony for the Eight Nights of Chanukah." *Tikkun* 14, no. 6 (November/December 1999).

Patai, Raphael. *The Hebrew Goddess.* 3d enl. ed. Detroit: Wayne State University Press, 1990.

Plaskow, Judith. *Standing Again at Sinai: Judaism from a Feminist Perspective.* New York: Harper & Row, 1990.

Rabinowicz, Tzvi M., ed. *The Encyclopedia of Hasidism.* Northvale, NJ: Jason Aronson, 1996.

Raddock, Charles. "Once There Was a Female Chasidic Rabbi." *Jewish Digest* 13, no. 3 (December 1967).

Raff, Jeffrey. *Jung and the Alchemical Imagination.* York Beach, ME: Nicolas-Hays, 2000.

Raphael, Simcha Paull. *Jewish Views of the Afterlife.* Northvale, NJ: Jason Aronson, 1994.

Rapoport-Albert, Ada. "On Women in Hasidism, S. A. Horodezky and the Maid of Ludomir Tradition." In *Jewish History: Essays in Honor of Chimen Abramsky.* Edited by Ada Rapoport-Albert and Steven Zipperstein. London: Peter Halban, 1988.

Rosen, Gavri. "Introduction: On Jewish Women's Writings." In *The Jews: A Treasury of Art and Literature*. Edited by Sharon R. Keller. Hong Kong: Beaux Arts Editions, 1992.

Rosenberg, Shalom. *Good and Evil in Jewish Thought*. Tel Aviv: MOD Books, 1989.

Rupp, Joyce. *Prayers to Sophia: A Companion to "The Star in My Heart."* Philadelphia: Innisfree Press, 2000.

Sabar, Yona, ed. and trans. *The Folk Literature of the Kurdistani Jews: An Anthology*. Vol. 23. Edited by Leon Nemoy. New Haven, CT: Yale University Press, 1982.

Sambari, Yosef ben Yitzchak. *Sefer Divrei Yosef*. Edited by Shimon Shtober. Jerusalem: Ben-Zvi Institute, 1994.

Schachter-Shalomi, Zalman M. *Gate to the Heart: An Evolving Process*. Philadelphia: Aleph Alliance for Jewish Renewal, 1993.

———. *Spiritual Intimacy: A Study of Counseling in Hasidism*. Northvale, NJ: Jason Aronson, 1996.

Schechter, Solomon. *Studies in Judaism: Women in Temple and Synagogue*. Philadelphia: Jewish Publication Society, 1938.

Scholem, Gershom G. *Major Trends in Jewish Mysticism*. New York: Schocken, 1961.

———. *Origins of the Kabbalah*. Edited by R. J. Zwi Werblowsky. Translated by Allan Arkush. Princeton, NJ: Princeton University Press/Jewish Publication Society, 1987.

Sered, Susan Starr. *Women as Ritual Experts: The Religious Lives of Elderly Jewish Women in Jerusalem*. New York: Oxford University Press, 1992.

Shar'abi, Mordechai. *Tefillah LeMoshe*. Jerusalem: Beit Midrash Ohr Hashalom, 1989.

———. *Tefillah HaMeyasher*. Jerusalem: Nahar Shalom, 1998.

Shlain, Leonard. *The Alphabet Versus the Goddess: The Conflict Between Word and Image*. New York: Penguin/Compass, 1998.

Simmons, Rachel. *Odd Girl Out: The Hidden Culture of Aggression in Girls*. New York: Harcourt, 2002.

Singer, Isaac Bashevis. *The Collected Stories of Isaac Bashevis Singer*. New York: Farrar, Straus & Giroux, 1953.

Singer, June. *Boundaries of the Soul: The Practice of Jung's Psychology*. Garden City, NY: Anchor Press/Doubleday, 1973.

Stein, Murray, comp. *Jung on Evil*. Princeton, NJ: Princeton University Press, 1995.

Teilhard de Chardin, Pierre. *The Phenomenon of Man*. New York: Harper & Row, 1959.

Tishby, Isaiah, and Fischel Lachower, arr. *The Wisdom of the Zohar: An Anthology of Texts.* With an introduction and explanation by Isaiah Tishby. Translated by David Goldstein. Vol. 2. Oxford and New York: Oxford University Press for the Littman Library, 1989.

Trachtenberg, Joshua. *Jewish Magic and Superstition: A Study in Folk Religion.* Cleveland: Meridian Books, 1961.

Tzadok, Ariel Bar. *Kabbalah 101: The Relationship Between Kabbalah and Halakha (Jewish Law).* 1995 [cited 14 May 2001]. Available at www. koshertorah.com/101.html.

Umansky, Ellen M., and Diane Ashton, eds. *Four Centuries of Jewish Women's Spirituality: A Sourcebook.* Boston: Beacon Press, 1992.

Vital, Hayyim. *Sha'ar HaGilgulim.* Edited by Y. Z. Brandwien. 15 vols. Jerusalem: n.p., 1988.

Wegner, Judith Romney. *Chattel or Person? The Status of Women in the Mishnah.* New York: Oxford University Press, 1988.

Weissler, Chava. *Voices of the Matriarchs: Listening to the Prayers of Early Modern Jewish Women.* Boston: Beacon Press, 1998.

Weiss-Rosmarin, Trude. *Jewish Women Throughout the Ages.* New York: Jewish Book Club, 1940.

Werblowsky, R. J. Zwi. *Joseph Karo: Lawyer and Mystic.* Philadelphia: Jewish Publication Society, 1977.

Wexelman, David M. *The Jewish Concept of Reincarnation and Creation: Based on the Writings of Rabbi Chaim Vital.* Northvale, NJ: Jason Aronson, 1999.

Winkler, Gershon. *Dybbuk.* New York: Judaica Press, 1981.

———. *They Called Her Rebbe: The Maiden of Ludomir.* New York: Judaica Press, 1991.

———. *The Soul of the Matter: A Jewish Kabbalistic Perspective on the Human Soul Before, During and After "Life."* New York: Judaica Press, 1992.

Wolfson, Elliot. *Through a Speculum That Shines: Vision and Imagination in Medieval Jewish Mysticism.* Princeton, NJ: Princeton University Press, 1994.

———. *The Circle in the Square.* Albany: State University of New York Press, 1995.

Zinberg, Israel. *A History of Jewish Literature.* Edited and translated by Bernard Martin. Vol. 7. Cincinnati, OH: Hebrew Union College Press; New York: KTAV, 1975.

NOTES

CHAPTER ONE

1. See *Encyclopedia Judaica*, s.v. "Ludomir, Maiden of"; Charles Raddock, "Once There Was a Female Chassidic Rabbi," *Jewish Digest* 13, no. 3 (December 1967); Gershon Winkler, *They Called Her Rebbe: The Maiden of Ludomir* (New York: Judaica Press, 1991).
2. Exodus 19:15.
3. Deuteronomy 12:2–3.
4. The goddess Asherah, for example, consorted with her lover, powerful El, and her daughter Anat coupled with Ba'al. The powerful feminine deities of the surrounding regions also had male consorts who aided the females and made them fruitful.
5. For one of many citations in the Torah, see Judges 3:6–7. The idolatrous practices decried by the prophets were much more popular than the sacred texts let on. Numerous archeological finds dating back to the time the Hebrew people arrived in Canaan through the First Temple period show amulets, figurines, and even female deities in the Temple. See Raphael Patai, *The Hebrew Goddess*, 3d enl. ed. (Detroit: Wayne State University Press, 1990).
6. See Jenny Kien, *Reinstating the Divine Woman in Judaism* (Parkland, FL: Universal, 2000), chap. 2.
7. Judges 4–5.
8. Nehemiah 6:14.
9. 2 Chronicles 34:22–28; 2 Kings 22:14–20.
10. 1 Kings 16, 18, 19, 21; 2 Kings 9.
11. B. Talmud Sota 20a–b. In Sephardic communities living in southern Europe, northern Africa, and the Middle East outside of Palestine, this passage was traditionally interpreted to mean that women should not be allowed to read or write. For more on the religious lives of Sephardic women, see Susan S. Sered, *Women as Ritual Experts* (New York: Oxford University Press, 1992), pp. 66–71.
12. B. Talmud Shabbat 33b.
13. Talmud Brachot 48b.

14. Such hateful comments draw attention to men's dramatic lack of comprehension of their female counterparts. Thankfully, they are few. More frequently, the rabbis of the Talmud mention women in reference to their legal status: which regulations they must fulfill and which they are exempt from.

15. B. Talmud Brachot 17b, 20a.

16. B. Talmud Brachot 45a.

17. B. Talmud Gittin 52a.

18. B. Talmud Shevuot 30a. This ruling has been cited as the basis for women's ineligibility to serve as community leaders or judges, although there is evidence that this was not always observed, as in the case of the judge Deborah.

19. B. Talmud Kiddushin 33b.

20. For a thorough study of this topic, see Rachel Biale, *Women and Jewish Law: An Exploration of Women's issues in Halakhic Sources* (New York: Schocken, 1984).

21. Rabbi David Ben Joseph Abudarham, in *Sefer Abudarham*, part 3. Quoted in Biale, *Women and Jewish Law*, p. 13.

22. See Tracy Guren Klirs, comp., *The Merit of Our Mothers: A Bilingual Anthology of Jewish Women's Prayers* (Cincinnati, OH: Hebrew Union College Press, 1992); Chava Weissler, *Voices of the Matriarchs: Listening to the Prayers of Early Modern Jewish Women* (Boston: Beacon Press, 1998); and Ellen Umansky and Dianne Ashton, eds., *Four Centuries of Jewish Women's Spirituality: A Sourcebook* (Boston: Beacon Press, 1992). For more on *ChaNaH*, see Ross Shepard Kraemer, *Her Share of the Blessings: Women's Religions Among Pagans, Jews, and Christians in the Greco-Roman World* (New York: Oxford University Press, 1992).

23. B. Talmud Shabbat 31b.

24. *Midrash Tanchuma*, ed. Salomon Buber (Vilna: Romm, 1885), beginning of Parashat Noah. Quoted in Weissler, *Voices of the Matriarchs*, p. 216.

25. See Klirs, *The Merit of Our Mothers*.

26. Biale, *Women and Jewish Law*.

27. Gershom Scholem, *Major Trends in Jewish Mysticism* (New York: Schocken Books, 1961), p. 229.

28. Exodus 25:8. The third-century commentator Onkeles rendered the verse: "Let them make before Me a Sanctuary that I may let My Shechinah dwell among them." Although Onkeles was most probably trying to translate out anthropomorphic references to God and never had any intention at all of assigning a feminine quality or persona to God, the term nevertheless stuck, and we find it next in use by the rabbis of the Talmud and Midrash.

29. B. Talmud Sota 17a; Shabbat 12b; Brachot 8a.

30. This is perhaps the same collective impulse that continues to push for gender equality and harmony within human societies too. Although the

movement toward women's equality is not yet global and is certainly not being achieved in a straight line, it is a reality.

31. See Lamentations Rabba 1:24, 32, based on Jeremiah 31:15, and B. Talmud Shabbat 33a.

32. Despite the intention to create wholeness, there is still scarce evidence of sensitivity to the feminine within traditional Jewish circles. The Orthodox sectors that are likeliest to recite the *yichud* prayer and hold an intention of melding masculine and feminine approaches to life are not known for any outward show of interpersonal harmony. Nor has there been any great rush on their part to include women or proponents of feminine consciousness or to extend the circle of their sacred acts and rituals to women, thereby "unifying" feminine and masculine on the material plane.

33. This prayer may be found in most Jewish prayer books that are Nusach Sephardi, i.e., in the Oriental style. See, for example, those by Art Scroll Publications (New York). This prefatory prayer refers to the secret name of God whose pronunciation has been lost to us, but whose four letters themselves, YHVH, represent the mystical marriage of the divine feminine and masculine energies. Simply put, the mystical letter *Yud* is identified with God the King and *Heh* stands for the Shechinah. The rupture in the Divine Name reflects the separation between the masculine and feminine parts of the godhead, and its repair represents the reunification of these archetypes in the world.

CHAPTER TWO

1. Beruriah was famous among the rabbis for mastering three hundred laws from three hundred rabbis in one day. See B. Talmud Pesachim 62b.

2. One of many examples of Beruriah's ability to compassionately apply her wisdom to the world around her was her confrontation of her husband, Rabbi Meir, when she found him praying for the death of a local gang of robbers. Surely God does not want us to use our powers in such a way, she explained. Instead, Beruriah taught him, with the use of scripture, how to pray that the sins of evildoers, not the evildoers themselves, fall away and die. Following her instructions, Beruriah's husband is said to have uplifted the souls of the robbers, who eventually came to lead holy lives.

3. B. Talmud Avoda Zara 17b.

4. B. Talmud Avoda Zara 17b.

5. B. Talmud Avoda Zara 18a.

6. Take, for example, the story of the devout man who enters the brothel and is about to disrobe before a beautiful woman when he is hit in the face by the four fringes of his prayer shawl. B. Talmud Menachot 44a.

7. B. Talmud Avoda Zara 18b.

8. Mishnah Sota 3:4.

9. Midrash Mishle 31:10.

10. Rashi on B. Talmud Avoda Zara 18b, explaining why Meir fled to Babylon. His story is included in the margins of the original Talmudic text. For more thoughts on this story and what we can learn from it, see Rachel Adler, "The Virgin in the Brothel and Other Anomalies: Character and Context in the Legend of Beruriah," *Tikkun* 3, no. 6 (June 2001). See also Ross Shepard Kraemer, *Her Share of the Blessings.*

11. It is interesting to contrast a similar story of temptation and testing by a spouse, this one from a woman's point of view and exemplifying a woman's sensibility: "Every time R. Hiyya fell upon his face he used to say: 'The Merciful save us from the Tempter.' One day his wife heard him. 'Let us see,' she reflected, 'it has been so many years since he has held aloof from me, why then should he pray thus?' One day, while he was studying in his garden she adorned herself and repeatedly walked up and down before him. 'Who are you?' he demanded. 'I am Haruta (freedom).' He desired her. Said she to him, 'Bring me that pomegranate from the uppermost bough.' He jumped up, went, and brought it to her. When he reentered his house, his wife was firing the oven, whereupon he ascended and sat in it. 'What means this?' she demanded. He told her what had happened. 'It was I,' she assured him, but he paid no heed to her until she gave him proof." B. Talmud Kiddushin 81a.

12. Many early Judaic prayers place God the father in heaven. Few people know, in fact, that long before it became a staple of the Catholic Church, the "Our Father who art in Heaven" was a prominent Aramaic prayer among the Jews of the first centuries.

13. C. G. Jung, *The Structure and Dynamics of the Psyche. Collected Works*, vol. 8, R. F. C. Hull, trans. Bollingen Series XX (Princeton, NJ: Princeton University Press, 1969), p. xx.

14. See *Zohar* 1:55:b.

15. C. G. Jung, *Memories, Dreams and Reflections*, rev. ed., ed. Aniela Jaffé (New York: Vintage, 1989), p. 355.

16. Abraham's birth date is unknown but is often assigned as 1948 B.C.E.

17. For more about this transformation of consciousness, see Leonard Schlain, *The Alphabet Versus The Goddess* (New York: Penguin/Compass, 1998). In it, the author brings strong evidence that the advent of alphabet literacy, which first became prevalent with the Israelites and their sacred texts, fundamentally reconfigured human brain functions on a collective level, diminishing the importance of right-brain functions and, with them, the feminine principle.

18. For a thorough exploration of this radical change of worldview as well as a brilliant overview of the history of consciousness through a religious and mythological lens, see Anne Baring and Jules Cashford, *The Myth of the*

Goddess: Evolution of an Age (New York: Penguin, 1993), pp. 281–298; and Jenny Kien, *Reinstating the Divine Woman in Judaism* (Parkland, FL: Universal, 2000), pp. 57–61.

19. Genesis 1:2.
20. Genesis 1:2.
21. See Jeremiah 7:18; 44:17–26; 2 Kings 21:7. Throughout Palestine and dating from all periods of Israelite history, hundreds of Asherah icons, small clay figurines depicting a woman with large breasts who is posted on a cylinder, have been found. Most probably versions of a household goddess in the form of Asherah, these figurines were women's talismans thought to promote fertility and ease childbirth. For more on the topic see Raphael Patai, *The Hebrew Goddess,* 3d ed. (Detroit: Wayne State University Press, 1990).
22. This more esoteric approach is hinted at in the Kabbalah when it points out that the numerical equivalence of the term for snake is the same as the term for Messiah.
23. See the curse of the snake in Genesis 3:14–15.
24. See Jacob's blessing to Joseph in Genesis 49:22–26.
25. Deuteronomy 7:1, 3.
26. 1 Samuel 25.
27. 2 Samuel 11; Psalm 51.
28. Song of Songs 7:9–10, in *The Song of Songs,* trans. Ariel and Chana Bloch (New York: Random House, 1995).
29. Song of Songs Rabba 1:11.
30. B. Talmud Yevamot 62b.
31. B. Talmud Brachot 24a.
32. See Exodus 21:10 and the Talmudic tractates based upon it, B. Talmud Ketubot 47b and 48a regarding a husband's obligations.
33. B. Talmud Brachot 57b
34. B. Talmud Gittin 70b
35. Jerusalem Talmud Kiddushin 4.
36. "Come and see. Where humans exist in a single union, male and female, and there is the intention to be sanctified, this is wholeness and called 'one' without any imperfection. When they are both together all is one, in soul and body: in soul, because they cleave to one another with a single will; and in body, as we have learned: that a man who is unmarried is like one divided, but when male and female unite with one another they immediately become one body" (*Zohar* 3:81a–82b).
37. With this perspective in mind, one reads passages in the *Zohar* like the following with tremendous appreciation for their wisdom: "The Blessed Holy One does not live in any place where male and female are not found together. Blessings are found only in a place where male and female are found" (*Zohar* 1:55b). The *Zohar* also picks up on the theme of our original

wholeness. A man and woman joined in marriage represent the whole and perfect human condition, whereas alone, they are imperfect, separated parts.

38. B. Talmud Sanhedrin 106b.

39. Proverbs 3:6. If you peel back the outer layer of these words you will find that the word "know" in Hebrew, *da* or *da'at,* is the same word used throughout the Torah for the passionate or carnal "knowledge" that lovers have of one another, the intimate knowing that comes from erotic connection.

CHAPTER THREE

1. Malkah's stories are often ancillary to those of her husband, the first Belzer Rebbe (1783–1855). Although we do not know Malkah's exact dates, we do know that she died some five to ten years before her husband, as the stories indicate that he was inconsolable at her passing and depressed thereafter. Traditionally, Malkah's *yahrzeit,* or anniversary of her death, is 27 Adar.

   Stories of Malkah and Reb Shalom Rokeach can be found in *Dover Shalom* (Hebrew; Vilna: n.p, 1882); Tzvi M. Rabinowicz, ed., *The Encyclopedia of Hasidism* (Northvale, NJ: Jason Aronson, 1996); and Jiri Langer, *Nine Gates to the Chasidic Mysteries* (Northvale, NJ: Jason Aronson, 1993) and Yitzhak Buxbaum, *Jewish Tales of Holy Women* (San Francisco: Jossey-Bass, 2002).

2. A play on words emerged among the Belzer Hassidim illustrating this point. Based upon three words of a biblical verse (Genesis 14:18), *Malketzedek Melech Shalem* means that because of the righteousness found in Malkah, Shalom became a perfected leader.

3. See Rokeach, Shalom, in Rabinowicz, *Encyclopedia of Hasidism.*

4. Rebbetzin is the honorary title given to the wife of the rebbe in eastern European Ashkenazic circles.

5. Psalm 119:105.

6. The *sandek* is one who holds the baby as the circumcision is being performed. Being asked to be the *sandek* is seen as a very great honor and for this reason is rarely turned down.

7. See B. Talmud Ketubot 62b and Nedarim 20b for basic tenets on this subject. Also see Louis Jacobs, *A Tree of Life* (Oxford and New York: Oxford University Press for the Littman Library, 1984); and Seymour J. Cohen, *The Holy Letter: A Study in Jewish Sexual Morality* (Northvale, NJ: Jason Aronson, 1993).

8. This idea was derived from B. Talmud Yevamot 63a: "Rabbi Eleazar said: Any man who has no wife is no proper man; for it is said, 'Male and female created He them and called their name Adam.'"

9. See Exodus 21:10, which enumerates a husband's legal duties to provide "her food, her clothing and her conjugal rights." Also see Moses Cordovero, *Palm*

Tree of Deborah (London: Mitchell Valentine, 1960), for a poetic discussion of a husband's performance of the marital act as religious duty (p. 104).

10. B. Talmud Kiddushin 30b.

11. *Zohar* 1:49a.

12. B. Talmud Ketubot 62b; Nedarim 20b.

13. *Zohar* 3:81a.

14. A traditional morning rite normally practiced by men, *neggelvasser*, or "knuckle water," was traditionally performed as a cleansing of spiritual impurities accrued during the night. It has an important secondary purpose of helping to call into focus one's intentions for the day and, particularly, to remind oneself of the spiritual function of one's hands.

15. An acronym denoting the three sacred obligations of every Jewish matron: baking challah, menstrual purity, and candlelighting. See Chapter 1.

16. From the Gaon's commentary on the book of Proverbs, quoted in Eliahu Ben Shlomo Zalman, *Commentary on Proverbs* (Hebrew; Warsaw, 1837; 23:30), quoted in David Kraemer, ed., *The Jewish Family: Metaphor and Memory* (New York: Oxford University Press, 1989).

17. Immanuel Etkes, "Marriage and Torah Study Among the Lomdim in Lithuania in the Nineteenth Century," in Kraemer, ed., *The Jewish Family*.

18. For more on the Tree of Life from a mythological viewpoint, see Anne Baring and Jules Cashford, *The Myth of the Goddess: Evolution of an Image* (London: Arkana/Penguin, 1993).

19. Genesis 2:9.

20. See B. Talmud Mas. Megillah 13b. In regard to Rachel as archetype of mother of the people and a personification of the Shechinah, see the famous midrash in Genesis Rabba 82:10.

21. The book of Psalms, filled with lofty and base sentiments alike, is classically ascribed to David. His dramatic story is told in the books of 1–2 Samuel and 1 Kings.

22. See Genesis 37–50.

23. See Genesis 39.

24. See also Natalie Angier, *Woman: An Intimate Geography* (Boston: Houghton Mifflin, 1999) for an anatomical and physiological landscape of the uterus and women's unique physiology.

25. Genesis, Chapter 38

26. Genesis 32:24–32.

27. 1 Samuel 1.

28. B. Talmud Mas. Brachot 31a, b.

CHAPTER FOUR

1. The term Tanna'it is the feminine form of *tanna*, Aramaic for "holy teacher," used in reference to the male sages of the Mishnah (oral law). In

a letter written to Asnat in 1664, Pinchas Harriri, one of Kurdistan's scholars and Kabbalists, refers to her with all the appellations reserved for the most eminent of rabbis.

2. After the destruction of the Temple and the Exile in 70 C.E., the pronunciation of the Divine Name, which used to be proclaimed by the High Priest from the Holy of the Holies on Yom Kippur, was lost. From the third century B.C.E. on, YHVH, considered too sacred to utter, was orally replaced with Adonai during the reading of the Torah and prayer, but even Adonai is reserved for sacred speech. See B. Talmud Kiddushin 71a on the Name of God, which represents God's essential nature and attributes.

3. *Avnei Zikkaron, Sefer HaDrashot, Sefer HaIyyun,* and fragments of *Sefer Charuzot* remain.

4. "Asnat Barasani," *Encyclopedia Judaica*, 2:204. See also "Kurdistan," 10:1298.

5. See Chapter 1 for the three *mitzvot* of *ChaNaH*, an acronym for *challah, niddah,* and *hadlakat nerot*, the laws of Sabbath loaves, feminine purity, and candlelighting.

6. For a remarkable firsthand story on this topic, see Haviva Ner-David, *Life on the Fringes* (Needham, MA: JFL Books, 2000).

7. Translated by Peter Cole. Quoted in Shirley Kaufman, Galit Hasan-Rokem, and Tamar S. Hess, eds., *The Defiant Muse: Hebrew Feminist Poets from Antiquity to the Present* (New York: Feminist Press at the City University of New York, 1999). For the entire collection of the original Hebrew documents from Jacob and Asnat Barzani, see Jacob Mann, *Texts and Studies in Jewish History and Literature*, vol. 1 (Cincinnati, OH: Hebrew Union College Press, 1931).

8. Interestingly, the ancient *Bahir* tells us that studying *lishmah* induces the sacred marriage of God and the Shechinah: "When a person studies Torah for its own sake, the Torah above unites with the Holy One, Blessed is He. What is this Torah? It is the Bride who is adorned and crowned... the Betrothed of the Blessed One"; Aryeh Kaplan, ed. and trans., *The Bahir* (York Beach, ME: Samuel Weiser, 1979), Mishnah 196. See also Elliot Wolfson, *The Circle in the Square* (Albany: State University of New York Press, 1995), chap. 1, "Female Imaging of the Torah."

9. *Zohar* 2:42b.

10. From the Mezricher Magid, 1704–55. Magid Devarav LeYaakov 54, in Aryeh Kaplan, trans., *The Light Beyond: Adventures in Hassidic Thought* (New York: Maznaim, 1981).

11. The verse from Job "From out of Ayin, Chochmah is found" (28:12) is retranslated to mean Wisdom (Chochmah) comes from Nothingness (Ayin).

12. "In the beginning..." (Genesis 1:1), or *B'reishit* in Hebrew, is translated by mystics to mean: "From out of Wisdom, God created...." The word *reishit* is really a code word for Wisdom.

13. For more on Wisdom as the conduit of God's essence, see also the second-century mystical treatise *The Bahir*, ed. and trans. Kaplan, pp. 92–93.
14. Genesis Rabba 1:1. See also Pirkei deRabbi Eliezer, chap. 3, on God consulting the Torah for advice on the creation of the universe.
15. Proverbs 8:29–31, Jerusalem Bible.
16. The feminine character of Wisdom (Heb., *chochmah;* Gk., *sophia*) is readily found in the Hebrew scriptures; depending on the translation, She is more or less obvious. See Job, Psalms, and especially Proverbs 1:20–33; 3:18; 4:5–9; 8:1–36; 9:1–6. In the Apocrypha, Wisdom is a central figure in Ecclesiasticus, also known as Sirach, the book of Wisdom, also known as the Wisdom of Solomon, and the book of Baruch. These latter works are available in Roman Catholic Bibles, but excluded from Jewish and Protestant versions.
17. See Job 28. The book of Job dates back to around the sixth century B.C.E.
18. Proverbs 1:22–23.
19. Proverbs 4:13.
20. Proverbs 8:35.
21. Proverbs 3:17–18.
22. As was said earlier, God's feminine presence as the Shechinah was not mentioned in Hebrew scriptures until the rabbinic teachings of the Talmud, between 200 and 500 C.E. The character of Wisdom makes Her entrance between one and eight hundred years earlier.
23. Elizabeth A. Johnson, *She Who Is: The Mystery of God in Feminist Theological Discourse* (New York: Crossroad, 1992), p. 87.
24. Only God (under various titles), Job, Moses, and David are treated in more depth. See Susan Cady, Marian Ronan, and Hal Taussig, *Wisdom's Feast: Sophia in Study and Celebration* (San Francisco: Harper & Row, 1989).
25. To answer these questions, we must understand that the ancient Hebrews had an enormous impact on Western civilization, on both Jews and Gentiles alike. It is arguable that the very foundation of Western society was born out of the theistic and democratic ideals of the ancient Jewish tradition. The ethics, laws, and codes that we take for granted today, along with our cultural mythology and morals, were drawn in large part from the stories and teachings of the Five Books of Moses.
26. Two popular books that demonstrate the use of intuition in the realm of creativity are Julia Cameron, *The Artist's Way* (New York: Jeremy P. Tarcher/Putnam, 1992); and Natalie Goldberg, *Writing Down the Bones* (Boston: Shambhala, 1986).
27. For examples of their partnership in Hebrew scriptures, see Deuteronomy 4:6, Exodus 36:1, and 1 Kings 5:9.
28. *Zohar* 3:290b.

CHAPTER FIVE

1. The Hebrew date recorded by her husband is 22 Kislev (November 15), 1196 (hence her *yahrzeit* is celebrated on 22 Kislev). See Israel Zinberg, *A History of Jewish Literature*, ed. Bernard Martin, vol. 3 (New York: KTAV, 1975). This early date has been debated. See Gustav Karpeles, *Jewish Literature and Other Essays* (Philadelphia: Jewish Publication Society, 1895); and Trude Weiss-Rosmarin, *Jewish Women Throughout the Ages* (New York: Jewish Book Club, 1940) for speculations as late as 1215. All dates place Dulcie's death between the Second and Third Crusades.

2. Dulcie's husband, Rabbi Eleazar ben Judah of Worms (1165–1230), eulogized her in the opening dedication to his book *Sefer Hachochmah*, published in 1217. Although the entire book has not been translated, the elegy, *Eyshet Chayil*, "Woman of Valor," has been. It is from this poem that we learn the details of Dulcie's life.

3. Usury was one of the few professions allowed the Jews of Dulcie's day. It is no puzzle that lending money at high rates of interest would only fuel the aristocratic classes' suspicion and hatred of the Jews: a harsh double bind.

4. At the time of their deaths, Dulcie's daughters Bellette, thirteen, and Hannah, six, were already proficient at sewing, spinning, and embroidering in addition to knowing the daily prayers. These skills were taught to them by their mother. See Judith Baskin, "Some Parallels in the Education of Medieval Jewish and Christian Women," *Jewish History* 5, no. 1 (1991).

5. Alternately spelled *vorsugerins* and *zogerkerins*, these women translated prayers into the vernacular for the less learned women and were "found in every synagogue in Poland, and known in London." Solomon Schechter, *Studies in Judaism: Women in Temple and Synagogue* (Philadephia: Jewish Publication Society, 1938).

6. Rabbi Eleazar's elegy to Dulcie enumerates the many sacred tasks she performed. See also Louis Zinberg, *A History of Jewish Literature*, ed. and trans. Bernard Martin, vol. 7 (Cincinnati, OH: Hebrew Union College Press; New York: KTAV, 1975), p. 23.

7. Known as *hachnasat kallah*, this *mitzvah* (Mishnah Peah 1:1 in Talmud Shabbat 127a) includes funding a bride's dowry through collections and catering her wedding. In hard times, helping an unmarried woman reach the bridal canopy was considered one of the greatest *mitzvot* because poor or orphaned girls often did not have the financial means to pay for the required dowry. The rabbis taught that for dowering a bride one enjoyed rewards in both this and the next world.

8. According to the records, she repaired forty scrolls in her lifetime.

9. The youngest age for a girl's marriage stipulated by Talmudic law is the Jewish age of majority, or the completion of a girl's twelfth year (B. Talmud

Kiddushin 41a). Records show, however, that medieval Jewish parents married off their daughters before the age of thirteen and sometimes as young as ten. The Talmud stipulation of the twelfth year was often overlooked in the Middle Ages due to the dark circumstances of Jewish society. One twelfth-century Jewish authority is recorded as saying, "As to our custom of betrothing our daughters before they are fully twelve years old, the cause is that persecutors are more frequent every day and if a man can afford to give his daughter a dowry, he fears that tomorrow he may not be able to do it and then his daughter would remain forever unmarried." For a more complete understanding of the topic of childhood marriages, see Israel Abrahams, *Jewish Life in the Middle Ages* (Philadelphia: Jewish Publication Society, 1911), pp. 166–70.

10. See Gavri Rosen, "On Jewish Women's Writings," in *Bikurim: The Torah Journal of Midreshet Lindenbaum 5759*, Internet ed. available at ⟨http://www.lind.org.il/bikurim.htm⟩.

11. This small elite of religious thinkers lasted for approximately one hundred years and began with the seminal teachings of Rabbi Samuel ben Kalonymous, whose youngest son, Rabbi Judah HaChasid (d. 1217) wrote the famous work *Sefer Hassidim* (available in English as *The Book of the Pious*, trans. and cond. A. Y. Finkel [Northvale, NJ: Jason Aronson, 1997]). Judah's relative and main disciple was Rabbi Eleazar of Worms, Dulcie's husband, author of numerous works, among which are *Sefer haRokeach* ("Book of the Perfumer," a book of Jewish law and custom), *Sefer Hilchot Teshuvah*, ("Book of the Laws of Atonement"), and *Sefer HaChochmah* ("Book of Wisdom"), in which his elegy of Dulcie is the introduction. None of Rabbi Eleazar's books have as yet been translated into English in their entirety.

12. One of the most sensual love songs to God was the "Hymn of Glory," written by Rabbi Eleazar's teacher, Rabbi Judah the Pietist, and sung at the end of Sabbath services in many synagogues around the world. For medieval angelology and amulet lore, see Joshua Trachtenberg, *Jewish Magic and Superstition* (Cleveland, OH: Meridian Books, 1961).

13. "The fear of God," wrote Samuel ben Kalonymous, "means that when an opportunity to sin arises, [the Pietist] is afraid and thinks to himself: If I do not observe this, I am not perfect in my love for Him...one is afraid of sinning because one wants to avoid being deficient in loving God." See *Sefer haYir'ah: Shoresh l-Yir'ah* ("The Book of Fear: The Root of Fear"); and Ivan G. Marcus, *Piety and Society: The Jewish Pietists of Medieval Germany* (Leiden: Brill, 1981), p. 29.

14. Mishnah Avot 5:23.

15. "God wanted me to be stricter with myself than others are," wrote Eleazar's teacher, Judah, "and I therefore added [restrictions] even when Jewish law does not require them.... Whoever adds safeguards *[gedarim]*

to what is already prohibited, thereby fulfills the will of the Holy One, blessed be He" (*Sefer Hassidim*, p. 28).

16. I am grateful to Rabbi Margot L. Stein for her research and insight into Dulcie. Her one-act play about Dulcie, *Woman of Valor*, exemplifies feminine scholarly research brought to life.

17. The Hebrew text is Israel Kamelhar, *Rabbenu Eleazar me'Germaiza, HaRokeach* (Rzeazow, Poland, 1930), pp. 16–19, based on a manuscript found in Oxford's Bodleian Library, Heb. MS Opp. 757 (Neubauer #2289), f. 25v–26v. This quote of Eleazar's has been beautifully translated by scholar and rabbi Margot Stein. For the elegy itself, an acrostic poem, see *Sefer HaChochmah* (1217), translated in Ivan Marcus, "Mothers, Martyrs and Moneymakers," *Conservative Judaism* 38, no. 3 (Spring 1986), and by Rabbi Margot Stein, as yet unpublished.

18. Isaiah 45:7.

19. The rabbis differ on this point. For instance, one legend (Genesis Rabba 7:7) tells the following story about the creation of evil. On the first Sabbath eve at twilight, when God was putting the finishing touches on creation, God turned to create the evil spirits, who, although part of God's plan, had been left for last. God had but finished creating their souls when twilight turned to sundown and the Sabbath commenced. God was obliged to stop working at once to sanctify the first day of rest. This is why evil spirits were created without bodies while their spirits are intact. See also Trachtenberg, *Jewish Magic and Superstition*. On evil as God's agent, see Isaiah Tishby and Fischel Lachower, arr., *The Wisdom of the Zohar*, vol. 2 (Oxford and New York: Oxford University Press for the Littman Library, 1989), pp. 804–7. "Even evil spirits were created for correcting the world" (*Zohar* 1:47b).

20. B. Talmud Yoma 69b.

21. Tishby and Lachower, *Wisdom of the Zohar, Zohar* 2:162b–63b on Deuteronomy 6:5, an injunction to love God "with all of your heart(s) [written in Hebrew so as to denote two hearts, not one], both the good inclination and the evil inclination."

22. *V'chof et yitzreynu l'hishta-abed lach.* Found in the prayer *Gomel Chasadim Tovim*, just after the morning blessings. *Authorized Daily Prayer Book* (New York: Joseph Hertz Bloch, 1963), pp. 26–27.

23. For an in-depth study of Jewish beliefs about evil spirits, see Trachtenberg, *Jewish Magic and Superstition*, pp. 25–60.

24. Numerous books and monographs on Lilith are available and a feminist magazine is named after her. See, for example, Barbara Koltuv, *The Book of Lilith* (York Beach, ME: Nicolas-Hays, 1986); Raphael Patai, *The Hebrew Goddess* (Detroit: Wayne State University Press, 1990); and Alejandro Terriza, *Isis, Lilith, Gello: Three Ladies of Darkness* (http://www.ccat.sas.upenn.edu).

25. Not claiming the light aspects of our holiness is equally common. In this case, we tend to project our inner goodness onto others. We see this most commonly in the unreasonable projections that are placed on rabbis, ministers, and other spiritual leaders. This is often an uncomfortable and seductive experience for clergy, who know themselves to be real people! Yet, all too often, spiritual leaders become an externalization of the holiness that their students and followers have not yet come to recognize as their own.

26. Lilith's name stems from the same root as "night," *lilah,* in Hebrew.

27. For the story of Abraham, see Genesis 12–49. Miriam is spoken of, albeit briefly, in Exodus 15 and Numbers 12 and 20. The legend of Miriam's well may be found in Midrash Shemot Rabba 26:2; Midrash Bamidbar Rabba 1:2, 19:26; and Louis Ginzberg, *Legends of the Jews,* 7 vols. (Philadelphia: Jewish Publication Society, 1909–38), vol. 3, pp. 50–54.

28. Many studies and books are now available on the unintegrated Din side in girls and women. See Margaret Talbot, "Girls Just Want to Be Mean," *New York Times Magazine,* March 3, 2002; Phyllis Chesler, *Woman's Inhumanity to Woman* (New York: Avalon, 2001); and Rachel Simmons, *Odd Girl Out: The Hidden Culture of Aggression in Girls* (New York: Harcourt, 2002).

29. Genesis 22.

CHAPTER SIX

1. Her *yahrzeit* is 21 Shevat.

2. One can find photographs of and books by Rabbi Shar'abi, considered a saint to the Mizrachi community, in stores and holy sites throughout the Jerusalem area. His books include *Tefillah LeMoshe,* a collection of stories, prayers, and mystical practices (Beit Midrash Ohr Hashalom, 1989) and *Tefillat HaMeyasher,* a book of prayers (Nahar Shalom, 1998).

3. A quote from a Kansas City paper. What did the paper know about Kabbalists? Leah's husband hailed from the noble Shar'abi lineage; he was the great-grandson of Shalom Shar'abi himself, one of the greatest Kabbalists who ever lived.

4. Rabbi Mordechai Shar'abi established his *yeshivah* in 1949, naming it Nahar Shalom, "River of Light," after his great predecessor Rabbi Shalom Shar'abi's mystical opus of the same name. Rabbi Mordechai taught only men; however, he was known to welcome groups of women to his study to discuss their questions regarding Kabbalah. Women's sessions were held after his Kabbalah class for men. See Ariel bar Tzadok, *Kabbalah 101: The Relationship Between Kabbalah and Halakha (Jewish Law)* (www.koshertorah.com/101.html).

5. I thank my teacher, Rabbi Zalman Schachter-Shalomi, for this concept.

6. For a full accounting of these and other escapades, see my memoir *With*

Roots in Heaven: One Woman's Passionate Journey into the Heart of Her Faith (New York: Dutton, 1998).

7. For more on the kabbalah of the soul's composition and journey, see the *Zohar* 1:83a–83b, 205b–206a. Also see Simcha Paull Raphael, *Jewish Views of the Afterlife* (Northvale, NJ: Jason Aronson, 1994); Gershon Winkler, *The Soul of the Matter: A Jewish Kabbalistic Perspective on the Human Soul Before, During and After "Life"* (New York: Judaica Press, 1992); and Zalman Schachter-Shalomi, *Gate to the Heart: An Evolving Process* (Philadelphia: Aleph Alliance for Jewish Renewal, 1991). For a personal approach to these concepts through guided meditations, listen to my audio program *The Woman's Kabbalah* (Boulder, CO: Sounds True, 2000).

8. The laws of *niddah* stem from Leviticus 15:19–33. For a thorough analysis, see Rachel Biale, *Women and Jewish Law: An Exploration of Women's Issues in Halakhic Sources* (New York: Schocken Books, 1984).

9. For a well-researched fictional portrayal of these customs based upon biblical stories of the Jewish matriarchs, see Anita Diamant, *The Red Tent* (New York: Picador USA/St. Martin's Press, 1997).

10. Women's groups are growing in popularity throughout the world. Among Jewish women, there is a current revival of an ancient monthly ritual known as the New Moon, or Rosh Chodesh, celebrations. See Penina V. Adelman, *Miriam's Well: Rituals for Jewish Women Around the Year* (Sunnyside, NY: Biblio Press, 1986). Also, Kolot: The Center for Jewish Women's and Gender Studies (kolot@rrc.edu) is a resource for all kinds of Jewish women's learning, including promoting girls' moon rituals. Their sourcebook for leaders is called *It's a Girl Thing!*

11. See *Zohar* 1:83b; and Aryeh Kaplan, *Jewish Meditation* (New York: Schocken, 1985).

12. The first published text to discuss reincarnation is the *Bahir*, published around 1176 by the Provence school of Kabbalists. The first printed edition appeared in Amsterdam in 1651. See Aryeh Kaplan, *The Bahir* (York Beach, ME: Samuel Weiser, 1979).

CHAPTER SEVEN

1. Sixteenth-century Safed abounded in sages and mystics of the highest order: Rabbi Joseph Karo (1488–1575), *halakhic* authority and author of the standard code of Jewish Law, the *Shulkhan Arukh*; Rabbi Moses Cordovero (1522–70), author of *Pardes Rimonim* ("The Pomegranate Orchard"); Rabbi Solomon Alkabez (1505–74), author of the Lecha Dodi hymn; and Rabbi Hayyim Vital (1542–1620), author of *Sha'arey Kedushah* ("Gates of Holiness"), *Sefer Gilgulim* ("The Book of Transmigrations"), and *Sefer haHezyonot* ("The Book of Visions"). Vital was the chief disciple

and scribe of the great Kabbalist Rabbi Isaac Luria, also known as the Holy Ari (1534–72), who lived in Safed for the final two years of his life.

2. It is a time-honored Jewish belief that the burial sites of the ancestors and saints hold special power and that the souls of the dead can facilitate the fulfillment of one's prayers. One example is the grave of Rabbi Shimon bar Yochai, the second-century mystic traditionally believed to be the author of the *Zohar*, which lies just a few kilometers below Safed. His grave is the site of huge annual pilgrimages to this day.

3. Rabbi Hayyim Vital in his book *Sha'ar HaGilgulim* ("Gate of Reincarnations," ed. Y. Z. Brandwien, 15 vols. [Jerusalem, 1988]), tells of his master, Rabbi Isaac Luria, who saw the departed souls "with his eyes" (vol. 10). For Luria, the dead mingled with the living everywhere. My thanks to Jeffrey H. (Yosi) Chajes for his elucidation of this era and its mystical texts in his remarkable doctoral dissertation "Spirit Possession and the Construction of Early Modern Jewish Religiosity" (Department of Philosophy, Yale University, 1999; Ann Arbor, MI: UMI Dissertation Services, 2001).

4. In his diary, *Sefer haHezyonot*, Rabbi Hayyim Vital tells that Francesca was present in the House of Study when he taught his students in Safed in 1594 and at a lecture he gave commemorating the deceased during that same time. See the English translation of Vital's diaries: Morris Faierstein, trans., *Jewish Mystical Autobiographies: Book of Visions and Book of Secrets* (New York: Paulist Press, 1999), p. 50.

5. Yosef ben Yitzhak Sambari, *Sefer Divrei Yosef*, ed. Shimon Shtober (Jerusalem: Ben-Zvi Institute, 1994), pp. 364–66.

6. From the *Malleus Maleficarum* ("The Hammer of Witches"), a widely distributed manifesto published by Catholic Inquisition authorities in 1485–86 for the purpose of routing out the evil of witchcraft. Quoted in Stephen Katz, *The Holocaust in Historical Context* (New York: Oxford University Press, 1993), vol. 1, pp. 438–39.

7. "The witch-hunts can be seen as a case of 'genderized mass murder," writes Katz in *The Holocaust in Historical Context*, vol. 1, p. 503. See also "The European Witch Craze of the Fourteenth–Seventeenth Centuries: A Sociologist's Perspective," *American Journal of Sociology* 86, no. 1 (July 1980); and *http://www.gendercide.org/case_witchhunts.html*. A dramatic documentary on the topic is "Burning Times," available through the Public Broadcasting Society.

8. Exodus 22:18.

9. See 1 Samuel 28. One other passage (2 Kings 23:24) infers a kind of witch-hunt, not necessarily of women, however. In about 600 B.C.E. King Josiah expunged the country of its "mediums, wizards,...and all other abominations that were found in the territory of Judah and in Jerusalem" of his day.

10. Vital's *Sefer HaHezyonot* was recently translated into English and intro-
    duced in Faierstein, *Jewish Mystical Autobiographies*.

11. Each of the women discussed in this chapter are referenced in Vital's
    diaries. Vital did not mention the women of Safed because of their spiri-
    tual expertise in and of itself. Rather, their dreams and visions tended to
    support his self-image and his mission as a national redeemer.

12. Faierstein, *Jewish Mystical Autobiographies*, p. 50.

13. Vital's diaries report at least two other encounters with groups of women
    in or around the House of Study and Prayer.

14. However, Francesca is the only recorded woman who had maggidic revela-
    tions. See Yoram Bilu, "*Dybbuk* and *Maggid:* Two Cultural Patterns of
    Altered Consciousness in Judaism," *Association for Jewish Studies Review,*
    21, no. 2 (1996): 362, n. 72.

15. For a thorough examination of Karo's mystical revelations as well as the
    phenomenon of maggidism in general, see Zwi Werblowsky, *Joseph Karo:
    Lawyer and Mystic* (Philadelphia: Jewish Publication Society, 1977).
    Werblowsky makes clear that others of Karo's mystical colleagues in Safed
    also had *maggid* experiences, such as Rabbi Moses Cordovero and Rabbi
    Joseph Taytazak. Later examples of sages who conversed with a *maggid*
    were Rabbi Moses Hayyim Luzzato (1707–47), whose *Voice Without an
    Image* appeared in 1727. The *maggid*'s words were dictated in Hebrew and
    published as the *Zohar Razin Genizin, Tikkunim Hadashim,* and other
    works. The *maggid* of the famous Hassidic master Rabbi Pinchas of
    Koretz (1728–90) was known as the Angel of the Zohar and appeared
    whenever he opened the pages of his beloved *Zohar*. According to legend,
    one of Rabbi Koretz's students was once determined to see if the *maggid*
    was authentic. He hid himself in his master's study. When the rabbi
    invoked his *maggid*, the student was instantly blinded. When his sight
    finally returned to him, he saw the room ablaze with divine light pouring
    from the rabbi's face.

16. Karo's guidance from his maggid was recorded in *Maggid Mesharim,* first
    printed in Lublin in 1646 (New York: Jewish Theological Seminary, MS.S.
    11/158/5514, fols. 1–66). It has not yet been fully translated from its orig-
    inal Hebrew. However, sections in English are found in Aryeh Kaplan,
    Meditation and Kabbalah (York Beach, ME: Samuel Weiser, 1982), and in
    Werblowsky, *Joseph Karo: Lawyer and Mystic*.

17. See Mishnah Avot 4:13; Midrash Shemot Rabba 32.

18. The Ari taught that although the world is filled with these angelic beings,
    "most of the time, these *maggidim* [plural] do not reveal themselves to the
    individual, but sometimes they do. This depends on the nature of the per-
    son's soul, as well as his deeds." The Ari's teachings about the *maggid* were
    transcribed by Rabbi Hayyim Vital in his *Shmoneh Sha'arim* ("Eight

Gates"), vol. 7. A small section of *Sha'ar Ruach HaKodesh* ("Gate of the Holy Spirit") is translated in Kaplan, *Meditation and Kabbalah*, pp. 223–24.

19. Kaplan, *Meditation and Kabbalah*, p. 224.
20. More specific guidance is found on my audio program, *The Woman's Kabbalah: Ecstatic Jewish Practices for Women* (Boulder, CO: Sounds True Recordings, 2000; http//www.soundstrue.com).
21. Vital, *Shmoneh Sha'arim*, vol. 7, p. 47. It is important to note that not one of the stories or quotes of the women in this chapter comes directly from the women themselves. They come to us secondhand, filtered through the perspective of the men, who were unusually respectful of the women, but who had their own agendas in preserving their words. Although we rejoice that the lives of the women of Safed were recorded at all, we must also take note of the fact that neither they nor any of the women sages in this book were able to preserve their wisdom in their own words.
22. Chajes, "Spirit Possession and the Construction of Early Modern Jewish Religiosity," p. 249.
23. The radishes and lettuce are possibly symbolic of the scarce nourishment in the books he was reading.
24. Obadiah 1:18.
25. Vital, *Shmoneh Sha'arim*, vol. 7, pp. 133–34.
26. B. Talmud Brachot 55a.
27. *Zohar* 2:216b.
28. *Zohar* 1:183b.
29. B. Talmud Brachot 57b.
30. This particular nocturnal appeal comes from a collection called *Seguloth l'Petcihat haLev* ("Treasures for Opening the Heart") in a Bodleian MS. (Opp. 447, Neubauer 1833), fol. 164b. For more on this topic, see Werblowsky, *Joseph Karo: Lawyer and Mystic,* chap. 4.
31. A symbol of our Malkhut grounding.
32. The stories of the daughter of Raphael Anav are documented in two books of the day, Vital's *Book of Visions* and Y. Zemach, *Ranu LeYa'akov*, MS. Machon Ben-Zvi 203, 72b (Institute for Microfilmed Hebrew Manuscripts no. 26559).
33. *Dybbuks* are embodied spirits, often malevolent in nature, who were believed to cling to and take over a vulnerable living person's body to control his or her behavior. The remedy was exorcism, an art that was widely practiced among mystically inclined medieval and premodern rabbis. Stories of *dybbuks* are found throughout Jewish folklore. See Chajes, "Spirit Possession and the Construction of Early Modern Jewish Religiosity"; Bilu, *"Dybbuk* and *Maggid"*; Isaac Bashevis Singer, *The Collected Stories of Isaac Bashevis Singer* (New York: Farrar, Straus & Giroux, 1953; and Gershon Winkler, *Dybbuk* (New York: Judaica Press, 1981).

34. Although this benevolent form of spirit possession is generally regarded as a visitation to exclusively male sages by male sages, the term used in *Ranu LeYa'akov*, one of the two documents recounting this story, quotes the spirit speaking in the first person, claiming: "*Nit-abarti bah*" (first-person past passive tense of *ibbur*), meaning: "I became spiritually impregnated within her [the daughter of Anav]." See Chajes, "Spirit Possession and the Construction of Early Modern Jewish Religiosity," appendix 2, case 11.

35. Faierstein, *Jewish Mystical Autobiographies*, p. 65.

36. From Vital's *Sefer HaHezionot*, in Faierstein, *Jewish Mystical Autobiographies*, pp. 67–71. Translated above by Chajes, "Spirit Possession and the Construction of Early Modern Jewish Religiosity," p. 242; appendix 2, case 11a, part 2:21.

37. Fioretta of Modena was another learned woman who lived in Safed, an exceptional scholar of Torah, Maimonides, and the *Zohar*. We know of Fioretta because her grandson, the Kabbalist Rabbi Aaron Berechia of Safed (d. 1639), paid tribute to her wisdom in his book entitled *Ashmoret HaBoker* ("The Morning Watch"; Mantua, 1624), p. 3a. Other remarkable women named in Vital's *Book of Visions* include Sonadora, a dream interpreter and "an expert in the art of oil gazing" (i.e., lecanomancy, oil-water divination); the visionary Mira, sister of Rabbi S. Hayati; and Mazal Tov, whom Vital sought out for her expertise in hearing internal voices.

38. Chajes, "Spirit Possession and the Construction of Early Modern Jewish Religiosity," p. 255.

39. Psalm 45:14.

40. Psalm 40:9.

41. 1 Kings 19:12.

42. Jeremiah 31:33; Psalm 51:11.

43. Mishnah Avot 1:3; traditionally translated "The world exists by way of three principles: Torah, Work, and Acts of Kindness."

44. The term *eco-kashrut* was first coined by Rabbi Zalman Schachter-Shalomi in the late 1970s. Practice of *eco-kashrut* involves only eating foods and using products that are healthy and nondamaging to ourselves and to the planet, and elevating all our consumption decisions to be in accord with sacred values and ethics. For a more detailed discussion of *eco-kashrut*, see Arthur Waskow, *Down-to-Earth Judaism: Food, Money, Sex and the Rest of Life* (New York: Morrow, 1995), pp. 117–29.

RESOURCES

Aleph: Alliance for Jewish Renewal
7000 Lincoln Dr., #B2
Philadelphia, PA 19119
215–247–9700
www.aleph.org

Bat Kol: A Feminist House of Study
P.O. Box 4047
Philadelphia, PA 19118
215–242–5075
www.batkol.org

Bat Shalom
A feminist peace organization
P.O. Box 8083
Jerusalem 91080
Israel
www.batshalom.org

Bayit Chadash
Rabbi Marc (Mordechai) Gafni
P.O. Box 53131
Jerusalem, Israel 91530
972–2–565–2222
www.bayitchadash.com

Bridges: A Jewish Feminist Journal
P.O. Box 24839
Eugene, OR 97402
888–359–9188
www.bridgesjournal.org

Chochmat HaLev: Center for
    Meditation and Spirituality
2215 Prince St.
Berkeley, CA 94705
510–704–9687
www.chochmat.org

Elat Chayyim: Center for Healing
    and Renewal
99 Mill Hook Rd.
Accord, NY 12404
800–398–2630
www.elatchayyim.org

HaMakom YeshivAshram
Rabbi Ohad Ezrachi
ezrahi@barak-online.net
www.hamakom.org

Jewish Women's Resource Center
National Council of Jewish Women
9 E. 69th St.
New York, NY 10021
212–535–5900

Kolot: The Center for Jewish
    Women's and Gender Studies
1299 Church Road
Wyncote, PA 19095–1898
215–576–0800
www.rrc.edu/departments/kolot.htm

Lilith Magazine
250 W. 57th St., #2432
New York, NY 10107
800–783–4903
www.lilithmag.com

Los Angeles Jewish Feminist Center
American Jewish Congress
6505 Wilshire Blvd., Suite 417
Los Angeles, CA 90048

Ma'yan: The Jewish Women's Project
   and Jewish Feminist Research
   Group
Jewish Community Center of the
   Upper West Side
15 W. 65th St.
New York, NY 10023
212–580–0099
www.mayan.org

Metivta: Center for Contemplative
   Judaism
Rabbi Rami Shapiro
2001 S. Barrington Ave., #106
Los Angeles, CA 90025
310–477–5370
www.metivta.org

Neshama: Encouraging the
   Exploration of Women's
   Spirituality in Judaism
P.O. Box 545
Brookline, MA 02146
617–965–7350

Sarah's Tent
Marilyn Berger
2461 Santa Monica Blvd., #319
Santa Monica, CA 90404
310–712–2615

Under Shekhina's Wings
Cross-cultural women's spirituality
   Web site
www.geocities.com/Athens/1501

Women in Judaism: A
   Multidisciplinary Journal
www.utoronto.ca/wjudaism

The Women's Kabbalah: Ecstatic
   Jewish Practices for Women
   (by Rabbi Firestone)
Original audio from Sounds True
800–333–9185
www.soundstrue.com